THE APPALACHIAN TRAIL:
A JOURNEY OF DISCOVERY

by

Jan D. Curran

RAINBOW BOOKS, INC.

Library of Congress Cataloging-in-Publication Data

Curran, Jan D., 1934-
    The Appalachian Trail : a journey of discovery / Jan D. Curran.
        p.   cm.
    Includes index.
    ISBN 0-935834-66-4 : $12.95
    1. Hiking—Appalachian Trail—Guide-books. 2. Appalachian Trail—
Description and travel—Guide-books. I. Title.
GV199.42.A68C87 1991   91-21920
917.4—dc20   CIP

The Appalachian Trail: A Journey of Discovery
By Jan D. Curran
Copyright © 1991 by Jan D. Curran
Produced by Ratzlaff & Associates
Cover design by Therese Cabell
Cover Background Painting by Jan D. Curran
Published by Rainbow Books, Inc.
P. O. Box 430
Highland City, FL 33846-0430

Printed in the United States of America.

CONTENTS

POEMS

MAPS

ACKNOWLEDGMENTS

I am deeply indebted to all the people I met on the Trail who shared their time and support in my adventure. Nick Sprague gave me encouragement during the critical initial stages of the hike. Jeff and Dorothy Hansen from Neels Gap helped with their advice and equipment. Buddy Crossman at the Rainbow Springs Campground provided terrific support when I needed a break. Levi and Jan Long, along with Kate Childress, were real friends to hikers, not just to me. Sutton Brown took a personal interest and generously offered his time to enrich my experience. Michael Joslin shared close spiritual insights when I was searching. Dan Dunford and Tim Evans introduced me to the natural world through which I was traveling. Cathy Morris provided comradeship and moral support at a critical time. Joe and Carol Stielper, John and Jane Blessing, and George Baty and his family generously shared food and company that averted crises.

I also wish to acknowledge the assistance of several people whose help was very instrumental in getting words on paper. I am particularly indebted to Tom Brantmeier who gave me extensive criticism and support, to Joanne Rainey for her insightful comments and support, Mary Foege who kept me focused, and last but not least, Nat Kaplan who also gave me excellent criticism and suggestions. Nat was kind enough to suggest that I was "the poor man's Hemingway," a lift that I truly appreciate.

Other Rainbow Books
in our highly acclaimed

The Appalachian Trail Series

by Jan D. Curran

The Appalachian Trail: How To Prepare For & Hike It

The Appalachian Trail: Onward to Katahdin

FOREWORD

The Appalachian Trail (AT) is a continuous 2100-mile footpath through the heart of the Appalachian Mountains. Its northern terminus is Katahdin in Baxter State Park, Maine, and its southern terminus is Springer Mountain, Georgia, about 90 miles north of Atlanta. (Katahdin is often referred to as Mt. Katahdin; however, the literal translation of the Indian word, Katahdin, means Mightiest Mountain.) In between, the Trail crosses or touches portions of 14 states. It lies within a day's drive of half the population of the U.S. Because of that proximity, it is visited by upwards of four million people yearly, all of whom seek to escape the steel and concrete canyons of our cities, to lift their spirits, to try to touch their primitive origins, or simply to experience nature for the sheer joy of it. Most come for only a few hours or days. Others spend much longer, some remaining for months.

According to the definition contained in the Comprehensive Plan for the Appalachian National Scenic Trail, the AT is:

". . . for travel on foot through the wild, scenic, wooded, pastoral, and culturally significant lands of the Appalachian Mountains. It is a means of sojourning among these lands, such that visitors may experience them by their own unaided efforts.

"In practice, the Trail is usually a simple footpath, purposeful in direction and concept, favoring the heights of land, and located for minimum reliance on construction for protecting the resource. The body of the Trail is provided by the lands it traverses, and its soul is the living stewardship of the volunteers and workers of the Appalachian Trail community."

Definition of the Appalachian Trail,
from *Appalachian Trail Management Principles (ACT)*

Although it is referred to as a footpath, the AT is more than that. From a physical standpoint, the terrain which it traverses is very mountainous with continuous climbs and descents. Many long stretches of the Trail are a rock scramble with no visible path; only the white blazes painted on the rocks to guide the way. The steepness of the Trail and the rough, rocky terrain require strength, stamina and dedication on the part of those who accept its challenges. The terrain by itself is difficult enough. But with the added weight of a 40-, 50- or 60-pound pack, the difficulty for the hiker is exponentially increased.

Many people view the Trail in terms of the glowing descriptions, written by writers who have romanticized this wilderness setting. To some, because of oft repeated tales and the descriptions of the fabled lands through which it passes, it has assumed a larger-than-life image. For other adherents and supporters, it conjures an almost religious aura conducive to zealotry — a True Belief for which no sacrifice is too great. In truth, the Trail is worthy of all that is said or written about it. To those who accept its challenge, it assumes an almost spiritual character, embodying the dreams and ideals of all whom it touches, giving back gifts of far greater worth than the dreamers imagined.

The Trail, however, should not be regarded only as a generous benefactor. It can be a beautiful, but demanding master, who exacts from those who would thru-hike it, an ever increasing measure of dedication and sacrifice. (Thru-Hikers are people who hike it in long stretches, mostly attempting to hike the 2100 miles end-to-end in one continuous hike.)

Meanwhile, the Trail becomes the catalyst for self-knowledge or self-fulfillment. The Trail helps with the learning process, and what the hiker learns will come from the ultimate source of all knowledge — from within himself. But, for each truth learned, he must sacrifice commensurately. In the end, he will understand that the Trail gives no quarter; it requires those, who truly want to know, to reach down deep inside, not only for wisdom, but also for the resolve to continue the quest.

Because of its physical and mental challenges, the Trail can be most effective in developing strength of character. Because of its natural beauty, it can sometimes affect our most intimate inner personal relationships with whomever or whatever we determine to be our spiritual source, and in so doing, can sometimes inspire greater spiritual awareness than our churches.

Each spring several hundred people, eager for the challenge and eyes bright with anticipation, start from Springer Mountain, or later from Katahdin, intending to hike the entire 2100 miles. Normally, fewer than 100 successfully complete the journey. Most cannot maintain the resolve needed to overcome the seemingly endless months of incredibly difficult conditions: treacherous climbs, extremes of temperature, rain and occasional snow, fatigue and the debilitating little injuries that seem to be a constant nemesis for the hiker. Some, if they are hiking alone, simply cannot endure the loneliness for such a long period. Others, who start with partners, find that the relationship gradually begins to unravel. With some, the split comes early; for others, it may come after several hundred miles. When the split occurs, most partners leave the Trail.

When I decided to hike the Trail, I had little appreciation for the physical or mental demands. Though I recognized there would be difficult times, I really didn't understand how severely the Thru-Hiker is tested. Focused only on the romantic Trail descriptions I had read in books, I created an unrealistic scenario which scarcely prepared me for the difficulties I encountered. In fact, had I known how difficult it would be, both physically and mentally, I might not even have started.

But start I did, and learn I did, and in the process, I made a commitment which kept me on the Trail. Day by day, I struggled as hard mentally as I did physically to overcome the obstacles. It became an endurance test, a battle of my will against the elements and the inner demons of anxiety and loneliness.

Originally, I looked at the Trail as a vehicle to help me make the transition from the structured existence of an Army officer to that of a private citizen. The hike became far more than a transition vehicle, and my part in it became more than merely overcoming physical obstacles or using the time to think about a transition in my life. I became intensely aware of a broader and deeper significance for my existence and of what had drawn me to hike the Trail. What I found was a priceless spiritual adventure which I could not have experienced in any other way. This book is about that adventure.

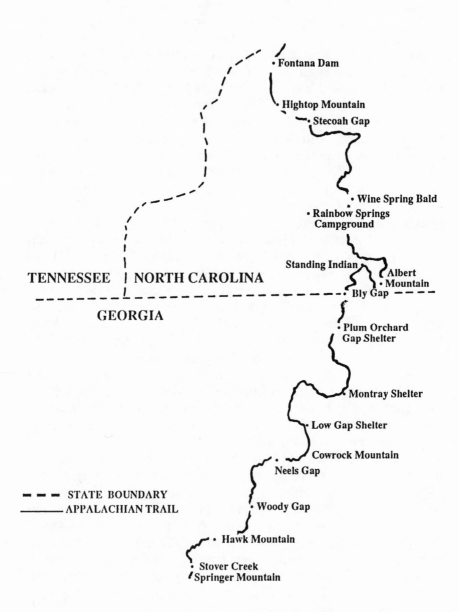

Springer Mountain, Georgia, to Fontana Dam, North Carolina

CHAPTER 1

Learning to Walk

My son, Rob shook his head as he helped me lift my pack from the luggage compartment of the car. He was wearing his "father" smile, the one he wore when my grandson was acting silly. "You sure you really want to do this?"

I nodded my head, not daring to look him in the eyes for fear of betraying my uncertainty. Instead, I pretended to adjust the pack straps. He watched silently as I struggled to get the pack on my shoulders.

The technique I had learned for getting a pack on my back was to lift it by the shoulder straps and rest it on my right leg just above the knee, slip my right arm through the right shoulder strap, then as I straightened up, to swing the pack around to my back and slip my left arm through the left shoulder strap. That put the pack on my shoulders. Then it was a matter of bouncing it a couple of times until it settled properly and cinching up the waist strap.

Unfortunately, this time, when I straightened up, the top-heavy pack slipped uncontrollably to the left and ended up hanging horizontally across my back. Slightly embarrassed, I manhandled it back to a vertical position and slipped my left arm through the shoulder strap. Then, feigning nonchalance, I threaded the tip of the waist belt through the locking buckle and yanked. Nothing happened. The belt had twisted and would not pull through the locking mechanism. Rob smiled even more broadly now as I straightened and rehooked the waist belt. When it appeared I had everything organized, he handed me my camera.

"Sure you can handle everything?" he asked.

"No sweat! It'll take a couple of times 'til I get the hang of it."

The physical effort of manhandling my pack and my anxiety over the unknown ahead of me caused my voice to tremor; I had to talk an octave lower to control it.

"We going to hear from you from time to time?" he asked as we shook hands.

"Yeah, I'll be in touch. I'll call and let you know how I'm doing."

I looked around the clearing known as Nimblewill Gap for the trail leading to Springer Mountain, the southern terminus of the Appalachian Trail (AT) and the starting point of my 2000-mile odyssey. On the north edge of the clearing was an opening in the forest where the earth had been worn bare. Just inside the forest fringe stood a tree with a pale blue blaze painted on the bark about head high. I remembered reading in a Trail guide that blue blazes were used to mark side trails and approaches to the AT. The AT itself was marked with white blazes. Beyond the tree, a well-defined path led up the ridge line. "Looks like this is it!" I said to Rob.

He leaned against the door, wearing the same smile, half laughing, half questioning. "Take care and don't forget to call!" He waved me away.

I waved back and headed into the forest, walking a little faster than usual. "Slow down," I said audibly as the strain of carrying 53 pounds strapped to my back immediately became evident.

The grade out of the gap was gradual. I covered the first 50 yards with tolerable difficulty. Then the trail steepened. I was surprised at how quickly the initial discomfort turned into real pain. Within seconds, the pack straps began burning my shoulder muscles, and the waist strap steadily and painfully pinched the loose skin on my hips. I stopped to relieve the pain and catch my breath, then turned to see how far I had come.

Peering through the foliage, I could barely see the car and my son still looking at the point where I had entered the woods. I doubted that he could see me, and I thought about taking the pack off to stop the pain. But what if he could see me? Why doesn't he just go on! I struggled on for a few more yards, then stopped momentarily when I heard the engine accelerate and the crunch of tires on gravel. Rob had departed.

When the sound faded, it was replaced by a frightening silence, and a rush of panic seized me. I was now totally alone. I started again. In my anxiety, I tried to climb too fast and was again forced to slow down. The pain in my shoulders and back increased to the point of agony. I tried to find relief by readjusting the pack straps, tightening first the left shoulder strap and then the right one, walking a short distance, then loosening them again. I lifted the pack higher on my shoulders. Then I lowered it. I loosened the waist strap and tightened it again. I leaned forward at the waist with my hands on my knees to catch my breath and to relieve the pressure of the straps on my shoulders. I climbed about 50 more yards, buying each yard with an increasing measure of pain. How long would the torture last? A day, two days, a week? Unconsciously, I tried to speed the process by climbing faster, and my pounding heart kicked in an extra beat in protest. That did it! I stopped, took off my pack and sat on a large log beside the trail to bury my head in my hands.

The afternoon sky was hazy from heat and condensation, but a slight breeze blew gently through the forest and, in the shade where I was sitting, it was pleasant. Some fix you've gotten yourself into! I said to myself. Here you are all alone, a jillion miles from any place, planning to walk 2000 miles with a pack that's way too heavy. Why couldn't you just retire and find a nice comfortable second career like a normal worn-out colonel? What, in God's name, are you trying to prove?

The thought of those army days caused my mind to wander back to Mainz, Germany, a beautiful old city on the Rhine River. I could see again the spires of its massive Romanesque cathedral rising above charming clusters of open-beam houses and the cobblestone market square. I desperately wished I could be back there — back where I knew what I was doing; and back where I had power, authority and responsibility.

My job had been to run the American Military Community (12,000 soldiers, civilians and family members — Mainz itself had a population of 180,000) as a combination, mayor/city manager and to interface with the German city and county administrations. As the Community Activity Commander, I had a staff of about 100 military and civilian personnel to assist in planning and executing the various functions and services. A 700-person-work force provided basic engineer, maintenance, construction, transportation and supply support.

The faces of the people with whom I worked daily to execute the programs were with me now, as if no time had passed at all. I wondered what they would think of the Boss, if they could see me now. I certainly wasn't the confidant, in-control figure they had known. But, I remembered, it was all over now.

No more short deadlines or budget cutbacks, or impact statements. No more budget submissions, budget execution reviews, or fights with civilian personnel and procurement bureaucracies. No more stress, trying to stay one step ahead of the bright ambitious brigadier generals. No more holding the hands of nervous German officials, passing on their constituents' outraged complaints about helicopter noise or tanks exercising in the local training areas on religious holidays. No more trying to control the uncontrollable.

Suddenly, it dawned on me that I was reviewing the litany of reasons why I had decided to hike the Trail. No longer was I a big fish in a little pond; as a matter of fact, I no longer had a pond. I was in a totally new environment in which I had little experience and which required a very substantial reordering of the priorities that governed my life. I was now a private citizen with no responsibilities or power and only the most tenuous of connections to the comfortable old support system of the past. I needed time just for myself, to think things through, to "peel back the layers of the onion" as an old boss used to say when he wanted me to get to the essence of a problem.

Just before retiring, I had received a tempting offer that promised excellent financial reward from a German automobile insurance company. I would administer their U.S. Forces private automobile insurance program countrywide. But I was concerned with the stress quotient and the hours I would have had to spend driving the autobahns. Something in my gut told me not to jump. I had the gnawing feeling that it wasn't something I would enjoy doing. I was faced with the old temptation of defining success in the terms with which I was most comfortable: money and material gain. It could have been easy to allow the acquisition of wealth to become an end in itself. I didn't want to fall into that trap. I had the disquieting feeling that I was already too keenly focused on the material aspects of life.

It seemed I now had a unique opportunity, free from material constraints, to make some of the most critical decisions of my life. I might be leaving the Army, but that didn't mean I had to leap immediately into another job like I was grasping for a life boat. Ultimately, I decided that the changes in my life were not something I could determine under the pressure of time. In fact, I recognized that I was embarking on a process, that I had completed one phase of my life and was about to begin a new phase, I needed time to complete the process, and what would drive my progress was the process itself without regard to time.

As my mind touched on memories of my career, I felt a loneliness I had never felt before. I thought about my concerns of being alone in the wilderness. It wasn't exactly scary. But it was downright sobering.

What if something happens? Suppose I get bitten by a rattlesnake? Suppose I fall and break an ankle or injure a knee? What if my heart goes into fibrillation? How can I get help?

I had entertained all those possibilities several times during my preparations. They were not a total surprise. But the way in which I reacted to them in light of my new aloneness was unsettling.

I felt the afternoon slipping away. Resolutely, I shouldered my pack. This time I put the pack on with no trouble. I simply took control of the thing, and, while muttering to myself about it being too heavy, slung it on my back and started off up the mountain. Eventually I made it to the summit of the mountain and looked around for some indication that I had reached the starting point.

When I couldn't find anything to reassure me that I had reached Springer Mountain, I panicked. My first reaction was to think that I had climbed out of Nimblewill Gap in the wrong direction. I fished the *Trail Guide* map from my pocket and noted, with a sigh of relief, that I had reached the summit of Black Mountain and still had another couple of miles to go.

It took another three hours to reach the summit of Springer Mountain. When I arrived, my back and shoulders throbbed with pain, and my hips burned to the point of numbness. Trying to walk on level ground again was a strange experience, much like the feeling one gets when walking on dry land immediately after spending a prolonged period at sea. I stumbled several times trying to maintain an upright position, since the pack tended to pull me forward. Finally in desperation, I wrapped my arms around a tree and hung on until a semblance of equilibrium returned.

I was still hugging my tree when I spied the summit sign about 15 feet away. It was a brown metal sign like those found in National Parks and informed all who cared to read that the elevation was 3820 feet and that it was 2000 miles to Mt. Katahdin in Maine.

So this is it, I thought. This is where it all begins. I felt as though I had performed a major feat in reaching the summit of

Springer Mountain. But the irony that I hadn't even begun my real hike was inescapable.

Near the sign stood a metal mail box which contained a Trail register. Beside it was a small wooden sign which read, SHELTER, with an arrow that pointed down the trail. (Trail Registers are usually 8"-by-10"-lined notebooks in which hikers write comments about the Trail, leave messages for one another or simply record what's on their mind. They make very interesting reading.) To my left, a small rock ledge opened to the mountains to the west. Embedded in the rock was a bronze plaque with the figure of a hiker in raised relief which read:

APPALACHIAN
TRAIL
Georgia to Maine
A Footpath for
those who seek
Fellowship with
The Wilderness

The Georgia Appalachian Trail Club

This was the real beginning, the place where the first step of a 2000-mile journey was to take place. I had read somewhere that it took five million steps to complete the trip. I wasn't sure of the significance of such trivia. Two thousand miles was mind-boggling enough without overloading my already reeling biological computer with five million more units of measurement. I shrugged off the thought. It was simply too vast to comprehend. I removed my pack and walked out on the ledge for a better look at the place where my great adventure was to begin.

It was now early evening, the time of day when the wind stops blowing, when the forest rests between the activity of the afternoon and the bustle of the night. It was uncommonly still and quiet. The view to the west, over purple mountains silhouetted against the reddish sky, was a feast of color. The ridge crests lay in massive ranks that stretched to a final silhouette on the horizon. As imposing as the mountains were, the silence that accompanied their march to the sky was even more imposing. It was a silence as gigantic as the land which it enveloped, as impenetrable as the mists which shrouded the valleys. It was a silence that imposed its will upon the scene, as awesome to the

Sign on summit of Springer Mountain.

Plaque on rock ledge on summit of Springer Mountain placed there by the Georgia Appalachian Trail Club.

listener as the mountains to the viewer. It seemed that the silence gave its power to the land and was in turn reinforced by the vision.

More immediate was the thought that somewhere in the distance, some 2000 miles away and across these same mountains, lay the summit of Mt. Katahdin. I would be crossing those mountains, totally alone in the sea of ridges, completely immersed in their silence. The thought was intimidating and a sense of powerlessness overwhelmed me. Suddenly I missed the narrow, comforting limits of the world I was leaving. And, yes, suddenly I was downright frightened by the immensity of the world I was about to enter. Then I remembered the quotation that "a journey of a thousand miles begins with a single step." That helped put the world I was about to enter back into a reasonable perspective; and now I felt slightly more confident.

After filling my senses one last time with the beauty of the landscape, I shouldered my pack and began again to make my way haltingly down the Trail toward the shelter. I passed a tree with a white blaze and wondered how may blazes I would encounter in my journey. I tried to calculate the number of blazes in a mile and multiply that by 2000. Blazes were supposedly painted every 100 yards. But I became depressed, until I applied my single-step theory to the blazes. It was then that I realized the significance of that first blaze. That was the first STEP and the first BLAZE!

I was still wrestling with the enormity of what lay ahead when three hikers, two fit-looking, lithe, muscled, teen-age boys about 16 years old, and a slender, delicate-appearing woman, with a gentle home-like quality that seemed out of place in the rugged mountains, came walking briskly up the path. We all stopped and looked at one another.

"You plan on stayin' at the shelter?" asked the lead boy.

When I indicated I was, he said they were planning to tent camp on the summit I had just left.

"We just come fer water from the spring. Ma don't like shelter mice," he said then.

The woman who was bringing up the rear introduced herself as Ginger and volunteered that it was her first backpacking experience.

"We're goin' back down to Amicalola tomorrow," said the boy who proved to be her son. He sighed wearily and the other boy nodded with a grimace.

Ginger, on the other hand, appeared to be ready for a shower and clean sheets. She was obviously tired, but in high spirits. "I did pretty good, I'd say," she said brightly, brushing wisps of brown and gray hair from her face. "I held up, though there were times when I wasn't so sure, 'specially that climb out of Amicalola. Why, I may even come back next year, if they'll have me."

When I learned that she had hiked the extremely difficult 11 miles from Amicalola State Park to Springer Mountain, my original impressions of her delicacy and gentility were tempered with admiration for her strength and determination. It made my puny three-mile hike from Nimblewill Gap seem insignificant by comparison.

"You're gonna have a real great trail tomorrow," said Ginger's boy wistfully. "It's easy walking. We hiked to Hawk Mountain yesterday so we know the trail pretty good. It's real pretty down by Stover Creek."

They became immersed in contemplation. "Maybe next year or the year after, we can go all the way," said the other boy.

"You can talk about that later," said Ginger. "Let's get goin'. I'm starved."

The shelter, like hundreds more I would see on the Trail, was a small, wood frame house, enclosed on three sides with an open side facing a forest clearing. The roof had an exaggerated overhang in the front which provided added protection from rain; on each side, smaller overhangs provided lesser protection for gear stored outside. The interior was completely bare except for a shoulder-high wooden shelf along the left side wall. Sleeping accommodations for up to about six people were provided by the rough board floor.

Hanging from the front roof support beam were several shoelace-length pieces of nylon cord used to hang packs to protect them from mice. Attached to the cords were jar lids or can tops which acted as barriers to any mice who might try crawling down the string to get at the packs and the goodies inside.

I unrolled my ensolite pad (sleeping mattress) and sleeping bag from my pack and laid them out on the sleeping platform. Next I removed my flashlight, stove, cook pot and food sack. I had planned well, because I was able to remove everything I required for the night without having to unpack anything I didn't need.

Before leaving Naples, Florida, my home, I had experimented with different menus and selected basic ingredients for breakfasts, lunches and suppers, which were all mixed together in the bag. With so many food items in one bag, it became a game of hide-and-seek as I tried to find the proper food for my evening meal. I immediately fixed that by segregating the ingredients according to meal and placing them in separate bags.

I had made my own snack food (gorp) from a mixture of granola, M&M candies, peanuts, raisins and cut, dried fruit. It proved to be a versatile food which I used for trail snacks, breakfast cereal and on occasions as desert. Later, because I wanted hot food in the morning, I switched almost exclusively to instant oatmeal for breakfasts.

For lunches I had packed cans of tuna fish and sardines along with peanut butter, crackers, candy bars, granola bars and raisins. I also carried powdered Gatorade which I mixed with water to drink with my meals along with instant coffee, sugar and powdered milk for occasional pick-me-ups.

For suppers I had created a tasty concoction of two bouillon cubes in two cups of water combined with one clove of garlic, one small onion, sliced, one small (4 to 6 oz.) can of tuna fish, ham or chicken and a handful of noodles. I added everything but the noodles to the water which I brought to a boil. About five minutes later, I added the noodles. A bag of Lipton Noodles and Herbs or Lipton DeLuxe Noodles and Sauce Parmesan added extra flavor. I then cooked everything for another eight to ten minutes until the noodles were soft, added salt and pepper to taste, and that was it.

Another supper I devised was very similar, except I added a dried soup mix consisting of dried beans and peas and carrots as well as pasta and salami chunks in place of the noodles and the canned meat. That had to cook longer, needing twenty minutes before the peas and beans were sufficiently tender. Both dishes were delicious, inexpensive and proved to be very nutritious. While experimenting with different menus before coming on the Trail, I had discovered that I could cook everything on my Coleman PEAK 1 MODEL 400 STOVE almost as efficiently as I could on my kitchen range at home.

I decided to cook my noodles and tuna fish casserole for my first meal on the Trail. I filled my two-gallon water bag from the nearby spring, hung it from a nail on the side of the shelter, measured out about two cups of water in my cook pot and started to work. It turned out to be a Class I meal, not only because it was delicious, but mostly because I was ravenous, and anything would have tasted great!

After supper, I opened my spiral notepad and began to record the day's events. I was determined, for once in my life, to keep a journal of my experiences. How I wished I had done that during the times I had been in Vietnam and later in Mainz. How much easier it would have been to identify exactly when it was that I first entertained the thought of walking the Appalachian Trail. As nearly as I could recollect, it was in early 1985 during a discussion with my boss, Brigadier General Glynn Mallory.

Mallory and I were talking about my impending retirement, and I said something about taking some time off to get away from it all — like walking the Appalachian Trail. I vaguely remember being intrigued by the idea, thinking it might be a "fun thing" to do, something to run up my mental flagpole to see if it would stay or come back down after my unconscious had sufficiently mulled it over. Gradually, the idea of walking the AT became an attractive option.

After convincing myself that hiking the AT would assist in my transition from the army to civilian life, I ordered a complete set of *Trail Guides* and maps from the Appalachian Trail Conference (ATC) in addition to a couple of books written by people who had walked the Trail. The more I read, the more excited I became. I began to look forward to the end of the day when I could curl up in a chair with a glass of beer and read and dream about camping on the Trail, imagining what it would be like in the shelters and in the mountains, cooking my meals over a wood fire. It was during those evenings that the real decision to walk the Trail was made. The romance had captured me. I had to do the Trail.

It was almost dark when I finished my journal notes, and the bugs were becoming a nuisance, particularly the mosquitos. I stumbled stiffly down to the spring and cleaned my cook pot and spoon, being careful to do it away from the spring so as not to contaminate the water. This practice should always be followed by hikers and campers, but, unfortunately, because of ignorance or fatigue, it is often ignored.

After washing, I drank a long draught of what tasted like the coldest, purest, sweetest water in the world, just like I imagined the water from a mountaintop spring would taste. As the evening shadows deepened, the forest began to hum with life. I sat silently breathing in the lung-cleansing freshness of the forest air and reveled in my closeness to nature. I listened with heightened awareness to the sounds emanating around me. But even as I did, my head began to droop. I crawled into my sleeping bag, and in no time I was overwhelmed by sleep.

REFLECTIONS ON SPRINGER MOUNTAIN

If viewed from on a ridge
These mountains show their friendly side.
Smooth topped and hazy soft,
The ranks of purple knolls
Fold into the distance
Like blankets mussed upon a bed.
At end a final silhouette where sky begins
Excites the wanderlust.
Here is where it all begins!
Beyond is where it ends!
Two thousand miles of silhouettes
And ranks of purple knolls
To carry me along.

If viewed from in a valley draw,
These mountains show a hostile side.
A savage growth of vines
And brush that weaves a tangled scape.
It blots out even sky.
A valley floor of tortured rock,
And awesome walls of mountainside
Suggest some questions to an anxious mind.
Here is where it all begins!
Beyond is where it ends!
Two thousand miles of mountainsides
Of growth and tortured rock
To harry me along.

The difference lies in where one stands
And also in resolve.
The need for courage has no doubt.
It's only more intense below.
Do I dare? Do I have the will?
Those are the thoughts
When facing up the first
Of two thousand miles of hill.

CHAPTER 2

Springer Mountain to Neels Gap
Getting Started

I awoke a short time later, drenched in sweat, a sharp, stabbing pain in my back from lying on the hard shelter floor. I relieved the back pain by rolling on my right side, and to escape the heat I lay outside the bag. (The synthetic fiber bag, manufactured by THE NORTH FACE company, was rated to 40 degrees Fahrenheit, much too warm for temperatures in the 70s.) After a few minutes, I became too cold and climbed back inside. I spent the remainder of the night trying to find a comfortable temperature by getting in or out of the sleeping bag, sometimes lying on top of the bag, sometimes lying directly on the ensolite pad with the sleeping bag draped over me like a blanket. That didn't work very well either, because it was a mummy-type bag, so narrow at the bottom that my feet became exposed whenever I turned on my side.

The ensolite pad, although good for insulation, lacked the cushioning property of even the firmest of mattresses; and if I remained in one position too long, the part of my body in contact with the pad ached so severely that I was awakened. Because I moved so often for relief, I became entangled in the sleeping bag fabric or threw it off entirely. Several times I awoke to find I had rolled completely off the ensolite pad and was lying directly on the floor.

Although the heat in the sleeping bag and the hard sleeping surface made sleep difficult, the racket made by the shelter mice made it nigh impossible. The first night in a new environment always has the potential for sleeplessness; the ear is sensitive to strange noises; and mine was an echo chamber that reverberated with each sound made by the mice.

The mice scampered all over the shelter, across the beams, up the walls, and on the roof. I could hear them scurrying across my pack, and in and out of my boots. They were incredibly loud, and I had visions of groundhog-size mice tearing at my equipment as they searched for food. Twice, I turned on my flashlight to see what damage was being done to my gear. But when I did, the night became perfectly still. Satisfied that my pack was still intact and my socks had not been dragged off for mouse mattresses, I turned the light off and laid my head back down again. The noise immediately resumed. I never saw one of the little rascals.

When I awoke to a murky dawn, I hurt all over, but particularly in my hips and shoulders. Muscle strain from the previous day was the obvious culprit, but I also hurt in places from the agonies suffered during the night as well. My senses were numb, and I felt listless and washed-out. I sat up and looked out into the clearing. The shapes of trees on the far side of the clearing were barely discernible. I fumbled for my flashlight and checked my watch, thinking it was about 5:00 a.m. It was 7:30 a.m. Where's the sun? I wondered. When I looked out again, I saw that Springer Mountain was enveloped in a dense mist.

I noticed then the sound of water drops falling from the foliage, making a distinctive splatter when they hit the ground. The mist had become so heavy that rivulets trickled down the side of the shelter's framework, forming suspended beads of water that built in size until their weight broke the binding tension, and they dropped onto the sleeping platform below. Minute drops of water covered my cushion-soled socks, creating the appearance of fine gauze, and the shirt and trousers I had hung from the main roof beam the night before felt like clothes removed from the spin cycle of a washing machine. Even the outside of my sleeping bag was coated with moisture. It didn't exactly correspond to the type of day I had envisioned in my reveries as the first day of my adventure. Missing was the deep blue sky, bright sunshine and crisp green forest filled with the songs of birds.

It was a shocking return to reality when I exchanged the comforting warmth of my sleeping bag for the chilling wetness of my clothes. It took about 30 minutes to eat breakfast, pack my gear and get ready to leave. When I heaved my pack onto my back, my shoulders rebelled. The pack straps pressed brutally against muscles not yet recovered from the previous day's punishment, and I winced with pain. I questioned the wisdom of my decision to hike the Trail, but even as I did, I knew I would have to walk out to the next road in any case, and that I might just as well get started. After a few steps up the hill, the pain subsided to a low-level discomfort, and I mumbled a silent thanks.

The Trail from Springer Mountain down to Stover Creek was not steep. There were few rocks, and the ground was soft and easy on the legs. After a short while, I became involved in the rhythm of the hike. The mist had the effect of turning my focus inward like it was compressing reality to fit within the limits defined by my feeling. I was sore and tired, the weather was miserable, and I reflected the conditions in my mood. I wondered how I would feel if I were to come off the Trail, to admit defeat. I had invested a considerable amount of time and money, not to mention self-respect, into my adventure. I became irritated with myself for even entertaining the idea. After less than an hour on the Trail, I was already considering failure. I pushed the thought out of my mind. I would not quit.

Now I became so absorbed with the implications of my journey that I paid little attention to my surroundings until movement on the Trail about 15 feet in front of me caught my eye. A large hen turkey destroyed the morning calm and my composure with a startling explosion of feathers. I watched, stunned, as the bird flew to the low branch of a tree about 20 yards to my right front. Then, before I could completely recover, a series of smaller explosions sent her brood of young turkeys scattering in blurs of feathers off the Trail in all directions.

Although I had been looking directly at them, the turkeys were so superbly camouflaged that I had not really seen them, and only their movement gave them away. The sudden release of adrenalin precipitated by the turkey sent my heart rate soaring, and I stopped for a second to let it return to normal. When I continued, the mother hen flew across the open forest in front of me, turned a long arc, and landed in a tree about 30 yards to my rear. From her perch, she commenced calling her flock.

Later, I thought how fortunate I had been to have seen those elusive birds so close. Had it not been for the poor visibility from the mist and the dampness of the path, they would have detected me long before I saw them and the opportunity would never have occurred. Stop complaining about the weather, I thought. Lesson number one: *There is opportunity in everything — we only have to understand or find it.*

It took about an hour for the sun to break through the mist.

It revived my flagging spirits. Despite the numbing fatigue and pain in my shoulders and hips, I began to enjoy my hike. A sense of confidence developed; I became less introspective, less concerned with my anxieties and pain. I began to look about me, to see the colors of the forest, and the birds and animals. In so doing, I became increasingly absorbed in the forest's beauty.

The spectacular colors of the wildflowers surprised me. One species, a fire-engine-red flower about an inch and a half in diameter with notches at the end of each of its five slender petals, grew in small clusters throughout the woods and provided brilliant contrasts to the dark greens, browns, and blacks of the forest floor. I later learned these were fire pinks.

The thought that I should carry a wildflower book never occurred during my preparations for the hike. Later, when it did occur, I hesitated to buy one; I didn't want to carry the extra weight. But I was remarkably successful committing to memory the colors and shapes of various flowers, so that when I had an opportunity later to look at wildflower books I was able to identify most of the flowers I had seen.

The fire pinks were certainly beautiful, but the flame azaleas were spectacular. They seemed to spring out of nowhere, blazing islands of fiery orange amid a sea of deep forest green. It was obvious where the name came from. They grew as bushes or small trees; although the majority of them were deep orange with a hint of red, they covered a spectrum of shades from subtle pale orange to almost blood red.

I also enjoyed the profusion of mountain laurel dotting the mountainsides. Its blossoms grew in clusters of tiny, cup-like, white flowers, each with ten bright red anthers, providing a contrast to the pattern of the white petals. At the center where the petals came together, a small segment of red added to the flower color. As a result, the mountain laurel often displayed varying shades of pink, depending on the size of the red anthers and segments.

At the end of the second hour, I took a ten-minute break. The sense of relief I felt when I removed my pack could be compared with gratification of the highest of sensual pleasures. It felt that good!

While admiring a nearby flame azalea, I reflected on the variety of color in the forest and congratulated myself on my great timing; I had arrived in the mountains when the late spring flowers and blossoms were at their peak. Then I realized that if the timing had gone as I originally planned in March, I would have been on the Trail by the end of April and probably would have missed the floral fire works.

I recalled my first preparations and how anxious I had been to get a taste of the Trail before I actually started my hike. I took the opportunity, while visiting family and friends in Northern Virginia, to talk with people about hiking and to visit various places along the Trail to see what it would be like. I stopped first at the Appalachian Outfitters, an outdoors sports store, in Oakton, Virginia, where I was assisted by Carl Friberg, a former Thru-Hiker. I must have asked him a thousand questions.

Carl suggested I buy a two-gallon collapsible water bag for use in camp. It weighed practically nothing, and I could fill the bag with enough water for all my requirements for the evening and still have enough left for breakfast and to fill my canteens the next day. That meant I had to make only one trip to the spring or other water source for the camp.

Many springs or streams were as much as half a mile from the shelters and some were hundreds of yards down the mountainsides which made getting water a major undertaking. When I arrived at a shelter after a strenuous day, the last thing I wanted was to make a 500-yard mini-hike down a steep mountainside and back up again just for water, and I certainly didn't want to be repeating the process during the night or in the morning. Once was enough!

He also advised me to take it easy in the beginning, until I had built up my stamina, and suggested I increase the mileage commensurately with my strength. He recommended I carry a pack cover which I later learned was an absolute must for keeping my pack dry in rainy weather. I also bought a lightweight flashlight and a lightweight aluminum Sigg fuel bottle in which to carry fuel for my stove. The Sigg bottle was particularly advantageous since it later served without modification as the fuel tank for my Whisper-lite camp stove. The Whisper-lite pump attachment simply screwed into the top of the Sigg bottle and was attached to the stove by a short rubber tube which conducted the fuel directly from the bottle to the stove. (In effect, the aluminum bottle became the tank.)

On the way from Washington to my family home in Berryville, Virginia, I stopped at Snickers Gap in the Blue Ridge where the Trail crossed Virginia Route 7. I climbed the pathway a short distance south towards Bears Den Rocks to get a feel for the Trail and learned that after 15 minutes climbing I was exhausted. I vowed to start a vigorous conditioning program when I returned to Naples. I also visited Paris, Virginia, where the Trail intersected U.S. Route 50, then traveled the Skyline Drive through the Shenandoah National Park, stopping occasionally to check it along the way.

In Georgia, I stopped at the Walasi-yi Center, a small rustic grouping of fieldstone and timber buildings in Neels Gap where the AT crossed U.S. Routes 19 and 129, about 30 miles north from where I now sat. (Walasi-yi is a Cherokee Indian word meaning "where the frog god lives.") The AT dropped precipitously down a narrow dirt path from Blood Mountain, crossed the highway, then followed a flagstone path which led directly to a stone archway that connected the family living quarters with the business premises. After passing the buildings, the Trail climbed out of the Gap towards Turkeypen Mountain.

From the steps of the building that day, I had watched a solitary hiker making his way slowly down the path from Blood Mountain. His pack was enormous with a sleeping bag and a canvas tarpaulin of some sort rolled up on top; in the back, tied to the pack, was a nearly full gallon can of Coleman fuel. Clearly, the man was tired. When he arrived, I asked how much his pack weighed. He told me he didn't know. I suspected he knew, but was too embarrassed to say. I tried to help him remove it, but it was too heavy for me to hold up with only arm strength, and it slid clumsily away before I could get a firm grip on it.

He had started from Amicalola Park five days earlier and was planning to hike to Damascus, Virginia. I had my doubts that he would make it to Damascus though; he said it in such a way that it seemed improbable that he would make it. With such a heavy pack, I was surprised that he had even reached Springer Mountain. I had read that the climb from Amicalola State Park to Springer Mountain was so difficult that many would-be Thru-Hikers, despite devoting months of preparation and hundreds of dollars to equipment became so disillusioned by the difficulty of the climb, they quit before ever reaching the start point.

Nonetheless, the man's jogging shoes excited my curiosity. Everything I had read indicated it was important to wear sturdy boots to provide as much support as possible. Jogging shoes didn't seem to fill that requirement, and I was eager to learn why he had chosen them.

"You can feel the trail with them," he said suddenly revived and enthusiastic. "Hiking boots don't let you get a feel of the trail. These let you feel the trail."

Jeff Hansen, the concessionaire at the center, said he preferred the traditional hiking boot for support. "But it's up to each hiker. Dorothy hiked in her bare feet sometimes," he said, shaking his head in wonderment. "She normally wore jogging shoes, though. She went through five pairs of 'em." He referred to his wife Dorothy's thru-hike of the Trail.

I smiled at the memory; a look at my watch told me that I had already extended my break by 15 minutes. I rose to resume my hike.

My legs felt leaden as I started the easy climb over Rich Mountain. The pain which had subsided when I removed the pack resumed with increased intensity. As I picked my way down the other side, I slipped while stepping off a rock and nearly fell. The incident impressed on me the need for a hiking stick, and I began searching the forest floor along the Trail for a likely branch or small tree. Eventually, I spied a ten-foot-long uprooted hickory sapling that I could envision as a hiking staff. I cut off part of the top and the roots. When I finished, I had a sturdy six-foot hiking stick. That tough, old piece of wood became a treasured possession.

The Trail followed Stover Creek through a magnificent stand of virgin hemlocks that towered like guardians of the forest over the younger hemlocks and other trees. Some of them had to be at least 300 or more years old. After gliding serenely past the relatively level stand of hemlocks, the creek crashed wildly down a steep, narrow, boulder-strewn gorge that cut through an impenetrable tangle of mountain laurel, then eddied in quiet pools as if rebuilding strength for the next run of boulders.

The Trail continued along an old logging road cut into the ridge above the creek until it reached a fairly level draw where it joined another abandoned logging road. The road junction, now smoothed by a carpet of thin grass and framed by trees and other vegetation, had been transformed over the years into a small, friendly wooded meadow. The Trail turned abruptly to the right and crossed a low, sturdy wooden beam and plank bridge which spanned the now gently flowing Stover Creek. Later the Trail crossed Chester Creek by Three Forks on another larger, sturdier wooden bridge.

Again, the scene was one of tranquillity, of sunlight reflecting from leaves heaving gently in the wind, while patches of

Wooden beam and plank bridge over Stover Creek.

shadow and sunlight swayed in unison on the forest floor. The creek sparkled with rare intensity as it glided gently in and out of the sunlight on its silent passage through the forest.

Perhaps the most beautiful spot of the whole day was Long Creek Falls. They were not high as falls go, maybe only 15 feet. But the water flowed smoothly over its rim, then tumbled down the jagged rock layers to land with a surprisingly loud splash in a large pool which reflected the pale bronze of morning sunlight. Although shallow and rocky, the pool provided ample room for floating and bathing. Since I was alone, I thought about stripping and skinny dipping. Unfortunately, I had left my pack back on the Trail about 100 yards, and I wasn't yet so confident that I wanted to tempt fate. I hurried away before the temptation of the pool became too great.

As the day progressed, the temperature rose and my pack became extremely uncomfortable. Even shifting the pack straps and the weight provided scant relief. By 1:00 p.m. when I arrived at the Hawk Mountain shelter, my shoulders felt as though they had been rubbed raw, and my feet ached. Recalling Carl Friberg's advice, I decided to stop for the day. I had hiked only

Long Creek Falls

seven and a half miles. But with my pack weight, fatigue and relative lack of stamina, the situation called for discretion.

It wasn't that I was unprepared for the physical rigors of the Trail. The difference was, I was now taxing my body beyond "conventional" limits. I was flat abusing it. I recognized the wisdom in Carl Friberg's advice and devised the simple plan to "do what my body would allow me." I would start off with five-to-ten-mile days, and as I increased in strength and stamina, I planned to increase the distance, depending on the difficulty of the terrain. I had learned another lesson from the mountains. Although I was in very good cardiovascular condition, nothing, but nothing, prepares one to hike long distances in the mountains, other than hiking long distances in the mountains.

Down the gently sloping ridge about 30 yards away from the shelter in open forest was an ideal tent site with level ground. A nearby fire pit was surrounded by three logs. I decided to erect my tent there and spend the night in it rather than in the shelter.

Although insects had not been a big problem the previous night, I wanted to take no chances. I also wanted to get away from the mice, and the mosquito net liner of the tent provided ideal protection against all the critters.

The tent was easily erected. Two Fiberglas rods, formed from a series of two-foot-long Fiberglas segments strung together by elastic cord, held the tent up; the floor was anchored to the ground by aluminum stakes.

I laid out my sleeping gear, then returned to the shelter to make something to eat. Because I had not eaten lunch, I made a combination lunch/supper meal. I dumped a full soup mix packet into half a pot of water along with lots of onions, garlic and salami. Soon the stove was going, and the aroma of bubbling food filled the air.

While the food was cooking, a group of three boys, 12 or 13 years old, arrived at the shelter. They were the fast hikers from a group of five Boy Scouts and a woman hiker from Tifton, Georgia, under the direction of Mr. Zorn, the Scout Master. They asked several questions about why I was hiking the Trail alone and how far I planned to go. When I answered, "Maine," one of them snorted that he only wanted to go home. "Where you all coming from?" I asked.

"Woody Gap," replied the biggest of the boys.

"We're headed for Amicalola day after tomorrow," chimed in another boy.

"You gonna spend the night here?" I asked.

"Nah, we're goin' up on Hawk Mountain," said the smallest one, who appeared to be the group leader.

"How far's that?" I asked.

He pointed up the side of the mountain. "'Bout a mile."

"Here come the slow pokes," said the biggest boy.

Two more boys came around the corner of the shelter and plopped their packs on the ground and themselves on the shelter floor.

"What took you so long?" said the smallest boy to the new arrivals.

The freckled-faced, strawberry blond with a pug nose slumped a little more. "Waitin' fer old man Zorn. What's the rush? We ain't goin' nowhere's 'til we git back."

"Man, I'm starved," one of them now said. "That sure smells good." He nodded to my dinner. "What you cookin'?"

"Salami and onions."

"Don't sound like much, but it sure smells good." He was about to say something else when someone said, "Shh, I hear somethin'."

Tent erected near Hawk Mountain shelter.

"It's Old Zorn. Don't get so antsy."

Mr. Zorn was a large man with a bandanna folded and tied around his head in a sweat band. It was difficult to tell which was redder, his face or the bandanna. He was sweating profusely, and when he arrived, he took off the bandanna and used it to mop the sweat from his face and arms. He was followed by a younger, well-proportioned woman who also was perspiring heavily. Mr. Zorn waited until he had regained his breath, then asked what I was doing, where I was going, and why I had stopped. I repeated what I had told the boys. "You're smart!" he said, wiping his brow again.

I didn't understand his comment and looked questioningly at him.

"I mean you're smart to be takin' it slow. Too many folks try to start too fast and end up with physical problems. Take your time and go slow, just like you're doin'." He looked at my pack. "How do you like the internal frame pack? Ain't it a little hot?"

"It's not bad," I replied. "'Course I haven't had much opportunity to test it."

"I've heard they can get awfully hot." He pointed to his pack at the place where the pack was attached to the aluminum frame. "See how this is open here? This lets the air get in and keeps you cool. If your pack starts to get too hot, you might want to think about getting an external frame."

"Talk about hot," I said, "It sure got hot in a hurry today. Good thing it was an easy Trail down from Springer."

"You sure had some beautiful scenery on your hike today. You go swimmin' at the falls?" Mr. Zorn's eyes lit up when he mentioned the falls. "When I get to the falls tomorrow, I'm gonna be peeling clothes for the last half mile. Hope I don't offend no one," he said, glancing provocatively toward the woman hiker. She averted her eyes demurely from his grinning face.

The boys began to fidget, indicating they wanted to be on their way, and Mr. Zorn suggested they get started up the mountain. He invited me to spend the night with them "up in the cool breeze on the mountaintop." I declined the invitation, but did follow them about 200 yards up the mountain to a spring of the "sweetest water around." It flowed from a small pipe sticking out of the earth and trickled down the rocks to start another of the mountain streams that bathed the area. Because of the extended dry spell, the flow was meager, and it took a long time to fill all our canteens.

Back at my camp site, I ate dinner, enjoying every bite. I was tired, but pleasantly content. The weather had been good, and physically I had been holding up well. I had not experienced even the suggestion of a blister on my feet, and aside from my sore shoulders and aching bones, I felt pretty darn good. A glow of satisfaction enveloped me as I reflected on my progress.

I slipped inside my sleeping bag and recorded the day's events in my journal. Impressions of Stover Creek, Long Creek Falls, the flame azaleas and mountain laurel all were documented as were my thoughts of self-analysis and physical condition. When it became too dark in the tent to write, I used my flashlight. After a while, I paused to reflect on the day, listening to the drumming grouse and the occasional hoot of an owl. It was my last conscious act. My notepad and pen were with me inside my sleeping bag when I awoke in the morning.

I had slept well. The tent had proved to be ideal protection from insects and mice, and the earth was softer than the shelter floor. I had none of the aches in my bones which I'd suffered the night before. Without dallying, I got up, ate breakfast, and was on the Trail in 30 minutes. The weather was perfect for hiking —

cool, crisp, not a cloud in the sky. Bright sunshine dappled the forest floor, occasionally bathing a flame azalea which took the sun's color for its own. After about 20 minutes of easy hiking, I arrived at Hightower Gap where two large square trash receptacles with heavy lids sat by the side of a forest service road.

I removed my pack, emptied the contents on the ground, then repacked what I thought were absolutely essential items and discarded what remained in the trash cans. I was ruthless.

I discarded a T-shirt; an old army fatigue shirt; two pairs of black, cushion-sole socks; a large cook pot; a ridiculous water filter that Carl Friberg had sold me while his boss was looking; and a small amount of canned food. I even got rid of some tent pegs. (I cut limb crotches from tree saplings for tent pegs and they worked very well.) After I shouldered my pack, I was tempted to retrieve half the stuff, because it felt as if I had not made a really appreciable difference in the weight.

The Trail was much more difficult than the previous day with two long and at times, extremely steep, climbs up Sassafras and Justus Mountains. They were not high in terms of elevation (3336 feet and 3224 feet respectively), but the Trail was very rough. In places I nearly had to go forward on all fours.

The climbs exhausted me, and it was after lunch when I experienced my first series of irregular heart beats. (I had recently developed a tendency toward atrial fibrillation.) I slowed down and the palpitations subsided.

Although I felt fine physically, the episode affected me mentally. I was experiencing my first really negative feelings about the trip.

I became aware of how insignificant I was in the impersonal pattern of life in the wilderness. In nature, life is impartially transitory and death is never far away. I was a part of that pattern now, reduced to the status of one of its elements. What made me different was that I could leave the pattern. I had the power to choose. It was a gift bestowed on me by virtue of my humanity. I realized in that instant that the choice of leaving or remaining with the Trail was totally in my hands. The more I thought about it, the clearer it became that I would have to maintain a positive attitude toward the hike if I were to remain on the Trail. It would be all too easy to find an excuse to come off the Trail, and unless I developed and maintained a positive outlook, it would soon be over.

I felt totally alone and wanted desperately to talk with someone, to feel kinship with another human being. My thoughts turned to my German girlfriend, Anna. I could see her face in my mind, her short black hair framing a tender smile. I remembered her eyes in particular. Mysterious and beguiling, they seemed to change color with her moods; sometimes they were a deep blue tinged with brown, and at other times they appeared green. And I remembered her strong, athletic legs, with long muscled calves and thighs like those of a runner.

We had talked several times about hiking the Trail together. But she had a job which made going all the way to Maine out of the question. However, we had planned that she would join me wherever I was on the Trail for a couple weeks in August. I wished it were August now. The more I reminisced, the more alone I felt, and, in the end, I was just plain miserable.

Besides being lonely, my back and shoulders seemed to hurt more intensely from the pack. Mr. Zorn was right: the pack was hot! Not only was it hot, it was downright uncomfortable because the bottom end of one side of the metal frame kept slipping out of its leather retaining pocket and digging into the upper part of my left buttock. Further, the pack was too short for my build, and I was forced to carry most of the weight on my shoulders.

The remainder of the afternoon was devoted to fighting depression and trying to establish and maintain a positive outlook. The continual physical and mental effort was draining. When I reached Gooch Gap, where I planned to spend the night, I was exhausted. After supper, I literally collapsed inside my sleeping bag.

The next morning I left the shelter at 7:30 a.m., which I decided would become the standard time to begin the day's hike. I had slept well and felt refreshed. I looked forward to a new day and new adventures. Soon after starting, I saw a magnificent scarlet tanager sitting in a tree just off the path. Later I stopped to watch several frolicking squirrels romp through the leaves on the forest floor. The woods seemed alive with wildlife, birds and chipmunks chirping and chattering everywhere.

All was not idyllic, however. A group of young people hiking ahead of me spent much of the morning shouting to one another. They interrupted the natural order of life in the forest. They also caught and killed a small timber rattler. The snake was draped over a tree stump beside the Trail, the blood still oozing from its wounds when I arrived. I had expected to see a giant snake from the description given me by a boy hiking in the other direction with his family. Not so!

At Woody Gap, I stopped to fill my canteens from a fast flowing spring located about 200 yards up a side trail from the picnic area. As I rested on a large rock at the edge of the clearing, a woman who had been admiring the scenery came up to me. "What are you carrying in your pack?" she asked.

"Feels like everything I own," I replied sarcastically. That was a stupid response, I thought. I answered her question directly: "Actually, sleeping gear, food, change of clothes and a tent."

"Where are you coming from?"

I glanced up at her and it registered through my fatigue that she was an attractive woman. She looked directly into my eyes when she spoke, her face smiling softly which made her even prettier. "I started at Springer Mountain, south of here. I'm walking the Appalachian Trail," I offered.

"Oh! I know where that is. Springer Mountain, I mean. How far are you hiking?"

"Depending on my luck, the weather and the Trail conditions, I hope to go all the way. To Maine."

Her blue eyes grew wide. "You really plan to go all the way? I think that's wonderful." Up 'til then she talked with curiosity. But when she learned I planned to thru-hike the Trail, she bubbled with excitement. "That's really marvelous. When do you plan to get there?"

"That's a good question. I'd like to make it by the end of September or the first part of October. It all depends on how much distance I can average in a day. If it gets too late in the season, I may have to come off the Trail and finish it next year."

"I'd really like to know how you are doing. My name is Sally Prestgard."

We shook hands, after which I took a business card from my wallet and handed it to her.

"Please write and tell me how you are doing. I'd love to know about some of the experiences you have," she said as she jotted her home address on the back of her business card before handing it to me.

"Do you come here often?" I asked.

"Whenever I can. I love these mountains. I'm from Michigan and I've just moved to Atlanta. Every chance I get I come to the mountains. I really envy what you're doing. I hope you'll write and tell me about your hike. It would be a vicarious experience for me."

I looked at my pack. I needed to get on with my hike. She nodded, understanding. "I'll stay in touch," I promised.

"Please do! And good luck!"

The Trail north of Woody Gap was fairly easy except for one tough climb up Big Cedar Mountain. Especially beautiful was Blood Mountain where the Trail wove through magnificent groves of mountain laurel bursting with blossoms. Interspersed among the mountain laurel were generous stands of flame azaleas and rhododendrons also in full display. In some places the Trail had been cut directly through the groves in such a way that the mountain laurel grew across the pathway at a height higher than a man's head, and I had the feeling I was walking through a tunnel of flowers. It was the most lavish display of color I had ever witnessed in the wild. Not only were the colors breathtaking, the Trail was sited so that it contoured the mountain and the climbing was not difficult. It really was conducive to stopping "to smell the flowers."

Blood Mountain is the highest mountain on the AT in Georgia, and being close to parking at the Walasi-yi Center made it a popular spot for day-hikers. I arrived on the summit to find a large number of people, several of whom found it necessary to shout to see if their voices would echo from the heights. The noise destroyed the peace and serenity and detracted from the personal closeness to nature one experiences when absorbed by natural beauty. It was really unfortunate, because the view, a magnificent panorama of mountains, forming a backdrop against which was set a massive display of purple, red and pink blossoms, was breathtaking.

Indian lore has it that Blood Mountain received its name from a great battle fought between tribes. It is said that the battle was so fierce that the whole mountain flowed with blood. Large numbers of spear and arrow points and other artifacts found there have undoubtedly added substance to the legend.

The shelter, an aging fieldstone house, sitting directly on the summit, contained a wooden floor with a sleeping platform and stone fireplace to comfort those driven to its protection by the skin-lashing rains which surely occurred during all times of the year. I thought briefly about setting up camp, but the number of day-hikers was discouraging. Then I thought about Neels Gap two and one half miles away, all down hill. I could easily make it in an hour, and there was a good possibility I could take a shower and sleep in a real bed between sheets. On the other hand, I was already tired from having hiked 13 miles. Another two and a half miles with a 45-pound pack was still something to be reckoned with. The decision was not difficult. After resting a few minutes at the summit and inhaling as much of the grandeur as I possibly could, I headed down the steep incline, hoping against hope that Jeff Hansen would have accommodations for the night.

LONG CREEK FALLS

No world class cataract
With thousands of gallons
Of water per minute
As in Niagara.
This is a fun waterfall.
The kind with a pool
At its base where kids can play.
Were one can strip
And keep an anxious eye
Hoping no one comes.
Where water drains the heat
And the aches from the muscles.
Small fish nibble at your toes.
You can shower under the falls;
The water stinging and chilling
Your head and shoulders.
Only the curious bird or squirrel
Can watch a man replay his fantasies,
Splashing with the abandon
Of a boy at the old swimmin' hole.

CHAPTER 3

Reflections On The Way To Montray

I was not disappointed. Jeff informed me that the hostel at the center was still not operational, but that I could almost certainly find a bed at one of the cabins down the road toward the east. I became conscious of feeling somewhat rubbery-legged as we talked; I wondered if I looked as tired as the hiker with the too-heavy pack in April. Evidently, I did. When the conversation ended, Grandpa Hansen immediately offered to drive me down to the cabin complex. Gratefully, I heaved my pack into the back of his pickup and climbed into the cab.

The road out of the gap was a series of hairpin turns. Although the cabins were not more than 300 yards away as the crow flies, they were probably double that by road. I also noted that there was very little room beside the road where a pedestrian could safely walk and that made me doubly appreciate Mr. Hansen's offer.

We stopped in front of a rustic wooden building that lay slightly downhill from a dirt parking area. The drive continued down a slight incline to a lower level, gravel parking lot, then turned to the left where it made a long loop through the forest past several widely-spaced wooden cabins nestled in a small mountain sag.

A young woman in her early 20's was skipping rope in the gravel parking lot in front of the porch, and Mr. Hansen pointed to her as I prepared to get out. "She's something, that one," he said. "Runs up Blood Mountain every morning, then lifts weights for an hour and skips rope for an hour."

I walked down the driveway, my eyes riveted on the young woman. She skipped effortlessly, her dark blond hair and breasts bouncing in rhythm to the cadence of her exercise. Her movements flowed with feminine ease, but there was also a firmness that hinted of power inside the fluid motion. She was intent on her exercise and did not see me initially, but when she did, she stopped skipping and walked towards me. I introduced myself and told her I wanted a cabin for the night.

"We generally put hikers up in the first house on the left up that road," she said, pointing to where the driveway disappeared into the forest. "It's $15 a night, and you might have company if any more hikers show up."

I nodded my head in agreement, then asked about her conditioning routine. "Mr. Hansen tells me you follow an ambitious exercise program," I said. "You look to be in great shape." Her eyes widened ever so slightly and her lips pursed. "I mean you look to be in great condition." Another Freudian slip, I thought to myself.

Her expression softened. "I try to stay in shape," she said with a smile.

"Are you training for athletic competition?"

"No. I just work out because I like to," she said somewhat self-consciously.

"You ever think of entering athletic competition? With your strength and conditioning you could probably do well in many sports."

"I thought about skiing, but I injured my knee a couple of years ago, and I don't think it would hold up under competitive conditions."

"If you couldn't handle skiing, how about running? Mr. Hansen tells me you run up Blood Mountain every morning."

"I don't run up the mountain," she explained, "just walk up at a fast pace. It isn't really for conditioning that I climb the mountains. I love these mountains and I just want to be in them, be a part of them. I think I could spend my whole life in them."

"Have you done any hiking?"

"Not too much. I hiked from Springer Mountain to here last week," she told me.

"How long did it take?"

She hesitated for a split second. "I don't want you to get the idea that I'm boasting or trying to make anyone feel bad." She looked down as she continued softly, "I did it in one day."

My jaw dropped!

"I climbed from Amicalola to Springer in the afternoon," she continued quickly, "spent the night in the shelter on

Springer, then hiked here the next day. I didn't carry much weight, though, only a little food and a sleeping bag."

I murmured something about her stamina and courage to hike the stretch alone. She had had to negotiate Sassafras, Justus, and Big Cedar Mountains plus a host of smaller climbs all in one day. It had just taken me three days, and I was not in bad shape. Of course, I was carrying a lot more weight than she had. Nevertheless, it was over 30 miles, and that was no small accomplishment for anybody. I was sure I could not have done the whole thing in one stretch, even without a pack!

It became awkwardly quiet as the impact of what she had told me began to take hold.

"Come on, I'll get you signed in," she said, turning toward the house.

I followed her mechanically to the stairs leading to the "lobby." It was not until she had almost reached the top step that I became aware of the effortless motion that carried her up. It was fluid movement, her skin undulating across the muscles of her legs with liquid precision. It was graceful, but also powerful, and I understood then how she was able to hike 30 miles in one day.

Inside, she pointed silently toward a frail, wizened woman hunched over an old wooden desk, a cigarette in her mouth, and a skeleton-like hand wrapped in skin resting lightly on a pack of cigarettes and a lighter. The woman looked up briefly as I approached, then convulsed into a fit of coughing that ended in a rale which left her gasping for air and holding on to the desk for support. When she recovered, she slid a pen and registration card across the desk, indicating that I should complete the top part.

I filled in the information requested, then slid the card back across the desk.

She tried to fill out her part but had difficulty controlling the pen. After silently expressing a sense of frustration, she turned slightly, and a woman companion, hovering anxiously behind her, gently took the pen and completed the procedure.

I watched the proceedings with discomfort. It was clear the older woman was in poor health. Her face wore a yellow pallor, and each breath was labored. Her body was corrupted and death was visibly present. I looked at her, then back to the young woman, trying to establish a familial relationship, but I could discern none. The young woman kept her distance, like she was afraid to get too close. The contrast in the stages of life was profound. I wondered if the older woman had, at the golden time in her life, also possessed a healthy body, glowing with strength and promise. I was intrigued by the young woman's actions and wondered if unconsciously she was trying to distance herself from death, or merely from the older woman's afflictions. Later I learned that the older woman was Dorothy Hansen's mother, and when I returned a year later she had passed away.

I reflected on the encounter as I walked to my cabin. Death was clearly present and everyone felt it; and everyone was uncomfortable with it — everyone, that is, except the one most affected. She appeared to be the least disturbed, as if she accepted the fact that her battle had been fought and lost. In a way, the older woman assumed a heroic image because of her seeming lack of fear while the rest of us were intimidated by the aspect of approaching death. I was in a somber mood when I reached my cabin.

Actually, the cabin was a rustic vacation house with a kitchen, bedroom, sleeping loft, and a living room with a fireplace. It also boasted a large bathroom with shower. By my recent standards, it was palatial.

Before doing anything else, I unpacked my toilet articles and headed for the shower. It took three applications of soap to remove the three-day accumulation of dirt, sweat, and grime. After washing, I remained for another five minutes, allowing the hot water to massage my back and shoulders as it carried away the pain and irritation from my bruised and aching muscles. It was a luxurious feeling that wiped the tensions and stress from my mind as well as my body.

All was not happiness and tranquillity, however. My feet had begun to hurt from the steady, day-long pounding and more importantly from the blisters that had developed on my heels. The leather inside my boots was disintegrating from the moisture and formed little balls which rubbed the skin on my heels with each step. Using the scissors of my Swiss Army knife, I removed the little rolls and applied a smooth adhesive material to the leather. The repair job was reasonably successful, reasonable, that is, until the next day when the moisture and friction combined to roll the adhesive material into a ball. Then, it was worse than the disintegrating leather. I finally removed the adhesive and just suffered. But this wasn't the only problem with my feet.

My right boot had rubbed the top of my toes raw at the point where it creased between the toe and the rest of the boot. I tried to fix this problem by treating the leather with a generous application of saddle soap I had borrowed from Jeff. It worked well for a couple of days, but eventually, after becoming wet several times, the leather stiffened up again, and I could only protect my toes by placing a strip of gauze and adhesive tape across the tops of my feet at the point where the boot rubbed.

Actually, my feet were holding up quite well, considering they were constantly wet — so wet, in fact, that I could actually wring the sweat from my socks at the end of the day. Since the shelters provided only partial protection from the damp night air, my clothes never dried completely. In the mornings, I dressed in damp clothes and damp boots which became even wetter from perspiration as the day progressed. As a result, my skin became soft and susceptible to blistering.

The next morning I headed up the hill toward the Walasi-yi Center. To save time and avoid the dangerously narrow road, I took a shortcut through the forest. I was surprised at the ease with which I made the climb from the cabin to the gap. I was getting in shape!

I intended to eat breakfast at the center, but the fare was limited. I settled for two large bran muffins and a styrofoam cup of basically bad coffee, which I drank while browsing through the store.

Jeff had an excellent inventory of camping equipment, including several types and makes of packs and pack accessories, survival items, trail food, clothing and comfort items. I experimented with several packs to get a feel of how they fit my build before settling on a Kelty external frame pack which felt noticeably better than the others. I borrowed it so I could pack it with my gear to see if it was large enough and to check how it felt with a load.

The important thing about selecting a pack is to be sure it is long or short enough so the weight is evenly distributed on the wearer's hips and not exclusively on the shoulders. The shoulder straps keep the pack balanced by the shoulders but allow the center of gravity to remain at hip level. In that respect, the Kelty was far superior to my other pack, and I bought it.

I also bought a pair of quick release pack straps and a lightweight one-and-a-half quart plastic water bottle. This bottle would carry half again as much water as my Army canteen. I used the pack straps to secure my tent and ensolite pad to the bottom of my pack and with the quick release feature, I could remove those items without having to go through a major buckling\unbuckling process every time I wanted to remove or add them to my pack. I had only to loosen the straps and slip the tent and pad out or slip them through the loop and cinch the straps to attach them to my pack.

My boot soles had started to separate at the toe. Jeff loaned me an electric drill with a small bit and some wire to repair them. I drilled two small holes at the point where the separation was, then passed the wire through the holes of the boot upper and the sole, pulled them together and secured the wire by twisting it. I then covered the whole mess with Shoo Goo, which I also bought from Jeff. It was one repair job that really worked. I never had any trouble with my boot soles again.

Doing laundry proved to be a more difficult chore. I anticipated that a washer and dryer would be available at the cabin or the Walasi-yi Center. Not so. I had to go to Vogel State Park, a recreation area with accommodations, about three miles down the valley to the north. I hitchhiked from the Gap and got a ride almost immediately in the back of a small pickup. The driver was kind enough to drive a half mile out of his way to drop me off at the park concession area. I finished my laundry in about an hour, and wash under arm, headed for Alexander's, a general store some four miles further north off Route 129 on a secondary road.

I started hitchhiking as soon as I left the concession area parking lot and within five minutes was picked up by two boys, probably in their late teens, in a pickup relic that long ago should have found its final resting place. The motor was missing on half the cylinders, and the muffler no longer functioned. Its totally rusted body was held together with pieces of wire, and the floor board in the cab had gaping holes through which the road was clearly visible.

The boys, a pair of young farm lads, looked like prospects from central casting for a movie about north Georgia. They excited my curiosity. I wanted to learn more about them, but the noise was so loud that it was almost impossible to carry on a conversation. I persisted, however. Despite the engine noise, the wind rushing through the vents and windows, and the whine of tires on the road, I learned that they were "ridin' 'roun' cause there warn't nothin' else to do on Sunday." They played the role of knowing mountain men, strong and silent, who answered most of my questions with nods of the head or short responses of a few words. I had the feeling I was in a contest to see how many questions I could ask that they could answer in terms of one syllable or not at all.

The road seemed to wander aimlessly as it curved down the mountain toward the valley, and the driver gave me the opportunity to marvel at his uncanny ability to keep the wreck under control while traveling through the ever tightening curves. Every time the truck leaned on a curve, I held on white-knuckle style to the door handle, hoping we'd make it, hoping that the tires would stay on and that the steering assembly would remain functional. After successfully negotiating a curve, I gave silent thanks and breathed freely until we hit the next curve. Finally we reached Alexander's. I gave the driver five dollars for gas and with considerable relief, thanked them and climbed out.

Alexander's store was, in every sense, a country general store. I could have purchased almost anything ever manufactured — from clothing and shoewear to food and groceries, hardware, building supplies, guns, ammunition and furniture. I selected a shopping cart and started through the grocery section, selecting items from the shelf, checking them off my list as I went.

An elderly gentleman occasionally walked by. When it appeared that I might be stymied, he stopped and asked if I had found everything I needed. I was looking for individual jam and jelly packets of the type found in restaurants and a small bag of sugar. (The smallest they had was a five-pound bag.) I told him what I wanted, and he turned directly away without answering, as though he were going to fetch some for me. After about ten minutes of waiting in vain, I continued on with my shopping. I saw him later in another part of the store, and he came over to me. I expected him to tell me they were out of jam and jelly packets.

"Find ever'thin' yore lookin' fer?" he asked.

I was about to ask about the jam and jelly, but since I was then in the hardware section, I decided to skip it. I nodded my head, and he doddered off.

After returning to my cabin, I spent the remainder of the afternoon experimenting by putting different combinations of items in different pockets of my new pack. (My old pack had no pockets.) I could now separate items that I used on a frequent basis, like the stove and toilet articles, from items, like my sweater, that I needed only occasionally. When I was satisfied with my efforts, I took the old pack and canteen out behind the building and stashed them in the small hollow of a tree stump and covered them with leaves. I intended to return for them after my hike. (I recovered the items still in serviceable condition a year later.)

Next I made myself a sandwich supper with bologna, cheese and hot dogs from Alexander's and thought about what I had accomplished. It had been a long day, but I felt "aces high." My heart was behaving well. My muscles had ceased to ache, and my feet no longer hurt. And I was positively elated with my new pack. I looked forward confidently to the challenges that lay ahead. At about 8:00 p.m., I repacked my pack for the last time and headed for the sleeping loft. It was not late by my normal standards, but normal standards no longer applied. My legs were heavy as I climbed the stairs, and my head no sooner hit the pillow than I was asleep. I must have been more tired than I realized; I slept the whole night through without interruption.

The Trail from Neels Gap to Low Gap the next day was reasonably graded except for one difficult ascent from Tesnatee Gap up Wildcat Mountain. The weather continued to be glorious, just as it had been the whole weekend, and the forest continued to abound with flame azaleas and other wildflowers. Once I encountered a flock of grouse that flew up in pairs or singly as I approached. They were so superbly camouflaged that had they not taken flight, I wouldn't have seen them.

The more I hiked, the more aware I became of my surroundings and the more I was able to see because I anticipated seeing something. I became more attuned to movement and color, and more attuned to walking and looking.

When hiking through rough terrain, a person has to know where to step; the trick is to keep an eye on the path but also to be aware of the forest about him, stopping occasionally to study things of interest. Just such a thing occurred below the summit of Cowrock Mountain where the Trail turned sharply to the left to avoid a large rock outcropping.

As I approached the turn, my eye caught movement on the rock ahead. I froze. A fox, its red and gray coat gleaming in the sunlight, crouched out in the open some 15 feet away, looking in my direction. The fox remained motionless but tense, in a pose that suggested energy at rest like a coiled spring. Then, the fox sniffed the air and shifted its head several times, trying for a better angle of sight through the vegetation. The fox remained exposed on the rock for what seemed to be a long time, then, after looking around as if it were trying to decide how to get down from the ledge, leaped silently down the face of the rock and disappeared into the underbrush below. What a glorious sight!

With a smile on my face, I hiked comfortably for the first time on the Trail. I was pleased with the way I had handled the climbs. I seemed able to move with much less effort, and the constant pain of the previous few days had mostly disappeared. I was sure my new pack made the difference. It was a big improvement over my old one; the weight was much more evenly distributed over my body, and my shoulders were spared the constant effort of carrying the bulk of it. That didn't mean I was completely comfortable, though. My shoulders were still tender enough that, after prolonged periods of wearing the pack, they informed me they were not completely healed from the damage suffered from the first four days. Even so, I felt quite good. As long as I took regular short breaks, the discomfort was minimized. I did learn, however, that I was still carrying too much weight. In the future I vowed to discipline myself and carry only the food required between resupply stops plus one day's extra rations for emergencies.

I traveled 11 miles before reaching Low Gap where I spent the night. It was not a hospitable place. The sagging shelter was in dire need of repair as was the half-rotted, rough board picnic table that stood (barely) about ten feet in front of it. The fire pit was mostly a rubble of rocks covered by ashes and blackened pieces of wood and contained an unsavory collection of discarded food containers, cans and wrappers. A horde of gnats and yellow jackets lured by the remainders of repasts left by careless hikers had established colonies somewhere in the vicinity. They swarmed over the fire pit and the picnic table. They were particularly bothersome while I ate; trying to keep them away from my food proved to be a major challenge. I had to brush them away from just about every spoonful before I put it in my mouth. Even then, I was concerned that one might have escaped notice and ended up in my mouth.

I had a shelter mate, the first on the Trail. Nick Sprague, from the Florida Keys, had passed me early in the afternoon. He was already at the shelter when I arrived. Nick was taking a summer break before returning to finish his senior year at Georgia Tech where he majored in chemistry. He was a very interested and interesting young man with a great memory and a lot of common sense. I liked his positive attitude and enjoyed his company.

Nick had bought a new pair of boots for his hike but had

been unable to break them in before getting on the Trail. As a result, he had developed two angry-looking blisters, one on each heel. They were so bad, in fact, that he was concerned he might have to come off the Trail. At that moment, he had on a pair of jogging shoes which he carried for the purpose of wearing around the camp. I remembered the hiker in April who wore jogging shoes and asked Nick why he just didn't wear the jogging shoes for hiking. He seemed surprised at the suggestion. But after thinking about it for a second, thanked me with the heartfelt sincerity one bestows on lifesavers.

Eventually, the conversation waned. Nick took a book from his pack, and I turned to recording my Trail notes. "I really hated to leave the comfort of the cabin," I wrote. "It was like beginning all over again to go back on the Trail." It was all the more difficult because it would be another seven days before I could shower again and resupply. I was still very much a creature of comfort, I noted.

Although I was very tired tonight, I felt a sense of accomplishment. The encounter with the fox had been a spirit-lifting experience. Up 'til then, the hike had been basically an effort to get over the next hill. Then, for the first time on the Trail, I began thinking about the hike and myself as part of it. Before, the Trail seemed to be an external challenge; now it seemed more like a personal part of me, and I wondered what it really meant to me.

I knew that my intention for coming on the Trail was to help me make the transition from soldier to private citizen and to help me determine what I really wanted to do with my life now that I had the luxury of time to think about it. It was a chance to reassess my values and decide on a new career. That was certainly important, but it seemed I was into something deeper than that.

I'd devoted much of the day to thinking about my adventure and its significance in my life. I wondered if the discomfort and the aggravation of the constant aches and pains, the psychological stress of my solitude, and concern about my heart condition were really worth any benefits I might derive. As of yet, I hadn't seen any benefits other than the beautiful natural surroundings to which I was exposed. That was important, though. I now had the opportunity to experience the wilderness, a vanishing part of America. I could now enjoy some of America's original splendors, in many places, still not too different from what the Indians and the first white men saw when they came to these shores. That was significant. But I had the feeling there was something of even greater significance waiting for discovery.

Perhaps, I thought, the real purpose of my adventure was personal growth. It would certainly be an opportunity to relax and take things as they came and not always be in control.

That could prove to be a major challenge. One doesn't just shed a 30-year habit in a night. One thing was sure; I would have to reorder the priorities that shaped my life. Much of what produced my life-guiding philosophy had now changed, and I needed to respond to that change. The fact that I recognized that imperative was an absolutely essential first step in making my transition.

Clearly, I was at the beginning of a new phase of my life, and one of the requirements for fully participating in that new phase was to let go of the old phase. I had to accept that, no matter how good, bad, rewarding or damaging it had been, that part of my life was over, and I needed to let it go. That could be difficult, because I had become very comfortable with my ways. Change on the order I was contemplating, was frightening. In my case, it could be especially difficult since I had become accustomed to power and authority. I liked being in charge, in control, and I was uncomfortable in situations where I was not in control. Clearly, I was at a point that would require an extensive adjustment in my approach to living. I would have to view events from a different perspective and alter my behavior patterns accordingly. I would have to meet the change head on and deal with it logically and patiently. Perhaps the development of patience was the first order of business. Patience had never been a virtue. In fact, patience was less than a virtue for someone who always demanded results in a hurry. I was still wrestling with these ideas when sleep overwhelmed me.

I started off at 7:30 a.m. again the next morning, about one and half hours before Nick. (Getting on the Trail early provided a greater opportunity to see wildlife.) I hadn't been walking for more than 15 minutes and was concentrating on my personal development when I was startled by a loud commotion in the underbrush about five yards off to the left of the Trail. Suddenly, a grouse popped out of the brush onto the Trail and charged toward me, holding its head sideways with the ground and hissing like a snake. It then retreated a step before resuming its menacing action, still hissing as though it were going to attack. I was dumbfounded.

Author in front of Tray Mountain shelter.

facing up to the changes in my life. My recognition for the need of patience notwithstanding, I had raced through the day. I was pushing too hard; perhaps unconsciously, I was trying to keep up with Nick. It was typical of me to focus on the time element and feel that once I had planned to be in a certain place, I had to be at that place and at the time I planned. This, of course, resulted in unnecessary pressure that caused me to miss much of the enjoyment in my hike. Clearly, I needed to focus on patience, not only with the pace of events, but with myself. I needed to slow down, to stop and "smell the roses." Again, that was easier said than done.

CHAPTER 4

The First Test

In the morning, I headed down the ridge behind the shelter to the spring where a pair of well-worn paths led in the direction I assumed would lead back to the AT. (The access trail to the shelter ran northward for about half a mile at an oblique to the AT, and I thought that by following the trails at the spring, I would reconnect with the AT.)

I selected the ridge line path that appeared most traveled. After a few yards, it evaporated into a tangle of thick growth, and I returned to the spring. I then tried the second path which headed directly downhill. Almost immediately, I found myself bushwhacking through the underbrush.

Disgusted, I thought about continuing down the mountain until I remembered an admonishment in the *Trail Guide* advising hikers to stay on the Trail because of the danger of becoming lost in the wilderness. A cooler head prevailed. I decided to return to the shelter and backtrack to the AT, a wise decision. A closer inspection of the Trail strip map showed that Montray shelter sat on a ridge spur far to the west of the main ridge which the AT followed. I would have had to scramble through several miles of uncleared mountains to reach the AT. Nick had already departed by the time I passed the shelter.

The weather was sunny but cool. The Trail was nicely graded, at least, for the first six miles until Addis Gap; and I made good time. After Addis Gap, it became difficult and the climbs strenuous. The hike across Kelly's Knob took what seemed like an eternity, and I again experienced several irregular heart beats when I tried to go too fast uphill for too long a stretch.

The physical effect of the irregular beats was negligible, but they had a disturbing psychological impact. My anxiety level increased. Still, I pushed on, silently expressing the determination to keep my fears under control.

I had been on the Trail much too long and was exhausted when I arrived at Plum Orchard Gap shelter that evening. Nick, who had arrived three hours earlier, was reading a book when I stumbled into the shelter clearing.

Given the lateness of the hour (8:00 p.m.), he was surprised to see me. I was numb with fatigue and barely responded to his greeting. Since it was so late, I decided to forego my casserole. Instead, I ate a pot of Campbell's Instant Chicken and Rice soup along with lots of saltine crackers. That was a mistake. I had pushed the limits of my physical endurance, traveling 15.2 miles for the day, not counting my ill-considered little excursion out of Montray. I gulped the soup and crackers down in huge swallows, not feeling at all satisfied. But I was too exhausted to cook anything else.

Generally, after supper I wrote Trail notes or puttered around with my gear until dark. This time, however, I climbed directly into my sleeping bag without even bothering to wash my cook pot. As I lay there in the twilight between alertness and sleep, I thought how foolish I had been to have pushed so hard.

I awoke about 4:00 a.m., my heart fibrillating with a vengeance. I bolted into an upright position to reduce the effect of the fibrillation and tried mentally to control the rhythm. But my emotional reaction to the irregular beats compounded the effects of fibrillation. My mind began imagining all sorts of irrational scenarios.

What does one do in the middle of the wilderness with no medical help for miles and a heart beating out of control?

I squirmed in my sleeping bag, concentrating on keep mentally strong. With every movement, the synthetic sleeping bag fabric scraped against the ensolite pad or brushed the floor, disturbing the silent darkness with incredibly loud noise. I wondered if I was disturbing Nick by moving around so much. If I was, he was sure hiding it well. He was breathing softly and regularly.

Now I began to wonder if I would be able to continue the hike in the morning. How can I hike when I can't even sleep? I thought. I also worried that when morning came, Nick would depart and leave me alone. That was an even more frightening possibility, and I tried to develop scenarios in which I could enlist Nick's help. Finally, common sense prevailed.

During other episodes, I had always converted by myself

after five hours. Why should this be any different? I asked myself.
Why should I burden another with something I can conquer!

I prayed for release from my torment and that quieted my
little panic. After a moment, I lay back down with my head resting
on my tent roll and dropped off to sleep. That little respite lasted all
too briefly. As soon as I dozed off, I was again awakened by a jolt of
another strong palpitation. I sat with my back against the shelter
wall until I felt comfortable enough to lie down. And so it continued through the early morning hours — praying, changing positions, exhorting myself to remain strong, and battling the frustration as my heart continued merrily in its mischief.

At about 7:00 a.m., Nick awoke. I took my pride in hand and
said to him, "Havin' heart problems, Nick. Don't know how serious it is. But I think it's not too bad." I tried to make it sound
routine by maintaining the pitch and volume of my voice at a
conversational level. It was no good. Christ, you didn't even let
the guy wake up before you dumped your troubles on him, I
thought. I had already told him I was scared by not even saying
good morning. I didn't want to give the impression of panic, but
I blew it and I recognized it, and I think Nick did, too.

Nick looked around for his glasses, put them on and eyed
me from across the shelter. He didn't say anything.

"Usually takes about five hours for this thing to run its
course," I added, trying now to reassure him and myself. "I
should convert about nine o'clock. I think it started somewhere
around four this morning."

"What're you going to do if it doesn't convert?" he asked.

"Good question. It'll be one tough job gettin' outta here.
Right now I'm pretty weak." Secretly, I was still hoping Nick
would stay until I could continue, but I didn't want to impose
on him or embarrass myself by asking for his help.

I was displeased by the clumsy way in which I had reached
out for support. Fear had taken control and I determined then
and there to get that control back. After all, I told myself, you're
not exactly helpless; where are your guts? I got out of my sleeping bag and headed down a slight incline to a small creek in
front of the shelter. The 30-yard walk proved to be an exhausting effort. When I reached the stream bank, I leaned against a
tree and waited for the dizziness to subside.

I gulped air into my lungs, trying to get as much oxygen
into my blood stream as possible. I felt much the same as I did
when I was in poor physical condition, and my throat and chest

had burned following a run or other demanding exercise. Even bending down to get water was an exertion, and I had to rest several times to relieve my lightheadedness. After getting the water, I started back to the shelter, walking very slowly and thinking about how I would handle the day. Then I realized I wasn't dizzy. It hit me like a thunderbolt. I had converted! My heart was beating at its normal rhythm!

I would have jumped and shouted for joy, except that I was still tired and subdued from lack of sleep and the effects of the attack. I couldn't believe my good fortune. I was on an emotional roller coaster. Five minutes before I had been wallowing in self-pity and battling anxiety, and now I was feeling the thrill of a new beginning. The sun was shining and, although I was tired, I was happy and confident, looking forward to whatever the day had to offer.

I considered staying at the shelter for the rest of the day to regain my strength. The voice of Carl Friberg kept ringing in my mind, telling me to go slowly at first. I should have listened to that yesterday, I said to myself. Much as the wisdom seemed to dictate resting, I just couldn't bring myself to accept losing a whole day on the Trail. So, I decided to move on, but at a very slow pace.

I left at 8:55 a.m. for Muskrat Creek shelter some 7.5 miles away over which, according to the map, appeared to be a stretch of reasonably graded terrain. I left ahead of Nick, but he caught up to and passed me after an hour. He was hiking exactly twice as fast as I, taking only half an hour to cover the same distance I required an hour to traverse.

When he passed, we shook hands and wished each other luck. We both thought it would be the last time we'd see one another on the Trail. I felt a touch of panic as I watched him disappear down the Trail, his dangling hunters' special boots bouncing from his pack in cadence to his stride.

I stopped at noon at Bly Gap and prepared lunch. Since I had eaten so little the previous night and had only gorp for breakfast, I decided to eat a big meal and prepared my casserole. I was so famished I ate half of the salami I had intended to add to the soup mix. But there was still plenty of meat left for the concoction. While my food was cooking, I took the opportunity to look around the Gap and admire the scenery. The state boundary between Georgia and North Carolina passed directly through the gap and was marked by an erect stone slab. I decided to "dine in North Carolina" in a grassy forest meadow with a clear view of the nearby mountains to the north. The food tasted good and I ate with relish.

As I ate, I realized I had hiked 80 miles to reach this point and felt that I had achieved a milestone of sorts which called for a celebration. Not having any champagne or noise-makers along, I recorded the event on film for posterity, taking photographs of the boundary marker and the mountain vista behind it. I also took photographs of an old, severely misshapened oak tree which stood forlornly in the center of the Gap. It was, in a grotesque way, a beautiful old tree with a bent and heavily gnarled trunk that grew horizontally for several feet before sending up its vertical branches. The twisted knots and knobs of the wood combined with its weathered gray bark suggested great age and character.

The climb from Bly Gap up Courthouse Bald was sheer agony. It was a steady, very steep climb for about a mile, which surprised me. The Trail profile didn't depict it as an especially steep climb. I mused cynically that the Trail clubs conspired to make Thru-Hikers pay their dues when entering a new club's jurisdiction by placing the Trail over the most difficult terrain in the most obnoxious way. There were no views or interesting terrain, and I found no reasonable basis for the Trail routing.

Although my pace was labored, my mind was bursting with energy. I reviewed and assessed the previous night's events and my reaction to the episode of atrial fibrillation. I was twice surprised: initially, by my panic; then, subsequently, by my control of the panic. Somehow, I had reached inside myself and found a source of strength. It was as if I possessed a reservoir of fortitude that I could dip into when the need existed. It wasn't a power I could prove existed by logic. It was something that became evident only during times of personal crisis. When the crisis passed, so, it seemed, did the conduit to the strength source, and I could neither identify it nor go directly to it as a matter of course.

I wondered if I could enlist the help of that power to conquer my fibrillation problem. I was convinced that the fibrillation had psychological origins and that if I could summon reinforcement from that reservoir of strength, I could defeat the problem. The question was: "What was the origin of that strength?"

I became oblivious to the Trail and my surroundings as I focused my energy and concentration on my question. As I relived the event mentally, one factor emerged clearly. When I had begun to pray, I also began to calm down. The question then arose: "Was this a spiritual strength?"

I had hit my recall button. Memories from my earliest religious experiences flashed through my mind. I saw again the nun pacing the aisles between the desks, watching for signs of inattention during catechism class. She usually carried a ruler in her left hand, (the right one held a pencil) which she used to rap the knuckles of boy students who talked or otherwise misbehaved during class. Only the boys were subjected to the knuckle-rapping treatment; the girls received verbal admonitions mostly.

Unexpectedly, I was a boy in school, the scene recreated in amazing detail. The nun intoned the question: "Why are we on earth?" The pause was pregnant with terror as she looked around the room. "Jan Curran!"

Everyone else breathed a silent sigh of relief. "To know and love God, Sister," I replied.

"Very good, Jan!"

I slumped back into a welcome oblivion, knowing I had gotten my question for the period.

That was a good memory. I had blocked out the embarrassing ones where I became confused and gave the answer to question six in the book when she asked me for the answer to question number five. In those cases, she asked disapprovingly, "Did you read the homework assignment?"

Later in life, I came to the understanding that my catechism experience was an indoctrination session. Until recently, I didn't realize that the words religious and spiritual were not synonymous. I had assumed that catechism was spiritual instruction. Since it was boring, everything spiritual was the same.

In school I was interested in "useful stuff" like geography and arithmetic. As I became older, the sophistication in the religious instruction improved and some of the classes in high school were interesting, particularly those dealing with the philosophical underpinnings of Catholicism. Still, I didn't understand the need for personal spiritual development. That had changed. I now recognized I had been missing something. I was missing an essential element from the whole person concept, like a body without a leg. I could exist, but I felt, in a way, that I was a cripple.

I concentrated on the concept of spirituality as I groped up Courthouse Bald. What is spirituality? How can it be defined? I stopped to let my heart rate subside and inhale more oxygen into my lungs. It's my relationship with the Higher Intelligence.

I answered myself, the Power that gives order to the universe. I continued to climb. It was the Law Giver that made things happen and looked on dispassionately as men fought their eternal struggle with the gods of their own making. I stopped again, though I had gone only a few yards. Was that it? No, that wasn't it!

I started again, as if my physical movements were tied to my intellectual activity. Why could I not bring myself to understand that faith had to enter the equation? Why was I holding back? I was looking all over the spiritual landscape trying to find a definition to hang on the Supreme Being without using the one I had been taught. Why didn't I just say it was my relationship with God? After I acknowledged that solution, I felt like I had solved some complex puzzle, and I climbed more easily.

It was early afternoon when I reached Muskrat shelter, an A-frame structure, much larger and different in style from the other shelters I'd seen. The roof came almost to the ground on both sides and the side walls were probably not more than a foot or two tall in front.

A little mountain stream, burbling about 15 yards away from the shelter, looked so inviting, so deliciously cool, that I considered stretching out on the bank and drinking directly from the smooth flowing liquid. I didn't. I had established a cardinal rule that I would drink untreated water only if it came from a spring directly from the ground. Otherwise, I would purify the water, either by treating it with iodine purification tablets or boiling it for seven minutes.

The danger in drinking unprotected water, even in an unpolluted wilderness region, comes from *giardia*, a common bacteria from animal feces which causes intestinal illness in humans. It affects different people to different degrees; some have very little problem with the illness while others become incapacitated by it. I couldn't take a chance.

I found a small pool where the water was deep enough to dip my cookpot. The reflection from the pool amazed me. As distorted as it was, I could see that my beard was getting heavy, and my hair shaggy and long. I had already resolved not to cut a single hair while I was on the Trail. I'd shaved every morning for 30 years and had my hair cut to military specifications every week or two for as long. Now I was going to cleanse my psyche, and that included the hair that covered it. I was rebelling!

After supper, I dutifully recorded the day's events in my Trail journal. Because it was so quiet while I wrote, a tiny mouse appeared and began foraging around the fire pit in front of the shelter. It appeared not in the least intimidated by my presence. Since I had missed my entries for the previous day at Plum Orchard Gap, I had a lot to write, and it was almost dark when I finished. In fact, I stopped writing because it became too dark.

I put my pad and pen away in my pack and climbed into my sleeping bag. I settled my head on my tent pillow and tried to pray. The last thing I heard before morning was the sound of the mouse running across the shelter floor.

It was June 20th now, and another spectacular day dawned on the horizon. The Trail was not too difficult. I covered the four miles to Deep Gap in a little less than two hours. The *Trail Guide* mentioned that the AT entered a wilderness region at Deep Gap and continued until just south of Albert Mountain. The word, wilderness, had an exciting, somewhat ominous ring to it and conjured visions of the virgin land faced by the early settlers and men like Daniel Boone. Here was a place where no human habitation existed, where the land existed as it had for centuries.

No roads existed, no havens were available in case of trouble. I pushed on, expecting to see a special landscape teeming with wildlife. But I didn't see anything different from what I had seen earlier. It was still mountains, rocks and trees and only occasional wildlife.

I stopped for a break at Standing Indian shelter and read in the register that Nick Sprague had spent the previous night there. He left me a note to "keep on truckin'." I also left a note, indicating that I was still "truckin'" and signed off, "Old Soldier."

Almost everyone who hikes the Trail for any distance adopts a Trail alias and many times becomes known only by that name. Some of the names were very good: Hike-a-holic or Caveman Dave or AT Believer. Nick signed his literary efforts, "The Ramblin' Wreck." He later learned that someone else on the Trail was using the same name and changed his alias to Keys Cruiser.

I reached Standing Indian Mountain shortly before noon and took a short 500-foot side trip to the summit. Standing Indian was my first 5000-foot mountain, and I was deeply impressed by the summit views of the Tallulah River Gorge and the mountains of north Georgia over which I had just come. Not only were the vistas beautiful, the mountain was a veritable palette of color with pink, red, purple and white rhododendron and mountain laurel blossoms, leaping from a backdrop of dark green foliage and gray rock ledges. The views and the color had an uplifting effect that I carried with me through the afternoon.

I had planned to tent camp when I reached Carter Gap shelter, but the only available tentsites were already taken. Two people, a tall, thin black man wearing Army camouflage trousers and a short, heavy, blond woman had erected their tents on the only two suitable tent sites. I made myself at home in the shelter about 50 yards away.

After supper, a large skunk ambled out of the forest and came so close to the shelter that I felt forced to run it off. I yelled and waved my arms energetically, but not so energetically that it felt too threatened. (I remembered a firsthand experience with a skunk in my youth, and I was not about to repeat the mistake.) The skunk headed into the forest, then reappeared after a few minutes, and I again ran it off. I was sure it smelled the food and was looking for a morsel.

The skunk acted with incredible indifference toward humans, almost like a pet that had strolled into camp. I eventually became more comfortable with the animal and watched it come and go until it was bedtime when I shooed it off again. It departed in a manner that could best be described as nonchalant if not reluctant. I didn't want the critter to be nosing about the shelter or fooling with my pack or food while I slept, so I made sure it left for good. I chased after it, beating my hiking stick on the ground while being careful not to get too close. It got the idea and began to run in an ungainly, sluggish lope down the hill to eventually disappear into the forest.

The tent campers never noticed the skunk. They were engaged in an animated conversation. I heard them laughingly mention the words "terrorist" and "hostage" several times. I guessed they were playing a game of some sort.

I saw much wildlife the next morning, which I attributed to being in a wilderness area. Just after leaving the shelter, I encountered a baby squirrel sitting on a low branch directly above the pathway. It was not more than seven feet from the ground. Though I walked directly under it and could have touched it with my hand, it remained sitting on the limb, watching as I passed. I was so close I could see the small swells of soft gray fur that covered the muscles in its haunches!

I also saw a grouse family with several very young birds. The young ones could fly. But they were so new at it mother grouse was unimpressed. She gave me the broken-wing routine until I was about 30 yards down the Trail.

At Beech Gap, I found myself being watched by two great horned owls sitting side by side on the highest branch of a naked, gray tree skeleton at the edge of a small clearing. One of the birds was almost twice as large as its companion. I watched them watching me for a few minutes until it was time to continue; then I arose from the log where I was sitting and picked up my pack. When I looked back up for one last view, the owls had disappeared. The huge birds had taken flight without making a sound or at least a sound that I could hear. I learned later that the wing feathers of raptors like the owl are constructed in a fashion that provides very little wind friction, which makes for silent motion, a great advantage in hunting their vigilant prey.

Just before reaching Albert Mountain, I met an older Atlanta, Georgia, couple who were day-hiking out of Standing Indian Campground. We talked a little about our backgrounds, and I mentioned that I had just returned from a five-year assignment in Germany.

"Did you do any hiking in Germany?" asked the woman.

"No! No hiking. But I did participate in some *Volksmarsches*. Those are walks of 10, 15 and 20 kilometers. Whole families participate — little kids, big kids, parents, and grandparents. Everyone seems to enjoy the countryside. When they're done, everybody heads for the fest tent. They spend the rest of the day drinking soda or beer, eating wurst, and enjoying the camaraderie. If you participate, and finish, you get a medal. It really is a great tradition, a great opportunity for whole families to do something together."

Eagerly, the man inquired, "What does the countryside look like?"

"In places it's very much like America," I told them. "It has many beautiful mountains from the Schwarzwald to the Alps to the Bavarian Woods, the Spessart and the Odenwald. But they're not nearly as expansive as the Appalachians or the Alleghenies. The whole country is full of hills with beautiful valleys and quaint towns. I really loved the German landscape."

"We've been coming here for years," they allowed. "We used to go to other places for our vacation, but we couldn't find a more beautiful spot than this, so we stopped trying and we've been coming here ever since." The man looked down as he drew circles in the earth with his hiking stick. "The southern Appalachians are as beautiful a place as there is. I don't see why anybody would go outside of America for a vacation. We have everything they have anywhere else and more."

"There's no question about that," I agreed. "There's no place like home!"

"There's no place like the mountains, like the southern Appalachians as far as I'm concerned," he repeated.

"You remind me of a girl I met at Neels Gap who told me she wanted to spend the rest of her life in these mountains because she loved them so much."

He looked at me with a strange expression. "Well, I don't know about that? I haven't been compared to a girl recently!"

I recognized the awkward comparison as soon as I said it. "Unfortunate example," I replied. "I meant only that you exhibit a love for the mountains, the same type of love for the mountains that I saw in this girl at Neels Gap. I'm impressed by how some people are taken with the mountains. It's like they become part of the mountains, or maybe the mountains become a part of them, like a close member of the family. The attraction is felt to such depths that life without the mountains would be no life at all. I don't know if you fit in that category, but I do know that you share some of the fervor. I think it's wonderful."

The man was still digesting what I said when the woman asked if I planned to climb Albert Mountain.

"I'm on my way there now."

"You be real careful, hear!" she said. "It's very steep. Take your time and watch your step."

The woman was right. Albert Mountain was steep, the steepest mountain I'd faced yet. It was a difficult climb that required me to maintain my weight well forward so that there could be no possibility for a shift in pack weight to pull me off balance to the rear, causing a fast trip to the bottom. There were few handholds to aid in maintaining balance, and where they did exist, they were difficult to reach because of the excessive vertical distances between footholds. I literally crawled up some rocks, hanging on to occasional laurel branches for support and balance. Sometimes, a low-hanging laurel branch caught the top of my pack frame and held me back, until my forward momentum disengaged it. Some of the branches were so large that they stopped my progress altogether and required me to slide back down to my previous foothold and try to get beneath them either by lowering my entire body profile or, if possible, by holding them up high with my arm while I tried to "limbo" under them.

The climb covered about 500 feet, which measures a little

less than the length of two football fields, one and two-thirds to be exact. Walking that distance over level ground is easy; but climbing it almost vertically with a 45-pound pack is very demanding, and having to negotiate the rock ledges and fight the mountain laurel branches compounds the difficulty. It took almost an hour to make the climb. Normally, the Trail over the tops of mountains or ridges becomes less steep as it nears the summit. But in the case of Albert Mountain, it continued at an almost vertical incline right to the summit. I was surprised when I reached the top.

The narrow summit contained a small cleared area with an abandoned firetower and a rock outcropping with a marvelous view over the valley to the east. A group of young people, all wearing black, tight-fitting biker's pants, were lounging on the rock outcropping. They were laughing and joking with one another and paid scant attention as I approached. But there was something wrong with the scene. I'd just knocked myself out climbing this mountain, and these folks in bicycle pants were up here "cleaner 'n spit" and partying.

I talked to a couple who were leaning arm in arm against the firetower, watching me with amused expressions on their faces. I learned that the north side of Albert Mountain had a much gentler slope than the south side. The bicyclers had been able to ride their bicycles almost to the summit. I also learned they were members of a mountain bikers' club from Atlanta.

I dropped my pack beside the firetower and removed my lunch from the top flap pocket. I became aware of a feeling of tranquillity as I ate, watching occasional clouds sailing above the mountains and basking in the midday sun. Even the continued banter of the bikers was comforting. They told me I wasn't alone.

A short time later three hikers — a woman and two men — arrived at the summit. As is normal with hikers, we exchanged information about the Trail: where we came from and how far we planned to go. I explained that I was thru-hiking the AT. Suddenly, everyone, even the bikers, became interested in me. The woman hiker asked how it felt psychologically to be alone on the Trail for such a long time. I told her I didn't have any pat answers to give, that I'd experienced a wide range of emotions and feelings with no one emotion or thought dominating for long.

Then, a flood of emotional interpretations were rolling off my tongue . . .

"I didn't appreciate how important other people were to me

until I was alone. Another thing I've learned is that it's imperative to maintain a positive outlook. I'm sure that if I began to dwell only on the negative aspects of my hike, the pain, the fatigue, the climbs, the insects and the shelter mice, it wouldn't be long before I headed for the nearest bus home. I've also learned that if you plan to stay on the Trail for any length of time, you'd better like yourself because, much of the time, you're your only companion. Those are some of the things that I have found are important in hiking alone. I'm sure you would get as many different answers to that question as people you asked. I think the only constant measure would be a positive approach. I personally have had to look within for the strength and will to continue. That's another thing which I've found to be personally important."

"Don't you get scared? Like, what about snakes? Don't you ever get scared being alone? Suppose you injure yourself." The woman was removing her hiking boots as we talked.

"I guess the *thought* of being alone is the scariest part. It's mostly psychological, though. If you stop to think about the dangers and look at them objectively and in terms of probability, the Trail is a pretty safe place. Look at the animals. They're all more scared of us than we are of them. They just want to stay out of our way, so they're not a problem. If I fell and broke an ankle, there are enough people on the Trail that I wouldn't have to wait too long until help came. The only thing that really bothers me is the possibility I might end up at a shelter with a screwball or someone strung out on dope. But that's pretty remote."

"I couldn't do it," she replied. "I'd be scared someone would hit me over the head or something."

One member of the bicycle group, a young man with a powerful build, wild shoulder-length hair and the look of a free spirit came up to me as they were leaving and offered his hand. "I really admire your guts, and I'm pulling for you to make it. Good luck!" I was surprised and touched by his statement of solidarity.

Just before departing, I climbed the firetower steps to the first level and looked back at Standing Indian Mountain, looming massively above a row of smaller hills in the foreground. In the other direction, the way I would be going, the ridge crest followed several undulations which I was sure contained onerous little climbs. The valley floor was mostly a patchwork green formed by the different stages of growth of individual hay fields. These were interrupted occasionally by a cornfield or a freshly plowed patch of earth, either awaiting seed or just having been seeded. A much darker green outlined the borders of the fields where the forest began and became progressively lighter in hue as the forest swept up the ridges. Here and there, a white house or a red barn interrupted the green schematic, suggesting an even more permanent human presence than that represented by the hay and corn fields.

CHAPTER 5

The Nantahalas
Getting in Shape

I fairly cruised along the ridge lines, arriving by midafternoon at Rock Gap shelter where I had planned to stay overnight. The *Trail Guide* and map indicated the shelter was barely a mile from Wallace Gap, and from the Gap it was only another mile to the west down U.S. Route 62 to Rainbow Springs Campground. Considering that Rainbow Springs Campground also had cabins for rent and that six days had elapsed since my last contact with real civilization, the prospect of a bed with sheets and a hot shower had great appeal. Another two miles seemed a small price to pay for luxury. Since it appeared all downhill, the decision was easy. It was amazing how important the little things in life became. Hot showers, toilets with running water, beds with sheets, and pillows with pillowcases became highly desired luxuries.

I arrived within the hour and, after checking the empty campstore, stood on the porch and called out over the seemingly deserted campground that spread down the hill before me. "Hello, anyone home?" The sound of my voice was swallowed by the silence. After several seconds, I called again but still no response. I sat on the porch steps to rest. Five minutes later, tall, slender Buddy Crossman came hurrying up the hill toward the store.

Buddy informed me that the rental price of a cabin had increased from $15 to $20 a night; that seemed a small price for a night of personal indulgence.

When I first saw the cabin, I wasn't sure I had struck a very good bargain. It was an old, wooden frame shack with weathered board siding and tarpaper sheet roofing and looked like the next strong wind might blow it down. It, along with two

Cabin at Rainbow Springs Campground.

similar structures, sat in a spacious mountain meadow that sloped gently down to a broad mountain stream. It was primitive compared to the cabins at Neels Gap, but functional, with an adequate kitchen, a soft double bed and a shower that appeared to have been added as an afterthought, and at that point, function was what really counted. Other than unpacking, the first order of business was a shower, and I headed for the bathroom.

I was shocked when I looked at myself in the mirror. I thought I had been disreputable at the Neels Gap cabin, but I was positively civilized then in comparison to now. My whisker growth was at the ugly stage; it was more like dirt than hair.

The face in the mirror reminded me of a Hollywood portrayal of an escaped convict who had been on the lam for two weeks. Streaked with dirt, the hair was long and pointing in every direction but the right one. Not only was my face dirty, my clothes were filthy and reeked of a combination of odors, mostly dried perspiration and body oils. I looked and smelled so bad that I was surprised Buddy rented a cabin to me at all.

After showering, I headed back to the campstore to wash my clothes and talk with Buddy. I had been impressed with his openness and congeniality during our initial meeting and the "good chemistry" was reinforced when we met again. His easygoing, friendly demeanor was enhanced by a perpetual smile and his eyes looked directly at me as he spoke, conveying a feeling of honesty.

While Buddy and I were talking, a man in a police-like uniform, complete with pistol, came into the store. Buddy introduced him as Jim Bowman and indicated we had something in common.

Jim was a retired Army major, and we slipped easily into the "Did you know Joe Schmedlap?" routine, trying to establish who we might know in common. He had been an airborne infantry officer with extensive Special Forces experience while I had been "straightleg" infantry, the term used to describe non-airborne infantrymen. Because of our divergent career paths, except for a few higher ranking generals, we were unable to establish any common acquaintances.

Jim, having grown up in the mountains of North Carolina, was very knowledgeable about the land and the wildlife, and I learned much that was of great interest. He asked if I had seen any coyotes, saying they had established themselves in numbers in the region and that hunters had killed several in the recent past. That was a surprise; I had thought of the coyote as a western animal. I was even more surprised to learn that some of them had interbred with domestic dogs, resulting in a mixed breed called "coydogs," and had proliferated to the point of becoming pests. He told me that beaver had also been reintroduced into the area and had become so numerous that their dams were affecting the ecology of the mountains. The fox population was also increasing. He said I stood a good chance of seeing one since they often followed hikers, looking for dropped food morsels. He suggested I sit quietly by the Trail for a while and one was sure to come by. I might have to wait a bit, he admonished, because the fox was a clever devil and allowed a fairly lengthy time interval to develop before starting to follow.

I asked about other animals and learned that the mountains were home to a large mink population. The mink were bad news to trout farmers; they were adept fishermen and could rapidly wipe out the trout in a stream. "They ain't the only problem," he said. "The biggest problem are fish poachers." They not only poached in streams but lately had taken to raiding the trout farmers' stock ponds. After Jim departed, Buddy told me he worked as sort of policeman/game warden for a group of property owners who had large holdings in the area.

John Wasilik Memorial Poplar.

The next morning, after dressing, I watched two rabbits cavort on the lawn in the early morning sun. I had never seen rabbits behave in the way these did. One rabbit would run around the other, then leap across the back of the other to the side from which it had just come. The leaps were peculiar. The rabbits extended their legs spread-eagle style in the air as they crossed over the back of the rabbit below. They swung their rear ends as they jumped and allowed the momentum of their rear ends to give a graceful arc to their leap so that it gave the impression they were soaring as they flew through the air. They continued their acrobatics for about five minutes before disappearing behind some bushes, and I didn't see them again.

I had decided to rest for another day, so breakfast was a leisurely affair. I fried six eggs and half a pound of bacon and toasted half a loaf of bread, which I smeared with copious amounts of butter and jam. I savored every mouthful, even while recognizing I was consuming a cholesterol bomb.

The day before in Wallace Gap, I had passed a side trail leading to the John Wasilik Memorial Poplar. It had a reputation as possibly the largest poplar tree in the world. According to a story I had read somewhere, originally there were two giant poplars.

Wasilik cut one down. It was so massive he nearly killed his team of oxen trying to haul it out of the forest. So, he decided to leave the second for posterity. The story so intrigued me that, after eating, I headed for Wallace Gap to look at the tree.

The trunk looked to be about 12 feet in diameter. I guessed it would take five or six men with arms outstretched to girdle the circumference. It dominated the other trees in the vicinity, most of which were gigantic poplars in their own right. Lightning strikes had stunted the giant's vertical growth at about 70 feet, and the scars were visible on the bark near the top. The top branches appeared to be dead, but below them the leaf growth appeared to be healthy. I spent about 30 minutes taking pictures and admiring the monarch before heading back to the campground.

In the late afternoon, I rested on the cabin porch watching swallows feeding on insects in the air. I couldn't conceive of a more beautiful or graceful flight than the aerobatics of the swallows as they dove and rolled and dipped, at times seeming to hold themselves motionless in the air. I especially liked how they pulled out of their dives and became motionless for a split second at the apogee before beginning their next swoop toward some hapless bug.

The Trail the next day, from Wallace Gap to Silers Bald, was fairly tough. It required concentration and considerable mental effort on my part to maintain a positive outlook. I thought I might again be suffering some psychological relapse related to going back on the Trail. I was leaving the comfortable, secure environment of the campground and embarking again into the unknown. I felt much the same as I had at Springer Mountain when I came on the Trail the first time and also when I had left Neels Gap. It was not terrifying, but the apprehension was uncomfortable.

After getting into the rhythm of the hike and being immersed in natural beauty, my disposition improved and I felt good again about the Trail. Near Silers Bald stood a grove of hemlocks that looked every bit as majestic as those I had seen at Stover Creek. I wondered if they too were virgin trees. I particularly enjoyed one scenic spot where, after a two-hour climb, I entered a high mountain meadow with grass-carpeted logging roads coming in from different directions like spokes to the hub of a wheel. The meadow sat in a ridge saddle surrounded by giant hardwood trees, oak and poplar mainly, with a few smaller hickory trees mixed in. The sunlight filtering through the tree branches created shafts of light through the forest, reminiscent of the rays of sunlight passing through high, stained glass church windows. The sun bathed the grass with light that shimmered and changed with the breeze, and the daisies and black-eyed susans bobbed their heads in unison, bending whichever way the wind last blew.

When I reached Wayah Gap picnic area, I stopped for the day and erected my tent on the grass behind a picnic table where the most level ground could be found. There was no water at the picnic area, but according to the *Trail Guide*, a spring was located another two miles further on. I felt I could survive with the water in my canteen until morning.

After supper, I sat on one of the cement picnic benches to soak up the last few rays of the sun and contemplate what I had accomplished. I was doing "damned well" I decided. I had racked up nine miles for the day over tough terrain and had regained control of my emotions and apprehensions with an ease that would have been unthinkable at the start of the hike. I had been able to increase my speed incrementally as well as the distances I climbed before taking short periodic breaks to catch my breath. I was getting pretty good at the hiking business, I thought. Another reason to feel good was that I had covered 115.5. miles since starting from Springer Mountain.

When it became dark, I crawled into my sleeping bag and listened to the grouse drumming, the owls hooting, and the other sounds of a forest heading into night. My mind took me back to Germany. I had left not quite three months before, but it seemed so remote now that the months could have been years. I realized then just how free I felt — free from the constant stress, free from the frustration of working with the intransigent bureaucracy. I became intensely aware of how structured my life had been then, each and every minute planned, my workday completely controlled by an appointment calendar. My entire life was structured about the entries on that little pad of paper and coordinating appointments and, resolving conflicts became a primary duty for my secretary. When I compared that existence to the basically unstructured, undisciplined life I was leading on the Trail, I began to sense for the first time that I was revising the perspective with which I viewed the world . . . And, of course, I thought of Anna and wondered how she would have reacted to the rigors of the Trail.

I thought back to the time Anna and I had hiked into the Grand Canyon; she had left me in her dust on the climb back to the North Rim. I was sure she could handle the rigors of the

Trail, probably better than I. We had fashioned an interesting history over the past few years, and even when we quarreled, we could always point back to our shared experiences and feel good again.

Early the next morning, after a fairly strenuous climb out of Wayah Gap, I came to a forest road where, thankfully, I found the spring described in the *Trail Guide*. After washing my cook pot and filling my canteen, I rested for a minute beside the road and remembered my talk with Jim Bowman. I wondered if any foxes might be following.

The flow of my thoughts was broken when a convoy of cars with Florida license plates, led by a black pickup truck, interrupted my reveries. The people, all older folks, waved and smiled as they rumbled slowly past. The road did not show clearly on the map. (Because of the gray monochrome coloration, I confused the road with a contour line. The poor quality and limited topographical coverage of the maps that accompanied the Trail guides was a major disadvantage. They were basically useless for land navigation.) Because of the confusion, I did not realize that the road led to Wine Spring Bald or to Wayah Bald. (Balds, in the southern Appalachians, are mountains whose summits are treeless, grassy meadows. The name, "Bald," can be deceiving, though. Many mountains, although still identified as balds, have, in fact, undergone or are in the process of reforestation.)

Shortly after leaving the spring, I met a solo Thru-Hiker from Maine. He was sitting in his tent beside the Trail getting organized for the day. I learned that he was completing the second leg of his two-summer hike and was looking forward with great anticipation to climbing Springer Mountain. I asked him to compare the difficulty of the Trail he was now traveling with what he had hiked over the previous summer. Except for a stretch in Maine, this was the toughest section he had hiked any place along the Trail. He had not been impressed by the difficulty of the section between Wesser and Fontana, which was reputed to be one of the toughest on the whole AT. I was glad to hear that. The terrain I was hiking was tough enough. I didn't relish the prospect of having to climb tougher mountains.

I arrived at Wine Spring Bald late in the morning, just as it was about to sprinkle. A work crew from the Forest Service was putting the finishing touches to a public toilet. I stopped for a minute to watch. They were cementing fieldstone siding to the outside walls to give it a "natural look." It didn't have running water, but it looked pretty. I thought I'd just as soon they spent the money on running water.

At first, I couldn't tell who was in charge. Most of the men appeared to be supervising. It was a typical government work crew and reminded me of descriptions I had heard of WPA work crews during the Depression.

There were eight mostly middle-aged men, seven of them white and one black, clustered around a pile of volley ball-sized fieldstones. The black man was preparing the wall with cement and setting the fieldstones in place. Another man had been detailed to pick up a stone from the pile and give it to the man putting it on the wall. The rest stood around laughing and joking. A third man, whom I guessed to be the boss, contributed to the effort by telling the guy picking up the stones which stone to pick up next.

I asked an ice-breaking question about the weather and received a direct answer from the boss. Then, when I asked other questions, he showed increasing reluctance to answer. After a third or fourth question, he ignored me altogether and began issuing very direct instructions to the stone picker-upper in such a way as to emphasize his importance. Obviously, the task at hand required great concentration, and I was interfering with the effort. I took the hint and headed up the hill. It was the first time on the Trail that I met someone who didn't want to talk.

On the summit of Wine Spring Bald, I found an elaborately constructed two-story stone tower which I reached just in time to escape a downpour. I spent the next 15 minutes sitting on my pack, listening to the patter of raindrops on the walkway outside the entrance. After it stopped raining, I climbed to the top of the tower for a view of the panorama. According to the *Trail Guide*, the view was spectacular. Unfortunately, mists shrouded even nearby trees. I climbed down and headed back to the Trail.

I had not gone a hundred yards when the rain returned. I slipped the pack cover over my pack and donned my windbreaker; then, almost as soon as I reshouldered my pack, the rain stopped. I walked for only a short distance until the windbreaker became unbearably hot and stopped again to remove it. I found it to be just as comfortable to walk in the rain and later let the air dry my clothes rather than become drenched in sweat from wearing a windbreaker. Either way I was going to be wet.

The sun broke through the clouds by the time I reached Burningtown Gap, and the evaporating rain water made the air

uncomfortably humid. I was surprised to see the gap full of
parked cars, which I recognized as the same cars I had seen earlier in the morning on the road to Wine Spring Bald. On the
climb out of the gap, I encountered the car owners coming down
the mountain in one long single file. Several stopped to chat,
and I enjoyed a period of notoriety. "You hear that? He's walked
here all the way from Georgia!" I could hear it pass up the line.

"How far's he going?" someone asked.

"All the way to Maine!" someone else responded.

Some tried to whisper the information to their companions.
But the level of hearing among many was so bad that people
ended up talking in a "stage whisper."

The last man in the file talked with a heavy German accent,
and I began talking to him in German. He was from the area of
Lake Constance in southwest Germany, had immigrated to
America in 1951, settling originally in New York, then moving
to Connecticut, and finally retiring to Henderson, North Carolina. He had been a machine tool engineer with a packaging
material firm. I enjoyed the opportunity to speak a little German, and so did he. He was astounded to find a German-speak-
ing American in the middle of the mountain wilderness in
North Carolina. He said again and again, "*Dass darf nicht wahr
sein!*" (It can't be true.)

After a time, his wife came back up the Trail to rescue him.
They wished me well on my adventure, then hurried down the
hill to the accompaniment of beeping horns.

Someone in the group had asked if I planned to stay overnight at Cold Spring shelter, which lay about another mile further up the Trail, indicating that it was empty. That was good
news. I wanted solitude to meditate. My thoughts of good fortune were premature, to say the least.

By the time I arrived, the shelter had been occupied by a
large group of Boy Scouts, none of whom were enjoying themselves. They were accompanied by two adult leaders who also
were not enjoying themselves. In fact, everyone was wet and
miserable and trying to outbitch everyone else. The adult leaders seemed to be interested exclusively in their own comfort and
had taken over most of the shelter (leaving a little space for a
couple of Boy Scout leaders) while the rest of the Scouts were
left to fend for themselves.

Everyone followed the example of their leaders, being concerned only with taking care of themselves. There was abso-

lutely zero cohesion or camaraderie in the group, and the only leadership I detected was negative at best. It was unfortunate; the boys were receiving a completely negative message. It was for many, probably, their initial experience with camping or backpacking, and the negative cast of the experience was bound to influence their reactions to future wilderness experiences. The vicious comments I heard while filling my canteen at the spring sealed my decision to move on and tent camp wherever I could find a place.

It required a little more than an hour to cover the two and two-tenths miles to the next available campsite listed in the *Trail Guide*. It was not an inviting place. The few worn tentsites were quickly turning to mud, but it was 5:30 p.m. and I was tired. I selected the most level place I could find and set up my tent. I was joined a short time later by Fred White and Les Rust. They too had planned to spend the night at Cold Spring shelter, but the Boy Scouts' behavior had also influenced them to search for a more tranquil spot.

I had met Fred at the Rainbow Springs campground during the afternoon of my second day there and had talked to him briefly, learning only that he was originally from Sarasota, Florida, but was now going to school in Boston. Les, a student at Berea College, a highly regarded college for economically disadvantaged students, was spending his last bachelor fling in the woods. He was leaving the Trail two days hence to get married.

Both Les and Fred were avid Boston Celtic fans and knew the names of all the players and their individual statistics. They told me that the Celtics had selected Len Bias from the University of Maryland as their number one pick in the NBA draft and that two days later Bias had died from a cocaine overdose. This was all news to me. I had not seen a newspaper nor heard a news broadcast since leaving Naples.

I was amazed, when I reflected on it, how personally unimportant television and newspapers had become now that I was totally involved in the adventure of my life instead of spectating at others who were involved in theirs. It was another lesson that helped me reorder the priorities I was now establishing in my life. I felt I had been too strongly influenced by events which, although apparently important, were really superfluous to the thrust of my life. Transitory events that glittered in the light of notoriety had influenced many of my previous decisions. Now I was learning that the really important events were those which contributed to my spiritual development. The other events were mere distractions, and I had to learn the difference.

I started off the next day feeling not very well because of a lack of sleep caused by Les' snoring. Having spent countless nights in the field and in barracks with thousands of men, I thought I had probably heard most of the Granddaddy snorers in captivity. After Les slipped into dreamland, I realized that he was in a class by himself. Will his bride be surprised! I thought as I made coffee.

The musky aroma of the woods refreshed by rain penetrated the air, and I breathed it deeply into my lungs, an elixir of life, as I strode along the Trail. The hiking was very good, and I made it over Wesser Bald in surprisingly good time, despite a long climb and a rocky pathway. Although it was listed as a bald, it had become overgrown and there were no views. The Trail then followed the ridge spine over many little "jump-ups" (minipeaks) and crossed areas where the path was no more than two or three feet wide with precipitous, but tree-lined drop-offs to either side.

Just before descending to Rufus Morgan shelter, the Trail led to a rock overlook with a magnificent view of the Great Smokies, Fontana Lake and the many hills and valleys in between. The Smokies were massive. I had just come over a couple of 5,000-foot mountains (Standing Indian and Albert Mountains, and Wayah and Copper Balds) during the past several days. But they seemed insignificant in comparison to the range I was seeing in front of me.

The Trail was basically a downhill slide from the overlook to the Rufus Morgan shelter. On the way, I passed several stands of pink rhododendron in full flower. I stopped for a break beside one of the more exciting floral displays and became captivated by the contrast in color between the lavish pink blossoms and the dark brown forest path that stretched down the green carpeted forest before me.

I reflected on what I had accomplished and how I had become conditioned to the rigors of the Trail, to the weight of my pack, and to the discomforts of wet feet and insect bites. I was pleased with the positive approach I had developed and resolved, no matter how difficult the Trail became, to retain that approach. I also felt I really had become "One with the Trail," that either I had become a part of the Trail or it had become a part of me, and that was a good feeling.

Being "One with the Trail" also had a broader significance. I identified the Trail as a guidepath for a spiritual journey. One in which I could find and touch my spiritual dimensions; a place where I could identify and understand God. It was to be an affirmation of a newfound faith. I realized I would have to devote extensive thought and effort to working out the basis for my newfound spirituality and reconciling it with what I had learned earlier. This was different from what I had learned as a student.

The "tapes" which had been programmed in my catechism classes and later religious studies would always remain with me and cause me to question any deviation from them. I knew I was formulating concepts which, I was sure, would have displeased my teachers. But I appeared to have something in my grasp. I didn't know exactly what it was yet, but I had the feeling that it would be exciting. It was as though I was on the brink of a discovery. I knew I had to pursue the quest.

I spent more than my allotted ten minutes and stepped out smartly when I returned to my conscious reality. I passed Rufus Morgan shelter without stopping for water since I'd heard that the stream there was polluted. I headed straight for Wesser and the Nantahala Gorge, which I reached at 3:00 p.m. I noted with pleasure that I had covered the 31-mile stretch between Wallace Gap and Wesser in under three days. I felt like a pro.

CHAPTER 6

Building A New Perspective
The Nantahala Gorge to Fontana Dam

Wesser, North Carolina, was basically a bend in the road beside a steel truss bridge that spanned the Nantahala River. It was a company town owned by the Nantahala Outdoor Center, a river/water sports company that offered white-water raft trips as well as canoe and kayak lessons and clinics. It also provided accommodations and meals for participants and tourists as well as occasional hikers from the AT.

The facilities consisted of a motel/hostel complex, a small administrative building, and a restaurant/equipment store building on the south side of the Nantahala River, opposite several houses, a meeting hall and a campground on the north side. The restaurant/store building was a dilapidated, weathered, wooden structure perched precariously on the river bank; it reminded me of the buildings in old western mining towns.

I planned to spend two days at the outdoor center to rest and do some white-water rafting. I hurried into the administration building to make arrangements for a raft trip the next day. The office was small, barely big enough for one person behind the counter and two or three customers in front. A young man repairing an air-conditioning unit was using the office desk as a work bench. The air-conditioning unit took up most of the desk space and with the man also behind the counter, very little room was left for the young female reservations clerk to do any work. The phone rang continually while the woman tried to conduct business, and I had to wait while she dealt with three calls from other customers. After the third call she directed her attention to me, and I asked if there might be room for me on a raft trip the next day.

The Nantahala Outdoor Center viewed from the bridge over the Nantahala River.

As luck would have it, the computer containing the raft bookings was down. "Should be able to tell you something by about 4:00 p.m.," she said.

At 4:30 p.m. I returned and was informed that all the rafts for the next day had been fully booked. I was disappointed, but not too surprised; it was the height of the rafting season, and the place was overrun by rafters, canoeists and kayakers.

I was halfway through the door when the man repairing the air-conditioner mentioned in passing that there might be space on one of the rafts of the Great Smokies Rafting Company, a rival which had just been purchased by the Nantahala company. I came back into the room.

The young woman allowed as how that might be the case, then abruptly dropped me to converse with a couple who had entered behind me to inquire about rafting. She simply turned her attention to the new people without comment or acknowledgment of any sort to me.

I was not accustomed to having a conversation terminated except on my terms; I couldn't remember the last time someone had consciously ignored me. The longer I waited for her to finish with the couple, and the more I thought about it, the more irritated I became.

When the couple left, I spoke in a loud authoritative tone that told her I was a customer and damned angry. "Please call the other company and book me a ride on one of their rafts!" I said bluntly.

The woman seemed surprised and made the call. Did they have any spaces available on any of their rafts the next day? Yes they did! "Good," she said, "Book one more at $18 a ride."

"Looks like I got lucky," I said, trying to soften the impact of my anger.

The woman nodded her head and turned to do something else.

I kept her attention. "Where is the Great Smokies Rafting Company?" I asked.

"About five miles down the road," she replied, waving her hand in the direction down river.

I explained that I was hiking the AT and didn't have a car and asked if the company had any transportation, or if she knew anyone going that way, or anyone I could hire to give me a lift.

The lack of a pause between my question and her curt response of "No!" indicated her lack of interest in helping.

"How can I get there?"

"Guess you'll have to walk or hitchhike," she said in a tone of voice that suggested irritation.

"Any taxis or buses around?"

"No taxis and no buses around here," she said. "Only way I know to get there is, like I said, hitch a ride or walk." She emphasized the "like I said" part.

My anger began welling up again. "Guess I'll just call it off," I said and started for the door.

The air-conditioner repairman saved me again. "They go right by here on the way to the starting point. Why don't you ask them to stop and pick him up on their way by?"

She was trapped and angry about it, but she was going to take her time about responding. She fiddled with some paperwork on her desk and answered the phone several times before my turn came up again, and she made the call. Could they stop by on their way by to pick up a rafter? "Good! He'll be out front of the store at 10:30 sharp." The deal was arranged.

The woman barely acknowledged my thanks, showing an indifference which I could only interpret as communicating the last "word" of displeasure. I tried to appear happy and congenial as I left. "I hope it sticks in her craw!" I hissed to myself as I crossed the road to the equipment store.

The women behind the cash register in the store dealt with customers in much the same way as the reservations clerk had dealt with me. One woman, checking inventory behind the counter was as much absorbed in animated conversation with the other employees as she was with her work. It didn't bother her when other employees interrupted her, but when a customer interrupted, she responded with a snappiness that bordered on rudeness. The other sales clerks talked to customers in condescending tones with a hint of sarcasm that quickly turned to impatience when customers persisted in trying to get their questions answered.

After watching the clerks for a few minutes, I decided to seek help elsewhere. I found a young man working in the rear of the store who was willing to talk with me. I explained that I was having problems with my stove flaming up and asked if he could recommend a safe, lightweight backpacker stove. He was very helpful and demonstrated how the Whisperlite backpackers' stove worked. Not only that, but because the price sticker seemed not to be correct, he took it upon himself to check it out and reduced the price some $30 from what it had been marked. I also bought a pair of Birkenstock sandals for wear around camp during evenings so I could get my feet out of my wet boots.

After experimenting a few minutes with my new stove, I packed it away and headed for the restaurant. Fred White was sitting by himself when I entered; he invited me to sit with him. (Les Rust had chosen to remain at the Rufus Morgan shelter.) We talked about the stretch of the Trail between Wesser and Fontana having the reputation as the toughest section of the AT outside of parts of Maine. As if to attest to its reputation, the *Philosopher's Guide*, quoted graffiti written on a guardrail in Stecoah Gap:

> "Throo-hikers beware — only 1 in 30 make
> it all the way. The test of staying power
> is here. The Smokies are vacation land."

Not only did the *Philosopher's Guide* mention the difficulty, the *Trail Guide* map profile showed the climbs to be both steep and long and that was reinforced by the written descriptions in the Trail guides themselves. When I mentioned that to Fred, he told me he had seen enough of the Trail anyway and that he would be getting off soon; he planned to do more hiking in the fall, probably in Vermont. It became quiet when our food arrived.

I was picked up by the bus from the Great Smokies Rafting Company at 10:20 a.m. the next morning. After driving the winding banks of the Nantahala River for an hour, we arrived at the starting point just below the dam. The guides struggled to unload the inflated rafts from the top of the bus while the people, not knowing what to do with themselves, milled about in nervous groups trying to stay out of the way. After unloading the rafts, the trip leader separated the people into raft groups and instructed the groups to carry their rafts to the river bank. I was assigned to the trip leader's raft along with a physician from Miami, Florida, named Levy and his girlfriend, Maureen.

The scenery in the gorge was in a class by itself. The walls of the mountains rose almost vertically hundreds of feet from the valley floor and here and there were strewn boulders that sometime in the millennia before had come crashing down, probably during the last ice age, or when the mountains were being formed. Some exposed mountainsides were composed of many layers of rock compressed into a multitude of angles that reflected the sunlight in a variety of colors.

The base of the mountains along the river was clothed in heavy growth while at higher elevations only a few spare tree skeletons clung precariously to their root holds in the cracks and crevices. Mostly though, the mountains were clothed in a verdant mantle of soft vegetation that draped over the shoulders of the ridges and flowed down to the water's edge where it was fringed by a dazzling display of wild flowers and occasional rhododendrons.

The rapids, although not dangerous, still required considerable skill to negotiate. With the leader in my raft, the paddling was easy. I thoroughly enjoyed the exhilaration of careening down the churning, rushing waters, slipping past boulders and dropping down minicascades into the whirling foam-coated pools. The others were not so fortunate.

There were six other rafts in our flotilla with people of varying degrees of inexperience at the helm. As a result, the river was soon strewn with wayward rafts, some broached on rocks in the middle, some caught in eddies along the bank, some caught in the low branches of trees that extended out over the water, and some floating down the rapids backwards while the occupants flailed at the water in a vain attempt to get the bow pointed downstream.

The trip leader stopped repeatedly to gather the gaggle together, reassert control, and account for everyone before again proceeding downstream. After one monumental snafu, he asked if I would take over the raft so he could assist another raft whose occupants were in complete disarray. Fortunately, the assistant trip leader arrived with her raft at that point and volunteered to take the "miscreants" in hand, and I was thereby relieved of my responsibilities even before I had the opportunity to display my incompetence. I faded back into the comfort of anonymity and talked with Levy and Maureen and paddled occasionally, when told to.

The climax of the trip was a minor waterfall of about four or five feet. The leader directed everyone to a sandy stretch of river bank about 100 yards upstream from the falls. We beached our rafts and proceeded forward on foot to make a visual reconnaissance of the falls. (As the people were assembling, I overheard the leader whisper to his assistant that ours was the worst group he had ever led down the river. After watching the morning's activities, I could believe it.) When we reached the falls, the leader pointed out the best approach to the falls, and we returned to our rafts.

A photographer stationed on a rock out in the water, just downstream from the falls, took pictures of the people as they came over the falls. Later he offered them for sale to whomever wanted a record of the event. The yelling and screaming that accompanied the rafts over the waterfall reminded me of the excitement I had experienced many years ago during my first ride on a roller coaster.

That evening I shared my hostel room with three other people, a woman from Alaska named Jeannie and two unaccompanied men from somewhere in the South, all enrolled in a kayaking clinic. (I had been "bumped" from the room I had been assigned the previous night.) Although tired from the day's excitement, I did not sleep well. Jeannie spent half the night reading and her light, coupled with some noisy adolescents in the room adjoining the wall where my bunk was located, combined to produce a fitful sleep. Getting proper rest is important for anyone doing the AT, even for 20 year olds. For me, however, it was imperative. At 52, I no longer had the reservoir of energy which the younger people had at their disposal. It was tough getting out of bed the next morning, and I felt drained even before I started on the Trail.

The hike out of the gorge was basically an eight-mile climb which ended on the 5,000-foot summit of Cheoah Bald. It was a demanding climb, and my heart told me so on a couple of occasions by palpitating noticeably in protest. At one point, in the middle of the climb, I asked myself if I wanted to continue that effort for another 2,000 miles. My answer was an emphatic, "No!" I immediately recognized the danger in my response and vowed not to quit, silently chastising myself for the way in which I answered my question. At the same time, I hoped fervently that it would be easier hiking in the Smokies. (It was a well-founded hope because the trail elevation profiles on the *Trail Guide* maps showed the Trail in the Smokies to be more gradual in ascent and descent.)

In the early afternoon, while climbing between Sassafras Gap and the summit of Cheoah Bald, I heard thunder booming in the distance. Although it sounded ominous, I didn't pay much attention. The sun was shining, and I suspected it was caused by heat. When I realized that it was coming steadily closer, I began looking for shelter. I wanted a rock overhang of some type for protection from the rain but more importantly as a place to get away from lightning. I hoped the storm would pass me by. That was not to be.

As I neared the summit, the sky suddenly became black, the wind began blowing in powerful gusts, and the crack of lightning became louder and increasingly closer. That lasted for only a short time, then it became absolutely still. I could feel the electricity in the air. Several seconds later, the mountain erupted in a flash of light followed by a torrent of water.

The explosion that followed the flash of light was exceedingly painful, and I wondered if it had burst my eardrum. There followed a series of lightning flashes, some in my vicinity, some further up the ridge, some below me. One lightning bolt struck a small tree about 75 yards down the hill. I watched in horror as the little tree virtually exploded, sending tiny shards of wood and bark in all directions.

Initially, I reacted in panic, looking frantically about for some place to hide. There was no place to go. I struggled with my fear, realizing that circumstances were beyond my ability to control or even influence. With that, I regained my composure and took what protective steps were available. I took off my pack, laid it down on the Trail, and backed away from it gingerly. I backed away as though it were a dangerous animal. (In a way it was dangerous because it had an aluminum frame which I feared might attract lightning.) I selected a place in a small mountain laurel thicket off to the side of the path, a good distance away from any large trees, and hunkered down. About five minutes later, it began to hail, and I watched numbly as ice balls the size of marbles bounced and rolled around the forest floor. Fifteen minutes passed before the lightning strikes moved on and soon all that remained was the rain, occasional hail and decreasing thunder in the distance.

In the meantime, my thin cotton summer shirt had quickly become rain-soaked, and the combination of moisture, wind and the sudden drop in temperature sharply reduced my body heat. I began to shiver uncontrollably. After the lightning departed, I removed my tent from my pack and draped the rain fly over myself for protection against the wind and to conserve body heat. The rain continued for about another half hour, then it too moved on. I was so cold and miserable I didn't want to sit down, so I stood and shivered while the rain poured down.

As I was contemplating my good fortune or misfortune, both of which could be claimed at the moment, movement on the forest floor about ten yards away caught my attention. A small cottontail rabbit, its damp fur matted against its body, hopped about contentedly munching tender shoots of new growth amid the leaves. It stopped and looked directly at me, then continued feeding, all the time edging closer to me.

First it moved in one direction, then reversed direction, then went on another angle and finally zigzagged a roundabout way until it ended up directly at my feet. I remained motionless the whole time. It sniffed the ground like a dog as it neared me. Then it sniffed directly at my feet. When it became clear that I was not a tree stump, it bolted in panic back in the direction from which it had come. "To each his own terror!" I laughed.

I was astonished by the contrasts of emotion I had experienced in the space of less than an hour. First I had been so concerned with the difficulty of the climb that nothing else mattered much. Then I had become terrified of the lightning strikes. Now I was feeling a warm glow of kinship with a tiny forest creature. There has to be a lesson in this somewhere, I mused.

After the rain stopped, I rolled up my tent and headed for

the summit, a large mountaintop meadow awash in sunshine. I removed my clothes, which, along with my tent, I spread out over some low bushes to dry. I also removed my boots in a vain attempt to dry them out. (They would require at least half a day to dry and even then I wasn't sure they'd be completely dry.) I sat completely naked on the edge of the bald waiting for my clothes to dry and feeling strangely good about it.

What if somebody comes? What will I do? I wondered. I couldn't think of a graceful explanation or escape in the event of that possibility. I decided to trust in Providence.

The warming sunshine felt good as I gazed across the summit meadow at the mountains in the distance and felt the confidence one always feels after surviving a dangerous event. The view was somewhat hazy, bluish with patches of light and dark on the mountains. The wood line at the farthest corner of the field was faintly screened by a thin, gauze-like veil of evaporating moisture. It was a tranquil scene with the gentle wind tugging occasional clouds across the sky, which in turn dragged their shadows across the landscape. I was content.

The wind picked up slightly and my clothes waved with the bushes, and the tent fly began billowing like a flag. Flags belong in the wind, I thought, unfurled and with their streamers waving brightly in the sunlight; and I was reminded of the flags in my office in Mainz.

They were office flags, flags that never waved in the wind. I suspected I had been like that in spirit, confined to a constrictive environment, functioning within the limiting parameters of the bureaucracy. Now, I experienced the freedom of release, as though I had been unfurled and set free to wave joyously in the fresh air. Then, I realized that I no longer had the nagging ache to be back in Mainz, to be at the seat of power. I was concerned now only with the adventure of the Trail, almost totally focused. When I did relate to the past, it was always within the framework of the present. For the first time, I had broken out of the psychological confines imposed by 30 years of discipline and bureaucracy. Clearly, my priorities were changing.

That night, I used my Whisperlite stove for cooking and was pleased by its efficiency and simplicity. Almost as soon as I finished eating, the rain started; it arrived as a steady downpour. I rough-scrubbed my cookpot and set it in the rain. Then I scrambled into my tent. This was the first prolonged heavy rain in my 15 days on the Trail.

As I drifted off to sleep, I realized how fortunate I had been on Cheoah Bald. I was thankful to have survived the lightning and vowed to be more attentive to approaching storms in the future. I had always thought of life in terms of strength and vigor. Now that I reflected on it, I realized life was impossibly fragile and susceptible to countless dangers.

The morning after this personal breakthrough, I encountered a wild dog on the south ridge crest above Stecoah Gap. From the rear, it looked similar to a malamute with a tail that curved up and over until the tip touched its back. Its attention was entirely directed downhill, and it did not sense my presence until I purposely hit my hiking stick against a rock. At first, I thought it was an ordinary dog until it bolted in panic like a wild animal. I wondered if it might have been a coyote or one of the "coydogs" Jim Bowman had talked about. Whatever it was, I observed it only briefly. It raced headlong in flight downhill and disappeared among a jumble of rocks at the base of a small cliff.

After walking a short distance down the ridge toward the Gap, I realized why the wild dog hadn't seen me. Coming up the Trail from the other direction was another dog and behind it, two day-hikers. The dog, a male German short-hair pointer, wearing a leather collar with a metal nameplate, stopped to sniff at my feet and pants' legs for a second before continuing up the hill. His clean, white and liver-spotted coat stretched smoothly across bulging chest muscles and down his back to his powerful haunches. His ribs showed clearly on the sides, and he was very thin at the point where his back joined his haunches. When the couple passed me, I congratulated them on owning such a beautiful dog.

"Oh, no," said the woman. "We thought he belonged to you."

I had gone only about 50 yards when the dog came racing back down the hill. I stepped off the Trail to let him go by, thinking he was headed back to his owner in the Gap. After he passed me, he slowed to about my pace, staying on the Trail just in front of me and stopping occasionally to allow me to catch up before resuming his gait. I was not interested in canine companionship and tried several times to shoo him off. Each time, he would slink off into the woods for a few yards and after a few minutes come bounding back through the brush, returning to the Trail in front of me. I concluded it was hopeless. I had been adopted, and there wasn't much I could do about it. He stayed with me the entire day.

Since we were going to be Trailmates, I decided he needed a

name and called him, "Stecoah Sam." Sam was long on conditioning, with seemingly boundless energy and zero discipline. The skin around his eyes seemed stretched at the corners, giving his face a mongoloid cast, and his eyes had a vacant, transparent quality that suggested cerebral deficiency. He wore a collar with a metal plate on it. I checked the plate; it contained the following information:

Gerald Garland
Robbinsville NC
479-3798

I resolved to call his owner when I reached Fontana.

Frequently, Sam would catch the scent of some animal or bird and go bounding off with his nose to the ground. He would run excitedly back and forth through the leaves and bushes until he had a clear scent, then streak off in a straight line to disappear into the forest. He always returned after a short time. Although apparently unsuccessful, seemingly he wasn't in the least discouraged. He seemed to have been blessed with the eternal optimism of a happy idiot. Needless to say, I saw no wildlife during the entire day.

Sam stayed with me all the way to Cable Gap shelter, a distance of ten miles. It was still fairly early when we arrived, but I was tired from the climbs. Since the next shelter at Fontana Dam was six plus miles away and over yet another steep mountain, I decided to stay for the night. While I rested after supper, Sam ran with tireless abandon through the forest, searching for a scent of something, streaking off to return a short time later to start the process again. Eventually, he wore down or became bored or both and remained at my side while I cooked supper.

I had not given him anything to eat at lunch; I didn't want to form an attachment with him. But at supper time, my pity overwhelmed my good judgment, and I cooked an extra portion of food for him. Evidently the macaroni, cheese and tuna was too rich, and he chucked it up, then ate it a second time. He then sat in front of me while I ate, his pleading eyes following every mouthful until it became unbearable. I yelled at him and he lay down in the leaves beside the shelter with a final grunt. I couldn't have given him anything else if I wanted. I was out of food. All that remained in my food sack was a small bag of gorp that Fred White had given me at Wesser, and I needed that for breakfast.

Cable Gap shelter was primitive as far as shelters went. It

"Stecoah Sam."

had three sides and a roof, but the floor was dirt, and instead of a sleeping platform, four chain-link fence bunks had been attached to the walls. The place had the disagreeable odor of damp, decaying vegetation, and I would have pitched my tent if a decent tentsite could have been found. Unfortunately, there were none and I settled in for the night. The shelter was deep in a heavy forest draw, and the light faded quickly. By 6:30 p.m., it was already twilight. Sam was snoring in his bed of leaves beside the shelter when I crawled into my sleeping bag.

During the night, I was awakened by the familiar crack of a thunderbolt. I was not pleased to be sleeping on a steel fence section under a tin roof in an electrical storm. But there wasn't much I could do about it, and I curled a little deeper into my sleeping bag and hoped for the best. I had trouble sleeping now with the noise from the thunder and the rain pounding on the shelter roof; and as if that wasn't disruption enough, the storm had driven Sam inside the shelter and he whined, groaned, chewed and scratched throughout the night.

As a result of these distractions, I didn't sleep well and again awoke the next morning feeling groggy and washed out. Sam, however, bounced around the shelter clearing in obvious high spirits. Maybe he expects food, I thought. When he realized I wasn't going to feed him, in resignation he lay down and went to sleep. Sam never stirred a muscle when I left. I wasn't even sure he knew that I had gone. As far as I know, Sam could still be sleeping there. I never saw him again.

I wondered why he was running loose; he was certainly a beautiful dog. Possibly his owner had moved out of town and left Sam with a friend, or abandoned him, or perhaps Sam had simply gotten lost. At any rate, Sam now had to fend for himself. He had a great bird dog's nose, but as a hunter he had about as many brains as a rock, and I wasn't sure he could survive in the wild. I suspected Sam lived by mooching from hikers or picnickers. When I arrived in Fontana, I put in a call to the number engraved on his collar plate only to learn the line had been disconnected.

The weather and the hiking were miserable; the sky was dreary and the forest wet. I became completely soaked from the wet grass and bushes that lined the pathway up High Top Mountain; if that wasn't discomfort enough, my heart palpitated with increasing frequency as I climbed higher. About half way to the summit, the mountain became shrouded in mist which prevented me from seeing the exceptional views of Lake Fontana and the Smokies mentioned in the *Trail Guide*. In fact, at times, the fog was so thick I could barely see the Trail ahead.

I had now come to a mental phase of the hike and had to "psych" myself to keep going. Until now, the Trail had been interesting because of its scenic beauty and because of my desire to become immersed in the experience, to become "One with the Trail." Now the walking was beginning to get old. I was tired of climbing mountains for what seemed to be pointless reasons. The hike had become a psychological as well as physical endurance contest.

I wondered how many more climbs I would have to make to complete my "Appalachian experience." I knew I would have to dig down deep inside to find the resolve to keep going, that it could be very easy to come off the Trail at Fontana. The temptation to leave the Trail became strong when I was in the vicinity of "civilization."

My desire to become "One with the Trail" did not matter much initially, but now it was a decisive factor in achieving a positive outlook. I tried to concentrate on that theme, hoping that by identifying with my surroundings, I could achieve a positive outlook despite being miserable. I succeeded for only short periods of time in feeling anything positive; I was basically in a very negative mental posture. I was unhappy with the physical demands of the climbs, the wet weather, the personal discomfort, and most of all I was disappointed with my attitude. Perhaps my sour mood resulted from fatigue.

As an antidote, I tried to envision myself as part of nature, as part of the Trail. I understood intellectually that I was a part of the Trail because, at that moment in time, I was part of the experience. I tried to rationalize that I was experiencing the Trail in another dimension which was as completely natural to the Trail as the sunshine and the vistas. Now the Trail consisted of rain and mist and gray skies with no views. It was beauty of a different kind, and I had to learn to accept that part of the Trail as well as the wildflowers and sun-dappled forest. I needed to accept that what I felt about the hike was my responsibility, that I could not blame external conditions for the way in which I chose to react. The choice was mine; the weather and the climbs were neutral elements which I could not change; I could only accommodate myself to them. It occurred to me that in a certain sense I already was "One with the Trail."

I concentrated on thinking only positive thoughts. I repeated to myself positive encouragement. You will make it! I told myself again and again. Nothing very good or very bad lasts for very long, remember that! I could hear my father's voice as he said these words to me many years ago during one of my "counseling" sessions. He was talking about the Army then. But I was trying now to put the idea into practice on the Trail.

It was 1:30 p.m. when I reached Fontana Village two miles west of Fontana Dam and rented a room for two nights. (I planned to rest for one full day.) I spent the remainder of the afternoon shopping, doing laundry, and studying the *Trail Guide* for the Smokies. According to the map, the Trail in the Smokies appeared to be difficult, but the descriptions in the *Trail Guide* did not indicate such severe conditions. The question was, "How was it graded?" If it was constructed with switchbacks and graded so that the vertical ascent was reasonable, it would be no great problem. A 1:24,000 scale topographic map on the wall at the Inn showed the climb to be very steep. I decided at that point that I would just follow my own advice; take it easy, hike at my own speed, and be happy with making it to the shelter at Birch Springs Gap, a total distance of five and four-tenths uphill miles for the first day. That climb would put me on the main ridge of the Smokies and from there the changes in elevation would be less severe than the climb out of Fontana.

The next morning, I rode the shuttle bus to Fontana Dam to arrange for my passage through the Smokies and to get my overnight camping permit from the Rangers. I anticipated saving time by solving first any bureaucratic contingencies which might arise. The bus stopped near the junction of the Fontana Dam access road and North Carolina Route 28 to pick up four teenaged boys hiking from Dicks Gap, Georgia, and deposited us all at the dam at about 11:00 a.m., the time I anticipated from my previous day's calculations.

I searched in vain for a Ranger, finally going to the gift shop concession where I was given the Ranger's telephone number. There was no answer at the number, so I walked back up the access road to the office of the security guard for the dam. I learned that two Rangers were assigned to the Fontana area, but both were indisposed. One was on vacation, the other was occupied "hauling a load of hay across the lake."

The security guard gave me the number of the National Park Service in Gatlinburg, Tennessee, headquarters for the Great Smoky National Park. I returned to the dam and started dialing. (He wouldn't let me use the office phone.)

When I reached the number, the person on the other end referred me to another number which I called without success. Either there was no answer or the line was busy. I tried about five times, then called back to the first number and was informed I had to talk with the people at the second number, the Backcountry Registration Office. The voice on the other end was very polite, in a bureaucratically firm way. "They're very shorthanded. Let the phone keep ringing until someone answers it. They will answer it. They're just shorthanded."

Where have I heard that one before? I asked myself sarcastically.

After about five minutes a woman answered, apologized for the delay, and told me again they were "extremely shorthanded." I explained the purpose of my call, and we developed an itinerary which she entered in the computer. I was informed that, if at all possible, I should contact the Ranger in the morning, and if that were not possible, to just begin my hike and if anyone questioned me, to have that person check with her office.

That evening, after supper I returned to my room and again inventoried and repacked my gear plus food. I wanted to be sure everything was in readiness for my hike through the Smokies. I had to make it through the entire 70 miles with what I carried on my back, because there were no places to resupply in the park.

As I lay in bed reviewing the day, I thought about the four teenaged boys who had boarded the shuttle at the junction of the dam access road and North Carolina Route 28 that morning and rode the last few hundred yards down to the dam. They had told me they had started from Dicks Creek Gap, Georgia, the prior Sunday. "Did a 100 miles," boasted one boy.

Shortly after that, I had visited the famous "Fontana Hilton," the elaborate Trail shelter on the high ground just south of the Dam, where I met two teenaged female hikers, also from the Dicks Creek Gap group. I caused a minor explosion when I inadvertently mentioned that I had met the boys on the shuttle bus. The girls were incredulous that the boys had stooped to ride the bus, while they, women true to the hikers' creed, had walked every last inch of the way. Needless to say, the boys took a vicious razzing when the girls caught up to them.

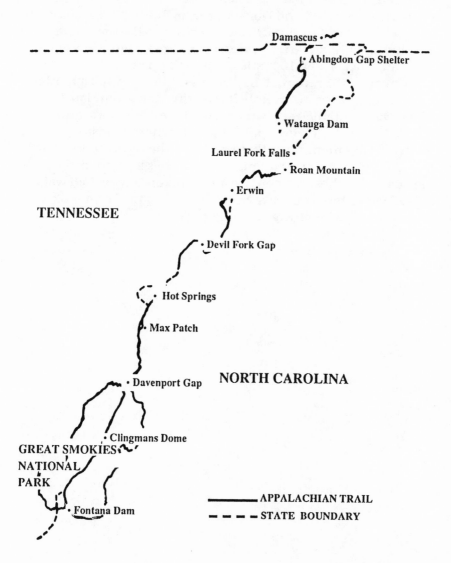

Fontana Dam, North Carolina, to Damascus, Virginia

CHAPTER 7

The Great Smokies
Birch Springs Gap to Clingmans Dome

As requested by the woman with whom I had spoken at the Park Service Headquarters, I telephoned the Rangers before starting from Fontana Dam the next morning. Ranger Mark Matsko apologized that he could not personally register me; an injury to his ankle the previous day had immobilized him. However, we reviewed and finalized my itinerary. After a short briefing on the Park Service rules, I was on my way. The itinerary I planned was:

> First night: Birch Springs Gap shelter
> Second night: Spence Field shelter
> Third night: Silers Bald shelter
> Fourth night: Mt. Collins shelter
> Fifth night: Pecks Corner shelter
> Sixth night: Cosby Knob shelter

The massive expanse of concrete known as Fontana Dam was awesome to behold. As I crossed, I was mesmerized by the desire to look over its sides. First, I was drawn to the side where the Little Tennessee River flowed from the conduits at the base of the dam. My eyes followed the smooth concrete walls several hundred feet down to the valley, and I felt the wrench in the pit of my stomach I always feel when looking down from great heights. The mountains framed the River on both sides, sending giant green-clothed ridge arms sweeping thousands of feet steeply down from their heights to the narrow channel where the river, resembling a silky, green ribbon, flowed smoothly for several hundred yards in a straight line west from the base of the dam, until it rounded a wide bend toward the north and disappeared.

On the other side, the low water level in Fontana Lake created a wide band of ochre earth and rock between the water surface and the vegetation level. An island near the dam reminded me of a caricature of an island drawn by a cartoonist. It appeared a bowl had been placed over the dome-like top of the island, then everything down to the water had been shaved.

The climb up Shuckstack Mountain was easier than I anticipated. I made good time, arriving at Birch Springs Gap shelter by midafternoon, much earlier than expected. I entertained momentary thoughts about continuing, but then remembered my itinerary.

I laid claim to a place on the wire mesh sleeping platform and began to record my Trail notes. About an hour later, I was joined by Melvin Wilson and his two pre-teen sons, David and Chris, from Bigstone Gap, Virginia, a small mountain community wedged into the extreme southwest corner of the state between Tennessee and Kentucky. They had started their hike from Clingmans Dome two days earlier and were spending their last night on the Trail before heading home in the morning.

I was immediately impressed by the atmosphere of respect and affection between Melvin and his two sons. It wasn't a coddling affection, though. Melvin set quite demanding behavioral standards which the boys willingly tried to meet. But it wasn't something that was ordered. There was no yelling or putting the boys down, no drill sergeant mentality, only patience and understanding. Corrections or suggestions, when necessary, were made quietly and with an appeal to the boy's sense of responsibility. Later, Melvin told me his father had taken him hunting and fishing when he was a boy and had taught him many lessons in woodsmanship which he was now passing on to his sons. I suspected that sometime in the future, Chris and David would be passing on those same lessons to their sons.

Chris mentioned excitedly that they had seen many deer and a fox during their hike, but then expressed some disappointment at not having seen any bears. I was surprised they hadn't seen a bear; I had heard that bears were numerous in the park and it was not unusual for a hiker to see one or two. In fact, many bears had lost their fear of man which made them somewhat dangerous nuisances.

I had been pointedly warned by the Ranger and others not to leave my pack unattended, even for a minute, because of the bear threat. At one time, people were not allowed to overnight-

Birch Springs Gap shelter in the Great Smoky National Park.

hike in the park without a rope of certain thickness and length. When camping for the night, this rope was to be strung between trees and packs hung from it at sufficient height to keep them out of a bear's reach. This ploy didn't work well. The bears simply climbed the trees and pulled the rope down and got the packs anyway.

Melvin mentioned that he had heard about instances of bears chasing people in an attempt to get them to drop their packs. I said I didn't think I'd drop my pack and Melvin said that any bear that tried to steal his pack would end up with a "knot on its nose."

Every shelter in the Smokies has a bear-proof chain-link fence from ground to roof across the entire open front. The recommended defense against bears stealing packs was for campers to simply bring their packs into the shelter and close the door.

While Melvin and I talked, the boys went exploring and found an animal burrow in a corner of the shelter between the sleeping platform and the fire place. "It's still in there!" yelled Chris excitedly.

Melvin and I went to look.

The boys slid the large rock away from the hole, exposing a

pair of beady eyes staring in the darkness. The eyes shifted positions occasionally, but never closed, and no sound of movement
could be heard. "Must be a ground hog," said Chris, slightly
spooked by the blackness and the silence.

"More like a skunk," said David.

No one could say for sure, not even Melvin, but the smart
money was betting it was a ground hog. I thought David was
right, that it was a skunk. I never saw a ground hog come near
the surface of his burrow when people were nearby. Of course, I
never saw a skunk do that either!

The shelter was infested with yellow jackets. Although not
aggressive, they were a colossal irritation, landing indiscrimi-
nately on people and equipment. It was impossible to sit anywhere near the shelter without two or three of them landing on
our shoulders or legs. After enduring the insects for awhile, the
boys ran out of patience and decided to solve the problem by
lighting a fire to drive them off with smoke. It may not have
worked on the yellow jackets, but it worked on Melvin and me.
The boys soon gave up that effort.

At about 7:00 p.m., two young men appeared on the scene.
The oldest one, a shirtless 20-year-old with shoulder length,
stringy blond hair, and a substantial belly that hung over his
belt, carried a small day pack. The other boy, a thin, quiet 18-
year-old with nervous eyes and curly brown hair, was carrying a
blanket or blankets rolled into a long bedroll. The two ends of it
were wrapped with rope, and it was slung over his shoulder like
a rifle. Neither seemed clothed nor equipped to spend much
time in the woods. Without saying a word of greeting to anyone,
the young man with the curly brown hair, acting as though he
owned the shelter, climbed up on the roof and walked along the
ridge beam to the chimney where he threw down a frying pan
and a box of salt that had been stashed there.

Initially, the two newcomers stayed apart from Melvin and
me. But a noticeable tension developed which made everyone
uncomfortable. After about 30 minutes, the blond boy ran up
the mountain as if he had an errand to do. I was impressed at
how easily he ran the steep incline, his excess weight seeming to
bother him not at all. When the blond boy disappeared from
view, I tried to break the awkward atmosphere by making conversation with the second boy. "Where's your buddy gone?"

"Fer a walk!" came the reply with a hostile curtness and nod
of the head.

I walked around to the other side of the fire next to Melvin.

"These are wild ones," Melvin whispered out of the side of his mouth.

The blond boy returned a short time later, and immediately both boys left the campfire and huddled off by themselves near the spring. The brown-haired boy watched me intently as they talked. After a few minutes, they returned to the fire, and the blond boy started talking about hunting. "You like to deer hunt?" he asked Melvin.

"I like deer hunting," Melvin replied. "Most always have two in the freezer at the end of the season."

"You like huntin' deer?" he directed his question to me.

"I've been a couple of times, but never got a deer," I told him.

The brown-haired boy took several large potatoes from the day pack and began peeling them, looking up at me from time to time as he worked. There was no hint of friendliness in his eyes, only suspicion and hostility. He paid no attention to Melvin or the boys and watched only me, which made me nervous.

"Gonna cook you some taters?" said Melvin cheerfully. I was glad Melvin and the boys were around. "Isn't anything as good as fresh fried taters over a wood fire," Melvin continued. "I like 'em with deer meat. I've spent many a night fryin' taters when I was your age."

"You want some?" asked the blond boy.

"No, you carried 'em, you eat 'em," Melvin replied.

"Y'all seen any b'ar?" asked the blond boy.

At first, I didn't understand him. I looked at Melvin and he shrugged his shoulders. Then the blond boy repeated himself. "No, we ain't seen nary a bear," Melvin answered quickly.

"We hunted lots of b'ar. His daddy probably killed more b'ar than anyone alive," said the blond boy, pointing to his companion.

The brown-haired boy looked up from the frying pan and entered the conversation for the first time. "Killed 129!" Then he looked back down at his frying pan and that was all he said.

"We used to go b'ar huntin' all the time, but there ain't many around now. I ate lots of b'ar meat, but I don't like it near as much as deer meat."

"You boys ever go after honey?" asked Melvin. "You know how to find a tree that's got honey?"

Everyone shook their heads.

"Watch how the bee flies. If it stays under the trees, it means the hive is close by, and you just follow in the direction the bee flew. If it has a long way to go, it flies over the trees. You need someone to stand on the ridge, and when he finds where the bees fly over, you just follow the line between you and where the bees flew over, and it takes you right to the hive. Then you got to get the honey out."

About that time, four teenaged boys from a summer camp in Brevard, North Carolina, came trooping down the shelter access trail, and the conversation waned, but not before the blond boy asked Melvin if he'd like to have some deer meat.

"Not so much that I'd do anything illegal to get it," Melvin replied.

After the new hikers settled in, the conversation picked up again. The blond boy talked incessantly about hunting and about how many deer he'd killed and how many bear his daddy killed and how to hunt bear. After listening to him describe how they hunted bear, I wondered that any bear remained in the forest. The technique, according to the blond boy, was to let loose a bunch of hunting dogs and follow them until they found the trail of a bear and treed it. The hunters had only to follow the sound of the dogs to the treed bear and shoot it.

"Some sport!" I murmured under my breath.

The blond boy dominated the conversation to the point of boredom. After about an hour, I climbed into my sleeping bag. Unfortunately, the conversation around the firepit continued and kept me half awake.

After they came into the shelter for the night, the two young men whispered intermittently in conspiratorial tones. Every time one of them moved, someone else shined a flashlight on the packs hanging from the roof support beams. Even Melvin, who was lying on a fence section next to mine, could not sleep soundly, and once I heard him swear and slap at a mouse that had run across his head.

The next morning, without even bothering to make breakfast, the Wilsons packed their gear and departed immediately for Fontana Dam. I cooked and ate breakfast, departing quickly. I didn't want to end up alone at the shelter with the two local boys.

The weather was cloudy but dry and very windy. But the hiking was pleasant. At about 11:00 a.m., a light sprinkle began which, after about 15 minutes, became a steady drizzle. The Trail followed the increasing elevation of the main east/west ridge spine of the Smokies for almost the entire morning, but it was well-graded and the walking as not particularly difficult.

The four summer camp boys overtook me three hours after I started. We stopped to talk. I mentioned something about the two local boys. The group leader made a funny face and the story came out.

After I had left the shelter, a young buck deer come to drink at the spring. One of the boys, using a rifle that had been concealed in their blankets, shot the animal. But the deer fled over the ridge with the two local boys in hot pursuit. One of them, I think it was the blond boy, his hands and arms covered with blood, returned to the spring a short time later to wash up. He warned the boys not to say anything, indicating he trusted them, but that he didn't trust me or Wilson.

Suddenly, I understood why the brown-haired boy kept looking at me. I was wearing long olive green fatigue trousers and a green poplin shirt with epaulettes and that resembled a Ranger uniform. They thought I might be a Ranger. I also understood why Melvin Wilson had departed from the shelter so early. I theorized that he suspected the two locals were up to trouble of some kind and probably wanted to be out of the area before anything happened. The four hikers said they were going to tell the first Ranger they saw, and I resolved to do the same.

I reached Russell Field shelter at 12:30 p.m., just ahead of a ferocious electrical storm. The metal shelter roof intensified the sound of the rain into an immobilizing wall of sound that all but drowned out the periodic thunderclaps. I found some dry kindling and a few sticks under the sleeping platform and started a fire in the small fireplace, then spread my clothes out to dry and prepared to wait out the storm. Eventually, the lightning passed and the rain receded in volume to a steady slow drum-roll beat on the roof.

As soon as the rain eased, I ventured forth again. I had not walked more than a hundred yards when I encountered a doe deer ambling down the Trail, feeding on the succulent vegetation beside the pathway about 20 yards in front of me. I saw her rump first, a sleek, tawny coat rippling across a roundly muscled flank as she sidled gracefully across the Trail. When she sensed my presence, she started and tensed into position for immediate flight. She craned her neck and cocked her head in several different positions trying to get a fix on me. I stood completely still. After a few seconds, she relaxed and began to nibble on the bushes again. Finally, she crossed the Trail on the left, wiggled her tail at me, and disappeared into the forest.

I spent the remainder of the day in the clouds. The wind whipped the mists in strange and somewhat haunting ways. Sometimes the wind seemed to blow in several directions at the same time. At other times, the mists floated gently one way until a gust changed their direction and swept them in swirls or sheets along the ridge, occasionally allowing them to pause before sending them spinning off again. At times, they reminded me of huge veils sweeping across a stage, hiding the scenery behind. The trees in the foreground appeared and disappeared frequently, and occasionally the slightest suggestion of a tree line appeared across the bald before the veil closed again. Sometimes I was able to glimpse the next nearest ridge line. Though I was wet, walking across Little Bald was a rare treat, and I sat on a rock for about ten minutes watching the wind work its magic.

When I arrived at Spence Field shelter, I met a Ranger on horseback and told him about the poaching incident at Birch Springs Gap. He wrote down the details, then rode off to report what he had learned. He returned about 30 minutes later to inform me that the Rangers had already been alerted by the summer camp boys, had located the truck belonging to the poachers, and had it under surveillance. He indicated that the poachers would not want the meat to go to waste and would, in all probability, try to carry it home in their truck. That's when the Rangers would nab them.

I learned that the Ranger was part of a "hog eradication" party engaged in a program to eliminate or at least reduce the wild boar population in the Great Smokies. The wild hogs were descendants of European wild boar imported years ago as hunting stock by a wealthy hunter. Some of the animals had escaped and, over the years, reproduced in such numbers that they now competed with native animals, primarily deer and bear for food. The Ranger explained that the hogs, in their search for food, tore up the sodgrass on the balds making the land more receptive to seeding by the trees from the nearby forest, which resulted in more rapid reforestation and a changed mountain ecology.

The weather was windy and still misty the next morning when I departed the shelter, and it remained that way until noon. At the top of Spence Field, I surprised a tawny-colored animal that ran off squealing in panic. It was 20 yards away when I first noticed the movement, but it was partially hidden by the tall grass and disappeared into the mist before I was able to get a good look at it. Because it appeared to have stripes or spots, for a moment I thought it might be a bobcat. Later, when I reflected on the incident, I realized it had probably been a young wild pig. A bobcat would not have made any noise.

I was still thinking about my "wildcat," when I came face to face with my first bear. We both saw one another at the same time and stopped abruptly — about 20 yards apart. I think the bear was as surprised as I. It filled the Trail, its flanks brushing the tall grass on either side. I didn't know if it was a he or a she bear, but I was certain it was a big bear. I quickly looked around to be sure no cubs were nearby. (Bears are most likely to be dangerous when they feel their cubs are threatened.) I was in luck. No cubs! And the bear blinked first!

The bear turned and started back in the direction from which it had come, then stopped, looked back at me, and before I had a chance to faint, turned off the side of the Trail and disappeared. I had not expected to see so large a bear, and it left me wide-eyed and slack-jawed. With some trepidation, I walked slowly to the point where the bear had entered the woods and peered through the underbrush hoping for, and at the same time fearing, another glimpse of the monster. It was much too dark and misty to see very far into the forest, so I continued on with slightly rubbery legs and a much keener awareness of my surroundings.

The climb up Thunderhead Mountain was not at all pleasant. First, it was a very demanding trail, steep, rocky and, in places, washed out. Secondly, because of the mist, I was unable to see any of the supposedly spectacular views from the open 5,500-foot summit. I continued without stopping toward Saddleback Ridge.

Shortly before Derrick Knob shelter, where the Trail passed through an open forest with a luxuriant carpet of thick, long grass, I encountered another deer. A whitetail buck lying in the grass about 20 yards downhill from the Trail either heard or smelled me, or both, and leaped from its bed, snorting with displeasure as it streaked down the mountain.

The buck was a magnificent animal with a beautiful rack of antlers that I guessed to have six or eight points. The power and the speed which the deer summoned from a dead stop were awesome. He had soared about 30 yards with his initial leap as his powerful hind quarters catapulted him into the air without discernible effort. When he had landed after his initial leap, it was like he compressed a spring that launched him a second time into a graceful short fight. And then he was gone.

The clouds had disappeared and the sun was shining by the time I arrived at Derrick Knob shelter. I undressed and spread out my clothes to dry while I ate lunch. Evidently, the shelter was occupied; a food bag hung from the rafters and a pair of moccasins had been neatly placed directly in front of the fireplace. Fortunately, the occupants did not return while I was sitting around in my underpants.

After returning to the Trail, I encountered a family of wild pigs. I saw the initial movement 50 yards away in fairly open forest to my left front. Although I couldn't discern the exact shape of the first animal, I could tell it was fairly large and at first thought it might be a bear. Then I saw the movement of other animals and was soon able to identify two mature pigs and six piglets.

I watched for several minutes as they grunted and snorted their way up the slight elevation toward me. They tore up the ground with their snouts, leaving it looking like a roto-tiller had churned through the forest. Then an interesting thing happened. When they came to within about 15 yards of me, they abruptly changed direction and headed at a right angle down the hill. I could detect no signal from any of the animals to show alarm or to cause them to change direction. Evidently, they all took their cue from one animal, and when it changed direction, the others followed automatically. Not once did any of them stop or raise their heads to look at me, nor did they race off in a panic.

After crossing Derrick Knob, I spooked two turkey vultures, one of which landed on the lower limb of a large tree to my right front. It was very large, about the size of an eagle, totally black, except for its ugly, naked, red head. The birds flew up from where they had been feasting on the bloated body of a dead hog which lay on its side with its legs sticking grotesquely in the air. Evidently it was one of the victims of the hog eradication program. I remembered the Ranger telling me they only killed the hogs; they didn't use the meat in any way or bury the animals. They left the hogs lying where they were shot, allowing the bodies to decompose in a way natural to all things wild. The vultures were beginning the process, and in time other life forms would complete the cycle.

Wanda and Bill Baker from Cincinnati, Ohio, were already

at the Silers Bald shelter when I arrived that evening. They were an interesting couple who did exciting things together such as sailing to Central America as part of the crew on a 44-foot sailing boat or sailing port-to-port in the Aegean Sea off the coast of Greece. They had been hiking parts of the AT in the Smokies and were leaving the next day for a week of kayaking on the Nantahala River. Bill was an engineer with the General Electric jet aircraft engine division, and I suspected his adventures provided free-spirited diversions from the pressures of his job.

After supper, I climbed to the summit of Silers Bald to watch the sun set. The dying sunlight bathed the hill in a frail light and cast the elongated shadows of the small trees and bushes far down the hillside. The green and yellow foliage, and the orange and reds from the dried and dead grass and leaves reminded me of autumn. The thickets near the top of the bald remained bright green in the sun light. But down the hillside, the light and shadow along the forest's edge created hues with varying intensities of green. The mountains in the distance appeared as if a soft, velvet green fabric had been draped over them, and if somehow it could be rolled back, a great surprise might be found.

I remained on the bald until almost dark. Then on my way back to the shelter, I passed a doe and her yearling feeding in a blackberry thicket. The yearling watched nervously as I approached but didn't run. The doe continued to browse without once looking up.

When I neared the shelter, a deer walking toward the rear of the building stopped to watch, then continued on without haste. A few minutes later, another doe ambled into the shelter clearing and came to within about five feet of me to feed on the leaves of the common plantain which grew in abundance there. Another doe approached the clearing from the ridge behind me and two more appeared from the other direction behind the shelter. I moved slowly so as not to alarm them, and they showed no signs of fear. Even when Wanda and Bill, who had also been viewing the sunset of Silers Bald, made their way back to the shelter, the deer watched without concern.

That evening while reflecting on the progress of my hike and my transition, I became aware that I was losing my fear of losing track of time. I was still aware of time and planned my day accordingly, but it had lost the all-consuming importance it once held for me. Initially, when I had started from Springer, if

I didn't arrive at a point as planned, I found myself becoming tense. I wasn't doing that now. If I wanted to be some place at lunch time and hadn't yet reached that location, I just waited until I arrived to eat lunch or I ate lunch when I got hungry. To someone who has not experienced the tyranny of time, the importance of that break may not be apparent. To me it was monumental.

On the Fourth of July, I awoke to sunshine. I was the first up, then Bill and then Wanda. The height of the upper level sleeping platform made it very difficult for Wanda to get down. Her short legs would not reach the ground, and it was too great a distance to just simply hop down. I suggested she lie on her stomach and inch over the edge of the platform to allow her legs to drop down until they reached the lower platform. (That was how I had done it.) Wanda's legs were too short for even that maneuver, and she hung balanced on her tummy with her legs swinging freely beneath her, trying desperately to find support for her feet. Just when it seemed her legs would swing underneath the platform and cause her to lose her balance, Bill came to the rescue and gently assisted her to the ground.

A flock of birds flitting through the bushes in front of the shelter intrigued Wanda. They were cardinal-sized birds with similar crests, but they were tan over all with a mask-like band of black that swept back from their eyes, and their tail feathers had a distinct yellow band near the tip. Wanda called our attention to them, asking if we knew what species they were. When neither Bill nor I could give her an answer, she retrieved a bird book from her pack and within a minute identified them as Cedar Waxwings.

The Trail proved difficult throughout the morning, particularly that part from Mt. Buckley to the summit of Clingmans Dome. The grade was very steep, and in places where it had been washed away, the footing was treacherous. Other parts were heavily overgrown; considerable effort was required to push through the thick underbrush. Despite the strenuous nature of the hike, I enjoyed the views, especially Clingmans Dome bathed in sunlight with people moving slowly up and down the trails. They looked like multicolored ants from the distance.

When I reached the point where the Trail joined the paved path from the parking lot to the summit tower, I felt like I had arrived at New York's Grand Central Station during rush hour. I fell in with the throng of tourists headed for the summit, ignoring the stares of those who looked at me as though I were from outer space.

I climbed to the circular observation platform and tried to identify the terrain features depicted on the panels attached to the railing at various intervals. But the weather was so hazy that I was unable to discern even one mountain peak in the distance. I didn't stay very long. The press of people made me uncomfortable, particularly those trying to impress others with loud and mostly inane remarks. I left the observation platform and returned quickly to the Trail and the welcome quiet.

About 100 yards down the hill from the tower, I found a log lying conveniently beside the pathway and stopped for lunch. A family on the way to Newfound Gap stumbled by, but other than that, I had the Trail to myself again and ate in peace.

MOUNTAINS

You can feel the magnetism of mountains.
To some, it is the power of granite crags,
Thrusting relentlessly against the sky.
To others, it is swirls of mist,
Dancing on the wind, flowing and ebbing;
Pirouetting along the ridge.
It can be the rush of pure emotion
That catches at your breath
When you reach the summit of Max Patch.
It can be the cathedral silence of hemlocks
That presses our spiritual borders;
Or perhaps the gardens of wildflowers,
Swaying in the sunlight across the balds.
To some, it is the closeness
Of the solitude of nightfall
As it creeps about the folds and draws
On its relentless climb up the ridge.
To all, it is a beckoning siren,
Promising escape from our desperation.
Our sensuous minds foolishly
Try to hold the raptures.
But, when we would possess the timeless,
It escapes into our memories,
Forever to be dimly savored;
And we poignantly hope that the morrow
Will bring fresh excitement
From another unexpected beauty.

CHAPTER 8

The Great Smokies
Clingmans Dome to Pigeon River
One with the Trail

I had traveled only eight miles for the day, but they were tough miles, and by the time I reached the Mt. Collins shelter, I was exhausted. Figuratively, I had been walking on the roof of the eastern United States, walking across mountains well over a mile in the sky. I had crossed Silers Bald at 5,607 feet; Mt. Buckley, 6,583 feet; Clingmans Dome, 6,643 feet; and Mt. Collins, 6,188 feet.

Clingmans Dome is the third highest of all the Appalachian Mountains, higher even than the infamous Mt. Washington in New Hampshire. Mt. Mitchell in North Carolina, the highest mountain in the Appalachians, is only 41 feet higher than Clingmans Dome.

In the gap between Clingmans Dome and Mt. Collins, I was stopped by a serious-looking, in-charge type Ranger who asked for my camping permit. I recited my story about not having a paper permit because the Ranger at Fontana Dam had injured his ankle, but that I was legal because my itinerary had been entered in the computer. The Ranger wrinkled his nose and narrowed his eyes like he expected me to offer him stock in the Brooklyn Bridge, then checked my story by calling his headquarters on a small, black, hand-held radio. The voice on the radio loudspeaker responded with my name and told him I had spent the previous night at Silers Bald shelter and was supposed to stay at Mt. Collins shelter that night.

I smirked ever so slightly when the answer confirmed my story and rubbed it in a little. "Can you give me a piece of paper so I won't have to go through one of these 'nut rolls' every time I meet one of you guys?" I asked smartly.

My refusal to be intimidated and the fact that he didn't have any permits with him unnerved the Ranger momentarily. But he quickly recovered and announced in an authoritarian tone of voice that a Ranger would be checking on the Mt. Collins shelter that night and he would give me a permit.

No Ranger appeared at the shelter. In fact, during my remaining time in the Park, I saw only one other Ranger. That was the next day at Newfound Gap, and he was in no position to check on anybody.

I had an audience that evening while eating supper. A reddish-brown ground squirrel, probably attracted by the smell of food, scampered from somewhere inside the shelter to the firepit and watched while I ate. It sat motionless in an upright position, its eyes fixed on me during the entire meal. When I finished eating, I returned to the shelter to clean and repack my utensils, and the squirrel went immediately to the log on which I had been sitting and sniffed about. Finding no food on the ground, it scampered up to the top side of the log, then leaped down and scurried back to the shelter, where despite my being no more than a couple of feet away, it inspected my stove and the ground in the vicinity where I had been cooking. When it became clear that no food was available, the squirrel made a beeline for a large tree stump on the edge of the forest.

After supper, I reflected on the events and important themes I had developed during the day, noting that I was still in the business of psyching myself for the Trail. I realized with renewed clarity that my attitude toward the Trail and my hike changed with my mood swings. Up to this point, I had done 200 miles of the Trail and now had less than 2,000 to go. "Whoopie!" I said sarcastically as I made a little circle in the air with my forefinger.

I recognized that the difficulty in remaining motivated and positive increased in proportion to my fatigue. I doubted I would ever get to the point where the physical pain and discomfort disappeared, and hiking, as such, became fun.

As much as I loved the animals and the scenery, and as much as I wanted to be "One with the Trail," I still missed Naples, beds with sheets, and bathrooms with running water. But most of all, I missed Anna. I was still very much a creature of comfort, and when I became uncomfortable physically, I also became uncomfortable psychologically.

I decided that four straight months of hiking would be long

enough and that I would come off the Trail on October 12. Winter is no time to be hiking alone in the mountains, especially without the proper equipment, I thought. I wondered how close I might be to my goal after four months. If I continued hiking an average of ten miles a day, I could expect to be somewhere around Delaware Water Gap by the middle of October. Maybe further north, if I can rack up 15- or 20-mile days, I thought. Then I remembered rule number one again: "Do what my body will give me."

I didn't want to make the hike strictly an endurance contest, although to this point that was exactly what I felt it had become. The physical challenge of the Trail was making it increasingly difficult to "smell the flowers" or to remain "One with the Trail." I could not ignore the rigors or the physical price which it exacted from my body.

On the other hand, despite the exertion and fatigue, I also felt good about myself. After all, hiking 200 miles through the mountains was no small accomplishment. I was proving I could hold my own in tough circumstances without the aid of a familiar support network. That was a confidence builder, and with it came the expectation that I would succeed. I was determined to succeed. But that was not all!

I also realized that I was learning to be flexible and realistic in my goals and that I would have to adapt to circumstances and realities, just as I was already doing. Clearly, I could not complete my hike by the end of the summer. I could not ignore my physical limitations; I could not hike 20 miles a day through difficult terrain. Twenty years ago I could have done it, but no longer. It was important to recognize that, and to accept that my physical strength and stamina would become increasingly limited and that I could not change that fact.

I had begun devoting periods of the day to meditation, trying to understand my relationship with God, and to develop a sense of spiritual confidence. The hike was giving me a unique opportunity to develop a new perspective to reorder the fundamental priorities that governed my life.

Every morning I tried to devote the first hour of the hike to pondering the essence and the limits of my spirituality. Sometimes I was able to concentrate for long periods of time; at other times, I couldn't retain my focus for more than a few minutes. On those latter occasions, I felt I had wasted an opportunity. Regardless of the outcome, I vowed to continue to press my spiritual development. I was convinced that with my spiritual consciousness in order, the real pattern of my life and my life's work would automatically coalesce.

When it was too dark for further writing, I climbed into my sleeping bag. So ends the Fourth of July, 1986, I thought; it really was a great feeling to be an American on Clingmans Dome. Then I smiled. I had a feeling of belonging. The other people I had seen on the mountain were there only for the day. When the day was over, they had gotten into their cars and left the mountains. I was alone now. It was me, the deer, the bears, the chipmunks and the mountains. At that moment, I became a part of those old hills. Sometime in the future, I might tell my grandsons about that July day on Clingmans Dome when I really was a part of the mountains.

On my way through Indian Gap the next morning, I met two young men "camped" beside a small overlook turnoff in front of their pickup truck. They were engaged in a mighty and seemingly futile effort to fire up their camp stove so they could make coffee. Feeling neighborly, I stopped, and using my Whisperlite stove, had the water boiling in no time.

We talked a few minutes about the Trail. When I mentioned that I was running low on Coleman fuel, they offered me enough to fill my Sigg bottle. I was so low in fact that the previous evening I had cut a notch near the top of my hiking staff to hang my pot from in the event I was forced to cook over a wood fire.

The young men were very interested to learn I was thru-hiking the Trail and asked many insightful questions. In addition to giving them some "expert opinions," I added some "local color" by relating my stories about the bear on Thunderhead and the two local boys who poached the deer at Birch Springs Gap shelter. I was surprised how vehemently the men responded to my story of the poaching incident.

"They ought to put scum like them in jail!" exploded one of them. "They need someone to get their attention! A fine won't do it."

His friend nodded enthusiastically in agreement.

The half-hour hike through the forest from Indian Gap to Newfound Gap was quiet and peaceful, and I became cloaked in an aura of serenity which was devastated by the carnival-like atmosphere I encountered a few minutes later at Newfound Gap. In the space of a minute, I stepped from a quiet, timeless, pristine wilderness environment into the noisy, ugly, machine-dominated civilization of the late 20th Century. I stopped for a minute to rest and watch the ebb and flow of people.

The parking lot, which had space for about 50 cars, was completely full and the overflow lined the sidewalks and the road up the mountain towards Clingmans Dome. A Park Ranger was totally occupied, trying to control a pair of book peddlers. Evidently, vendors were allowed to conduct business in the Gap but were required to remain within the confines of a yellow-lined square designated for their use. The problem was, the square was not large enough for both the peddlers and their cases of new books which overflowed beyond the yellow lines. The Ranger, smiling slightly, explained repeatedly to the peddlers that they were required by the Park Service rules to remain inside the square, and the peddlers responded vigorously that they were obeying the rules, even as they walked outside the square to plead their case. The Ranger, patiently pushed them back inside the lines as he might have pushed some wayward sheep.

The whole scene impressed me as one in which everyone was posturing for somebody, but no one was interested in looking, and so no one saw anyone else. There were proud new parents showing off their toddlers and proud grandparents with grandchildren who were taking full advantage of the opportunity to push the limits of allowable behavior. Teenage boys were trying to impress their latest girl friends with their newly-developed muscles. Several dark, grimy, and hairy motorcycle thugs, with black teeth to match their jackets, lolled about beside their bikes and ogled the women who hurried demurely by their blatant, penetrating stares.

A group of middle-aged motorcyclists arrived and dismounted their iron steeds with a stiffness that belied their posturing. The thugs laughed. Several older women wearing tight, gaudy, polyester pantsuits waddled by me on their way to the monument and behaved in such a manner that reminded me of the girls from my high school who walked the halls in small busy swarms, showing off their newly acquired feminine charms, confident of the safety their numbers afforded.

A young woman, about 19 or 20 years old, approached somewhat hesitantly and asked if I were a Thru-Hiker. When I responded affirmatively, she relaxed and explained excitedly that she and a friend planned to thru-hike the Trail the following year and asked how I liked my hike, how tough it was, and what I did to prepare for it. I told her it was a great experience, but very strenuous; that she needed to be in shape at the start and go slowly initially.

She turned to an older gentleman with a skeptical expression on his face, standing slightly behind her. "See, it's not all that bad, Daddy. I told you it wasn't!"

"I still say walking around the mountains with 40 pounds on your back is crazy," he snapped.

I mentioned something about it being a great character builder, and he retorted that there were other more sensible ways to build character. I mentioned the physical and spiritual benefits. But he remained unconvinced. I was sure my appearance made a negative impression on him. It had been three days since I had bathed or washed my clothes, and my beard and hair were shaggy and uncombed. No wonder the woman identified me as a Thru-Hiker!

After the father and daughter wandered away, a young woman named Dawn Stubbs from Miami, Florida, and her friend and business partner, Gail from Ft. Lauderdale, stopped to talk with me. They owned and operated a massage/health clinic in Miami; their clientele included several members of the Miami Dolphins' professional football team. We seemed to "hit it off" and when I departed, they decided to accompany me to Charlies Bunion, a rock formation four miles down the Trail to the east.

We started off at a medium slow pace, but it was not long before the Trail steepened. Dawn's friend, who was carrying a little extra on her spare frame, started to lag. Dawn slowed to wait for her friend, and I continued on, walking with the different groups encountered.

First was a group of young people from Charlotte, North Carolina, but they were faster than I and soon left me behind. (I passed them later when they stopped to photograph a deer feeding on the Trail.) Next was a middle-aged philosophy professor from the University of Tennessee at Chattanooga; he was hiking with a male friend of about the same age. He asked several questions about the Trail and long-distance hiking but had a disturbing habit of cutting me off in the middle of an answer. Once, as I was describing the difficulty in resupply on the Trail, he stopped me in midsentence to announce that he had identified a Catawba rhododendron bush. He called excitedly about his discovery to his friend, 20 yards ahead of us. His friend barely acknowledged him. They talked very little and the air between them seemed strained like the air between lovers after a spat.

After being rebuffed by his companion, the professor held a blossom out for me to admire. I couldn't think of anything to say except that it was beautiful and looked very much like an azalea. That was definitely the wrong thing to say. The professor responded with an emotional lecture on the differences between azaleas and the rhododendrons. I remained silent during the rest of the time we walked and listened to his agitated prattle.

At the junction of the AT and the side trail leading to Charlies Bunion, I removed my pack and walked unhindered to the rock formation. Although wide and easy to walk, the trail followed a ledge with a sheer drop of what seemed like a 100 feet to the left side, but which was probably less than 20.

The view from the rocks was spectacular. Across the draw to the right front, a wild and savage-looking ridge with great piles of rock interspersed with stands of balsam and pine along its spine, and steep sides covered with massive rock slides and sparse patches of low evergreen growth dropped precipitously to a rock and brush-tangled base. The ridge directly to the front appeared less formidable; it was more rounded and completely covered by forest, but it still looked rugged. The draws to both sides of Charlies Bunion were heavily forested and led to a great basin that was likewise heavily forested. I imagined the basin to look like the untouched, untamed wilderness that had greeted the first visitors to the region, and I remained on the rocks for some time to contemplate the beauty before returning to the Trail.

Horace Clemmons and his son, 16-year-old Jason, were already at Pecks Corner shelter when I arrived. They had started from Davenport Gap two days earlier and had spent the previous evening at Cosby Knob shelter. Horace was the owner and chief executive officer of a small firm called POST International. The word POST was an acronym formed from the first letters of the words Point Of Sale Terminal. They made and sold computer software that featured instant inventory data and automatic reorder capability for computerized cash registers.

Horace told me how he formed the company. Following service with the Marines in Vietnam, he went to work as a salesman for IBM. In the process of selling, he became aware of a vital software need that IBM refused to fill because, as he was told, "IBM is not in that phase of the business." He decided that if IBM wouldn't do it, he would start a business that would. He secured financial backing from a Cuban business partner and within three years built a three-man operation into a multinational firm, employing 54 people with operations in Canada, Australia and Italy. Evidently, the city of Wake Forest was

Charlies Bunion.

equally impressed because it floated a 1 1/2 million dollar bond for plant construction.

It had been three years of intensive, but exciting and satisfying work for him. I could imagine it was a source of great personal satisfaction. Talk about a story for the Fourth of July weekend . . .That's what this country is all about! I thought: the freedom to use your own initiative and take the risks for greater gain. It also meant the freedom to fail. It must have taken great courage, after 18 years in the IBM corporate womb, to launch a new life in a new environment where failure could destroy not only financial security, but self-confidence and self-esteem as well. But he had done it! He had accepted the challenge and was well on his way to winning it all. Another success story for the American Dream!

The one negative impact of his decision, he confided with a tone of regret in his voice, was that he did not now have as much time available for his family as he would have liked. Horace was a devoted father, and there was a very close bond between he and Jason, a sort of partnership based on love and respect as opposed to a superior/subordinate relationship. It was a natural, open relationship that reminded me of the Wilson family I had met at Birch Springs Gap. Both fathers treated their boys with respect and love, and the boys responded in kind.

Jason had recently turned 16, bought a car, and become interested in girls. His father teased him gently, saying they would probably not be doing much hiking in the future, now that Jason was more interested in girls than hiking with the "old man." That brought a vehement response of "Bull crap!" from Jason. He obviously was not about to give up hiking with his father for a woman. At least not yet!

As I contemplated my conversation with Horace and Jason, my mind reverted back to the Boy Scouts at Cold Spring shelter, and I could hear again the bitterness and the hostility in the dialogue among the adults and the boys. I shook my head at the "drill sergeant" mentality some men adopted toward their sons.

I was still tired from the previous day's effort when I started off the next morning. The weather was sunny and cool, and despite five miles of strenuous climbs, the hiking was bearable. During my climb up Mt. Chapman, I met Dave Walp (aka. Sonny Daze) from Wilkes Barre, Pennsylvania. He had started in Pennsylvania and planned to thru-hike to Springer Mountain, then get a ride north to Mt. Katahdin, Maine, and hike back to Pennsylvania, completing the trip all in one summer.

Dave had spent the previous night at Tri-Corner Knob shelter with a group of generous horseback campers who had shared their meal with him and then offered more food than he could carry. When I said that I could put up with a lot of weight if it was free food, he mentioned that his pack already weighed 50 pounds. I questioned how he managed such a heavy pack, and he told me that, by his standards, it was light, that it had weighed 70 pounds at the start, and that he had reduced the weight by mailing home several pieces of "unnecessary" equipment including his tent. He now slept only in shelters.

Near the junction of the side trail to Maddron Bald, I encountered parts from a military aircraft strewn about the mountain. Pieces of metal and wire lay beside the Trail and protruded from beneath the leaves and branches of the mountain laurel thickets down the hillside. The parts were obviously pieces of wreckage resulting from a plane crash, and I was surprised that no one had mentioned it during my previous conversations with south-bound hikers.

I had covered 13 miles by 4:30 p.m. when I reached Cosby Knob shelter. Despite having been tired at the start, I now felt very good and even better with the knowledge that my heart had shown no tendencies to skip or change rhythm. The Trail was now at a considerably lower elevation than it had been during the previous five days. That, along with the fact that much of it was downhill for north-bounders, probably accounted for my good physical condition.

In another six days, I would celebrate my first complete month on the Trail. Not bad for a 52-year-old tenderfoot, I mused. I was going to succeed! It was a marvelous feeling! I also realized that the number of times my mind flashed back to considerations of the Army and my former military life had radically decreased; and when I did flashback, the time durations were shorter. I now spent more time and effort thinking about the Trail and keeping myself pumped up psychologically for the challenge.

The sun was already shining when I awoke. The Smokies were magnificent in the cloth of summer. Everything was green, a deep rich green that permeated even the sense of smell. I was no longer seeing the Canadian forest of pine, hemlock or spruce as I had at the higher elevations. Now all the trees were hardwoods: oak, poplar, beech or maple.

It was my father's birthday, July 7th, and I thought momentarily about my father, comparing my experience with my father to what I observed with the Clemmons. Mine was different. My father, also a military man, was away more than he was at home. We tried to get close, but there was no common ground. He didn't hunt or fish or hike or play sports. There was only his work. When I grew old enough to drink, we would occasionally drink beer, and he would talk about the Army or raising horses. After a short time, our conversation would degenerate into generalities; neither of us knew the other well enough to say what was important to us. It wasn't that we wouldn't have tried if we had recognized the problem. We both wanted to know one another better but were both afraid to open up. Then we went our separate ways, feeling strangely unfulfilled, at least I felt unfulfilled and I had the impression he also felt a sense of estrangement.

I also thought about my relationship with my own son. It was not something I could point to with pride. I had divorced from his mother at the critical time when he was entering his teens. My job took me all over the world, just as it had my father, and except for a couple of times when I had coached little league baseball and basketball teams on which he played and a couple of times hunting and camping, we also didn't do much together. Lately, however, we had gotten on very well, despite our previously limited contact. But the gaps were there and could never be filled. What we had not shared was lost to both of us forever.

Much to my son's credit, he recognized that and was determined to break the poor role model chain his father and grandfather established. He was an outstanding father, devoted to his son in the same way I had observed that Horace Clemmons was devoted to his Jason. When my son and I talked about our Jason, I would mention what a wonderfully bright and happy child he was, and my own son often replied, "And now we just got to bring him up right." It was said without intention for me, but I could not help but get a message. Although it was painful for me, it was also painful for my son; he was determined not to perpetuate the hurt. I had not been so wise . . .

I was almost out of food and planned to reprovision at the grocery store in Mt. Sterling, a small settlement just down the road from the Ranger station. All that remained of my original 15-pound food sack was a small bag of instant rice and a bouillon cube, and that became breakfast.

I mused about the imagination required to make instant rice and bouillon edible at 7:00 a.m. as I walked outside the shelter into the sun. I had just turned the corner of the shelter toward the access trail to the AT when movement on the trail above attracted my attention. I wondered who might be coming to the shelter so early in the morning. My jaw dropped when a smallish black bear appeared from behind some bushes and headed toward me.

It was not nearly as big as the bear on Thunderhead had been. This was a young bear with a deep black muzzle, probably a two-year-old. It was three or four feet long and about two and a half feet high at the shoulder, approximately the size of a large labrador retriever dog.

The morning sun glistened from the coal black fur that rippled at the shoulders as the bear walked down the trail. It came towards me without haste, its brown eyes fastened on me. It showed no sign of fear.

When it came to within about ten feet, I said gently, "Well, and whom do we have here?" Evidently that was the wrong thing to say.

The bear replied, "GROWLL," and feigned a charge at me. It stopped almost immediately after starting, like a boxer who had thrown a jab, missed and reacted by recovering and getting back out of range.

I was taken aback by the aggressive behavior. Since this was my first really close encounter with a bear of any type, I decided to do the smart thing, which was to get my precious body as quickly as possible behind the protection of the shelter fence. I continued eating breakfast while the bear roamed the clearing in front of the shelter, probably looking for its breakfast. It disappeared periodically into the forest, then reappeared near the spring to eat a couple of bright red flower tips from the bee balm plants that grew profusely in the moist soil.

After about five minutes, it came to the shelter and watched me eat. This scene was all wrong. I was supposed to be the one on the outside looking in. The bear raised up on its hind legs to an erect position, leaning against the fence, trying to paw its way through the chain-link mesh, and knocking over a shovel that landed with a clatter on some rocks inside the shelter. It then spied my pack, leaning against the shelter wall in the corner next to the wire bunks. From that point on, ALL its attention was focused on the pack. It tried to dig under the fence, to pry the fence away from the wall, then tried to climb the fence, and in general just about wore out the fence. If it was becoming frustrated by its lack of progress, it didn't show.

I thoroughly enjoyed my good fortune at seeing a bear, but it was getting late, almost 8:00 a.m., and I wanted to be on the Trail. This was one determined little bear, however; it gave no indication of leaving. Clearly, unless I took some action, I faced the prospect of spending the day in the shelter, an unappealing thought. Still I waited, hoping the bear would tire and leave the shelter. After another 15 minutes slipped by, impatience got the better of me. Somewhere in the back of my mind came the old adage, "The best defense is a good offense." Then I remembered back to the *Principles of War*, particularly the Principle of Surprise and the characteristic of Armor — shock action.

With the bear's attention riveted on my pack, I quietly slipped out the door and tiptoed to where my hiking stick was leaning against the wall. The bear never ceased to "worry" the fence in front of my pack and didn't notice me. I then tiptoed up behind the bear, and with the best bloodcurdling scream I could muster, rapped the ground smartly beside its rump. The startled bear moved so fast in its attempt to escape that its feet slipped out from under it, and it rolled on its side and back. At that point, I let out another howl and again slammed my stick on the ground beside the struggling animal. I continued to yell and howl until the bear regained its feet, whereupon it ran to the edge of the clearing. It stopped and looked back as if it might have second thoughts. I was having none of that. I pressed the attack, screaming and howling and at the same time flailing the air and the ground with my hiking stick.

I'd heard that if you got into trouble with a bear, the best course was to run downhill because the bears' short front legs made it difficult to run downhill with speed. I was witness to a miracle. That bear fairly streaked down the hill! While I was mentally congratulating myself, the thought occurred: Don't be so smug, Buster! Suppose that bear was big like the one on Thunderhead? I moved out swiftly!

The Trail led downhill for a few hundred yards from the shelter to Low Gap, then climbed for about a mile to Sunup Knob. After that, it descended the main ridge spine due east until it reached Davenport Gap where it left the Great Smoky National Park. I did not go that far. I left the Trail about two miles before Davenport Gap, near the junction of the Mt. Cammerer Trail and descended toward the southeast via the Chestnut Creek Trail; this led directly to the Mt. Sterling Ranger station.

The Chestnut Creek Trail followed the creek for which it was named for most of the way down, and at the lower elevations the creek ran through a small gorge where some of the rocks, acting like small dams, created several pools of quiet water that offered the possibility for swimming. I was tempted a number of times to pause and go for a dip. Heaven knows, I could use one, I mused.

Seven days had passed since I last had been immersed in water. The only problem, the trail paralleled the creek so closely, there was no place private enough for "skinnydipping." I don't know why I chose that particular time to become concerned with modesty. Certainly, anyone hiking the trail would have understood and kept going. I was just about to take the plunge when a lone hiker came by. I allowed my inhibitions to dissuade me.

Before reaching the Park's boundary, I sat on a rock beside the creek and allowed myself a final few minutes to savor the beauty. I would not have the opportunity to enjoy such a great expanse of wilderness again soon. So, I sat in the sunlight, watching the water in the creek rush into a quiet golden pool, listening to the sounds of it intermingling with the other sounds of forest life. I felt as "One with the Trail" and the world, contented.

CHAPTER 9

Max Patch and Hot Springs, North Carolina
The Beginning of Understanding

A sign taped to the door of the Mt. Sterling Ranger Station indicated that the Ranger would return at 1:00 p.m. Just like a cop, I thought, as I glanced at my watch. (It was 12:50 p.m.) There's never one around when you need him!

I was beginning to get the impression that the Rangers were a phantom organization and appeared in public only when the taxpayers visited the Park on the Fourth of July. I had stopped because I wanted to learn about the plane wreckage by Maddron Bald. But the lure of ice cream from Mt. Sterling was too strong, and ten more minutes of denial was more than I could bear. I continued down the road.

Mt. Sterling was little more than a small cluster of houses near a crossroads. The general store was located on the ground floor of a two-story, white frame house, surrounded by white wooden sheds and small barns. The dusty remnants of two gasoline pumps poked up from a small cement island in the middle of a dirt and gravel driveway. Along the front wall sat a pair of well-worn, heart-shaped, wire-backed chairs and a church pew-like wooden bench with a straight, high back. A tired old screen door, its wood frame worn smooth from thousands of openings and closings, hung limply from its hinges. The only sign of real life, a bony mongrel hound lying in the dirt by the entrance, raised his head to look as I approached, then, with a grunt, laid out flat again as if the effort had been too much.

Inside an obese young woman, perched on a stool behind a 1930's vintage cash register, was absorbed in a romance novel. She barely acknowledged my presence when I said hello. The walls were lined with large, deep, white, wooden shelves that stretched from floor to ceiling. They were mostly bare except for a very limited variety of canned foods like tuna fish, sardines, Spam, beans and a few packages of macaroni.

After searching in vain for something exciting, like canned ham or chicken, I bought a couple of cans of sardines and tuna fish along with some macaroni and cheese, and a pint of ice cream. Outside again, I relaxed on the bench in the shade. The cool, creamy vanilla ice cream was the perfect treat for a lazy Carolina summer day. It tasted so good I bought a second pint to eat along the road.

I headed east toward the Pigeon River, following a blacktop road that changed to gravel after a few hundred yards. Several cars rumbled by, creating dust billows that coated the roadside vegetation with a layer of fine gray powder. I held my breath hoping the powder would settle before I needed air again, and most of the time I was successful. I ate the ice cream despite the dust.

Mostly, the drivers, oblivious to the effect of the dust on people walking the road, sped past without slowing. Once, a gray-haired old man in an empty pickup truck, heading in the opposite direction, slowed and waved a friendly greeting at me, smiling like an old friend. When he returned from the other direction about ten minutes later, I held out my thumb, anticipating a sure lift to the Pigeon River. He only waved again in the same friendly fashion and rumbled on, this time without slowing, leaving me hidden in the billowing cloud that followed.

I reached the Pigeon River at the site of a small, red brick hydroelectric plant that, despite the low river level, was humming with activity. From my map, I discovered that the water which powered the turbines was diverted from the Pigeon River about two miles further upstream where Walters Dam formed a small lake. The water was conducted from the dam through underground aqueducts to the hydroelectric plant, then released back to the river.

After skirting the plant, the road paralleled the river for several hundred yards to Davenport Gap, where it was intersected by the AT. I wanted to bathe but could not find a pathway down the steep river embankment until I had nearly reached Davenport Gap. I was not the only one to use the pathway. On a large flat rock beside the river, lay a small heap of clothes belonging to a couple who were swimming near midstream behind a pile of boulders. They were hidden from view but I could hear them.

I didn't realize they were skinnydipping until the man,

completely naked, came tiptoeing gingerly across the rocks to retrieve their clothes and returned to midstream where he disappeared behind a house-sized rock. A few minutes later, he reappeared, this time fully clothed, followed by a woman who was also clothed; they climbed the steep river bank back to the road where their van was parked.

Feeling much less inhibited now that I was alone, I stripped naked and slid into the river. The water, warmed from prolonged exposure to the sun in the shallow pools, imparted a sensual feeling as it washed over and caressed my skin. I wallowed in the broad, quiet eddy for about ten minutes, soaking the aches from my muscles before completely lathering my body with Dr. Bronners Peppermint 18-in-1 liquid biodegradable soap. I watched in amusement as the white lather turned gray at first, then almost black as it mixed with the layers of dirt from my arms and legs. I was surprised by the firmness of the muscles in my body. No longer could I grab liberal chunks of "love handles," the euphemistic term for the loose skin and fat at my waist. Just about all the fat had disappeared from my stomach.

The "peppermint" in the soap imparted its usually pleasant tingling sensation over most of my body, except for those more sensitive areas where it was just a little too tingly. Eventually, I slid out into the flowing water to rinse off and watched as the little globs of darkened lather drifted downstream to disintegrate. Then I lay in the shallow pool and allowed the gentle current to once again caress my muscles. It was, in a way, even more luxurious than a hot tub because of the closeness of the natural surroundings. It took considerable discipline to close the pleasant interlude and return to the effort of hiking.

At the point where the Trail crossed under Interstate Route 40 about 100 yards east of the Pigeon River bridge, I encountered a road survey team. The team members were heading for their truck as I approached, but an older man, wearing a khaki shirt and khaki trousers with light brown hunting boots and a blue bandanna kerchief sticking out of his left trousers pocket stopped when he spied me and intercepted me as I came through the underpass.

"Y'all hike up from Georgia?" he asked, rubbing the fine, day-old stubble of beard that covered his wrinkled, sun-bronzed skin. I nodded. "Used to hike myself," he continued. "In fact, used to help the Scoutmaster plan and take the Boy Scouts on hikes. Used to that is. I'm too old for that now."

Then he got down to business, telling me in an authoritative voice about the dangers of walking alone through the mountains. His pale blue eyes fixed me with a steady, serious gaze. "It's dangerous walking alone in these hills with so many snakes around," he said. "I remember a few years back, me and this other feller was doin' some work for the Interstate. It was God awful hot, and we run outta water. This other feller, he knew about this spring back in the woods, and we went to get us some fresh spring water. That spring was set back in a bunch of tall grass, and when we got there, we found it was guarded by the biggest copperhead I ever seen. That snake come after us like we was on his property. I climbed up on the truck, but my buddy, he got him a stick and went after that snake. I never seen nothin' like it. They fought like two men. First one would attack and the other would back up, then they'd change over and the other one'd attack. I watched from the roof of the truck scared to death."

He didn't say how the fight ended, but I imagined his friend won. Immediately after telling me the story, he said he'd better go. He smiled with a sheepish grin as we said goodbye, and I thought he might have been slightly embarrassed by his embellishment of the story.

Before we parted, however, I asked about the aircraft pieces I had seen in the Smokies. He said they were from an Air Force plane that had crashed a "few years back" while the pilot was practicing low-level flight techniques. "They flew in all kinds of Special Forces for that one," he said. "They had people runnin' all over that mountain for a month." I suspected the "Special Forces" were search and security personnel who had been brought in to collect certain important components of the aircraft and pieces within a certain radius of the crash site in order to conduct an investigation into the cause.

The campsite where I planned to spend the night was nestled in a small forest sag beside Painter Branch, a bubbling mountain stream that bounced gaily down the gently sloping draw. I erected my tent, laid out my gear, prepared a cup of coffee, and sat back to reflect on the day. I realized that I felt more peaceful and serene at this campsite than I had in the Smokies. I guessed it was because I felt a deeper solitude. I had come to enjoy the peace and tranquillity that came with solitude in the mountains and found that to be missing in the Smokies. The natural beauty of the Park wilderness was magnificent, but there were too many people and too much government presence. That inhibited the intensity of the experience.

After supper, I hung my pack from a tree to protect my food. Although I was still close to the Great Smoky National Park, I wasn't concerned as much about bears as I was raccoons. I searched the immediate vicinity of the campsite for two trees growing close enough together to stretch a rope between, but there were none. So, I selected a stout branch of a tree adjacent to my tent, threw my rope over it, and hauled my pack into the air, a safe distance from any marauders.

The idea of stretching a rope between trees is an ideal solution which in practice rarely works since it's difficult to find two trees of suitable height and distance apart in the vicinity of a campsite. Meanwhile, I found, trying to climb the trees to tie the rope is all but impossible. I decided that the pictures and diagrams in the books were written by people who had never backpacked or if they had, were lumberjacks who topped trees for a living.

The remaining climb up Snowbird Mountain the next day was less pleasurable. The Trail was steep, rocky, and difficult, and when I reached the summit, supposedly great views were obscured by mist. The fleas and gnats became a real distraction, particularly the gnats. They flew in circles in front of my face; no amount of waving could keep them away. So, I tied my bandanna to the top of my hiking stick. With every stride, I swung it ever so slightly so that the bandanna would sweep the air in front of my face. Nothing worked.

The gnats dove repeatedly into my eyes Kamikaze style. My reflex actions usually caught the critters in my eyelashes before they penetrated all the way to my eye. Then I brushed the carcasses away.

Occasionally, though, one would make it through my defenses. When that happened, it was painful, not only because it irritated the sensitive eye membrane like any other foreign matter, it also secreted a substance that severely stung my eye. It took a few seconds for my tears to neutralize the substance, and in the meantime, I was blinded which meant I had to stop until I was able to remove the invader from my eye.

About midmorning, I crossed the Lemon Gap and Max Patch roads and headed for Max Patch, a 4,629-foot mountain with awe-inspiring views of the Appalachians in all directions. I had read somewhere that Max Patch got its name from a man by the name of Max who almost single-handedly turned the mountain into a bald. The summit was already bald when Max started.

But working for seven dollars an acre beginning around 1840, he cleared the entire mountain over a period of several years.

Max was reputed to have been a giant of a man. He cut the trees and removed the stumps from about an acre a month. I wondered if perhaps Max saw the beauty he was creating and that kept him at the back-breaking labor. I doubt if there is a more beautiful place than Max Patch on a clear summer day.

After crossing the roads, the Trail meandered aimlessly through the forest for several hundred yards, then presented Max Patch like a surprise as the hiker emerged from the wood line. It reminded me of the rabbit that had approached me on Cheoah Bald after the electrical storm. The Trail zigged along the eastern side of the mountain inside the tree line before it turned abruptly left, climbed a small fence stile, and zagged along a narrow, old road before starting up.

At first, the mountain did not seem all that imposing. It wasn't until I came onto the side of the ridge that I began to get a feel for the immensity of it.

The day was gorgeous, the sky a bright blue populated by occasional clouds that marched in thin wispy ranks from horizon to horizon. The long grass swayed gently in a soft breeze, and millions of daisies, Queen Anne's lace, yarrow and other wildflowers grew in dense colonies that produced great swaths of white up the hillside. In other places, I found the wildflowers grew singly or in tiny groups, speckling the meadows as if some painter had splattered the green with his brush.

As I gained in elevation, the countryside fell away below me, and the mountains in the distance became more pronounced. On the ridge top, it was like having a grandstand seat from which could be seen magnificent mountain vistas unfolding in all directions, particularly the Smokies, which rose majestically out of the mists above the rest.

The view down the valley to the south and across to the lower ridges was inspiring. On one ridge, far below, an abandoned old barn gave the scene a hint of mystery. It sat in a hollow with the grass growing like a fringe at the base of its weathered gray metal siding. Its rough wall timbers leaned into the hill and long pole rafters showed through in places where the metal roof had rusted away. If I closed my eyes, I could imagine horses and cattle grazing on the rich grass in the draw beside it and down the ridge.

The sweep of the meadow below the barn was interrupted

Summit of Max Patch.

by differing shades of green created by someone who had harvested the grass. As the new grass shoots grew back, they displayed a lighter shade of green. The scene contained a pleasing mixture of wilderness, of virgin land and the presence of man, but not his domination.

The thick grass near the summit completely overgrew and hid the path that others on the Trail before me had made. Only the iron stakes with white blazes painted on their tops told me where the Trail lay. The soft, springy carpet cushioned my steps and eased the stress on my feet and legs.

When I reached the summit, I stood for a moment in awe of the panorama around me and felt a clutch of raw emotion as I reacted to the beauty. I was struck by the variations in the ridges that undulated down from the summit. To the northwest, an old road wove its way across the ridge line, then disappeared behind some low trees. Occasional boulders on the summit and the ridge to the west broke the softness of the bald before the grass again swept unhindered to the tree line far below.

I was able to see the barn again on my way down the other side. This provided a different perspective, a totally new scene.

Eventually, the Trail entered the tree line of a mixed forest, and Max Patch became another treasured memory.

Throughout the day, I continued with a sense of lingering euphoria. Then 16.7 miles later, I stopped at Lemon Gap to spend the night.

As I reflected on the day's activities, I realized for the first time how man had come to dominate almost his entire environment and how we seemed intent on bringing what remained in its natural state under control. Humans were in the business of "improving the land," of destroying the natural vegetation and animal habitat, and replacing it with infrastructure and housing along with so-called civilized vegetation, lawns and shrubbery.

What little remains of a once-magnificent wilderness has, in many places, become a battleground for conservation groups and developers, one trying desperately to retain as much of our wilderness heritage as possible and the other spurred by economic considerations or greed and the pressure of the population growth. I had the pessimistic feeling that eventually the United States would become as developed as Europe, that only the few pitifully overcrowded national parks would remain as symbols of a beauty that once stretched "from sea to shining sea." I hoped that Max Patch would endure as it was.

Perhaps, I thought, man, having already given up his efforts to colonize that mighty mountain, will have established the precedent necessary to save it. I surmised that what I found hopeful about Max Patch was that man had been there but, for whatever reason, had taken leave, the mountain rejuvenated as a result. Perhaps all was not lost after all. And for that we have the Appalachian Trail Conference to thank for bringing Max Patch under its protection.

A slightly overcast sky with a cooling breeze higher on the ridges kept the gnats away, and the hiking was good the following day. The scenery consisted mostly of trees and rocks until I reached a rock outcropping with views of Hot Springs and the French Broad River Valley. Other delights, though, made for interesting hiking.

Patches of blueberries with clusters of ripe fruit tempted me beyond endurance. I stopped frequently to stuff the juice-laden berries into my mouth, bursting them against the roof of my mouth with my tongue and savoring the sweet liquid.

My encounters with blueberries consumed more time than I realized. It was well past 4:00 p.m. when I arrived at Elmer

Hall's place in Hot Springs. The Inn, as it is known, is a large wooden house that had variously served as a resort hotel, a boarding house, a private mansion, and God knows what else. It had been abandoned for some time until 1979. Then it was rescued from the mice and termites by Elmer Hall and put back together to serve as a "resort" again as well as "way station" for hikers doing the AT. The Inn was widely recommended in all the literature I had read about the Trail.

Elmer was not home when I arrived. But a note taped to the kitchen door indicated he'd be back in an hour. After waiting in vain for two hours, I headed for the Alpine Inn Motel in the middle of town where I booked a room for $24 per night.

I felt a sense of accomplishment that evening as I lay in bed recollecting and recording the day's events before sleep overwhelmed me. For some reason, earlier in the day I had felt depressed and had to work diligently to create and maintain a positive attitude. Whenever a negative thought entered my mind, I countered it with a positive one. I had consciously thought myself into an atmosphere of mental strength. I had gritted my teeth and told myself, "I will succeed. I won't fail. I will remain strong." I repeated the words again and again, an affirmation, trying to etch their sense into my unconscious to combat the negative messages of fatigue, discomfort and loneliness. I had sought to turn my solitude into a strength. I had pushed aside anything that suggested failure. I was in a struggle with myself, but I couldn't back down. I had started the Trail with the attitude, "I hope I can make it." That had been replaced by the emphatic statement, "I will succeed."

I had also worked my psychological exhortations into the fabric of my meditation. I wanted to know and understand God. I wanted to build spiritual strength. I not only asked God for the gift of faith, I decided to help myself by devoting, not only my walking meditation to the effort but also by establishing a positive psychological climate.

As I formulated my approach to my spiritual awakening, I wondered if my desire to achieve spiritual confidence might not be so strong that it would force my unconscious to enter a spiritual state or apparent spiritual state without any other impetus. Would it become a self-fulfilling prophecy?

I had devoted much thought to the subject during the morning and could come to no conclusion as to how I could differentiate a self-fulfilling prophecy from any other spiritual experience — unless it was revealed to me in some way. Then, I thought, what difference does it make? If it works, if I have a stronger faith, if I feel closer to God, what difference does it make how I arrived? The important thing: I had arrived.

I was no longer so anxious about being alone in the wilderness. I did have some concerns about injury or snake bite, though. I was traveling some very rugged terrain and a snake bite, a twisted ankle or a broken leg could mean real trouble. I resolved to exercise reasonable caution but not be intimidated into being overly cautious. I needed to maintain my psychological as well as physical momentum. The fact that I was on the Trail alone was in itself a risk, but an acceptable risk, probably not greater than walking alone on the streets of any major city and probably a great deal less risky than walking alone in certain sections of those cities. The secret was to maintain an awareness of my surroundings and the Trail conditions and do nothing rash for the sake of expediency.

I looked forward to the end of summer when I could say I had completed my hike for the season, secure in the knowledge that I would return the following summer to complete the Trail. I simply could not reach Maine by the end of summer. But I could reach the inner essence of Jan Curran, and when I succeeded in doing that, hopefully, all the other things, like my search for spirituality and a second career, would fall into place. I was confident of success. I would succeed! I turned out the light and looked out the window at a town shimmering in the pale moonlight; then, it was morning.

Elmer Hall's place looked deserted when I returned the next morning. That was before I looked through the screen and saw a young woman in the kitchen drinking tea. She saw me peering into the kitchen and motioned me to come in. She introduced herself as Nancy and told me she was a guest. We talked a little about ourselves. She was a registered nurse, taking a sabbatical away from the stresses of her profession; she hoped to put her life into perspective as she put it. She was a delightfully unconventional person who fit perfectly into the atmosphere of Elmer's place.

It was Nancy's plan to wash some clothes at the laundromat. Since Elmer hadn't risen for the day, I accompanied her as far as my motel. I told her about the problem with my boots, that I was hoping I could get some advice or assistance from Elmer. Then, I gave her one of my business cards which contained my military rank and asked her to give it to Elmer when she got back. I'd contact Elmer later in the day.

That business card was probably a mistake, I thought, as I moved on. I had heard or read somewhere that Elmer had been a 1960's vintage social activist, antiwar, antiestablishment figure in the North Carolina universities' scene. (He was reputedly a chaplain at Duke University.)

Later in the morning, I returned to The Inn to a lukewarm, if not cool, reception from Elmer. He was polite. But I sensed an agitation that suggested discomfort. Nonetheless, I asked him if he could help me solve my boot problem.

"What do you want?" he asked coldly.

"I really don't know," I replied.

It was the perfect opening for a zinger. He turned to Nancy, drinking a cup of tea by the stove, and announced loudly with malice, "He doesn't know what he wants!"

My first reaction was anger at myself for not being prepared for the personality I faced. Knowing Elmer's background, I should have realized that my rank and former position was likely to place me in an adversarial position. It had to stimulate a conditioned response or at least rekindle some smoldering passions. My response to his question was just too tempting. My second reaction was to stifle some equally angry response. I was trying to get help. I thought of the old joke, "When you're up to your armpits in alligators, it's awfully hard to remember your objective was to drain the swamp!" In my mind, Elmer became a hairy-faced alligator with glasses who looked more comical than threatening.

I ignored the comment, and with an unemotional voice, explained that I didn't know what type of boot I wanted. I said that I thought his experience could point me in the right direction, something comfortable without a long break-in period. Then I praised his reputation for helping hikers.

I also remembered the old story of catching more flies with sugar than vinegar. Finally, I mentioned something about New Balance and Hi-Tec as some I had seen being worn by several hikers along the Trail.

Although his voice and composure became less confrontational, Elmer wasn't inclined to do anything beyond giving advice. However, the more we talked, the more relaxed we both became.

Elmer had hiked much of the Trail, those portions of the Trail that were of interest to him. He had not hiked the parts in

New York, New Jersey or Pennsylvania, they were too urbanized for him. But he had done Maine, New Hampshire and the southern Appalachians. Except for Maine, Elmer felt I had been over the toughest parts of the Trail.

We also talked about a young man hanging around the town who looked like he might be about to get into trouble. He had arrived about a week and a half earlier and tent-camped on the outskirts next to the French Broad River, staying there at night and spending the day sitting or lying on the cement platform of a vacant store in the town center. He wasn't doing anything illegal. But he was acting strangely. Elmer was afraid some of the local boys might try to convince the boy to leave town.

Meanwhile, the local police had checked on the boy in Ohio where he came from. His record was clear. Since he was not involved in anything illegal, there was no action they could take.

When I went to the restaurant that evening for supper, the boy was standing in front of the entrance looking at the door. At first, I thought he might be waiting for someone to come out. But when I passed in front of him and said hello, looking him in the eyes as I spoke, his brown eyes stared blankly back at me as if he didn't comprehend or didn't see me.

A growth of beard made his face appear even dirtier than it was. Shaggy curly hair peeked from underneath an olive-green knitted cap, similar to those issued to soldiers during WWII and Korea for wear under their helmets. He was slightly taller than I, about six feet with strongly muscled arms and legs. He appeared in excellent physical condition, well-fed, and his clothes, although dirty, were fairly new.

Inside, the waitresses were arguing about which of them would wait on his table if he came in. "I hope he goes away," one of them said.

My salad had already been served before he entered.

He took a table in the center of the room beside a low partition which separated the counter from the dining table area. He studied the menu for a long time before putting it aside and ordering nine hard-boiled eggs.

"Anything else?" asked the waitress.

He mumbled something . . .

The waitress bent her head to better hear him.

He lowered his head to his chest and slurred his words so badly the waitress could barely understand him.

"Iced tea?" she asked.

He nodded his head.

When the eggs arrived, they were served in a large soup plate. He picked up one egg, then motioned the waitress over. He again mumbled something which the waitress couldn't understand, and she bent her head to listen.

Finally, she asked, "Something wrong with the eggs? You want 'em hot? You want me to eat 'em for you, too?"

He threw his head back and laughed long and hard.

The owner, who had been watching the scene from the rear of the restaurant, hurried over and offered to take the eggs back to the kitchen and heat them. The hiker refused the offer. The owner was clearly concerned and talked in soothing tones diplomatically, trying to offer him other food. The boy only shook his head. Then, he ate the eggs, peeling each one very carefully with grimy hands, and stuffing the whole egg in his mouth, all the time with his eyes riveted on the waitress cleaning tables. He definitely had an eye for the girls.

Earlier in the day, while I was at the small grocery store across from the restaurant, the woman at the cash register told me he gave her the creeps.

"He come in the other day, mind you, and told me he wanted to marry my daughter. About knocked me over! I told him, 'You're just a day too late! She got married Saturday!' I don't trust him at all. I hope he gets out of town." She said this with a pronouncement of finality that ended the conversation.

I often wondered what happened to the boy. He was obviously strung out on dope, or mentally disturbed, but seemed harmless enough. The local ladies would not have agreed to him being harmless, particularly as it applied to their daughters.

After supper, I walked down to the old buildings that had once housed the hot springs for which the town had been named. In its glory days, the town was one of the most popular resorts in western North Carolina and boasted a beautiful thousand-bed hotel as well as spa buildings and a spring house. Unfortunately, with the advent of modern medicine, the popularity of medicinal baths declined and with that ensued a decline in business for the town. Now most of the spa buildings had disappeared or fallen into disrepair.

Hot Springs deserves a brighter future, I thought, as I went off to my motel, sight-seeing at an end.

MAX PATCH

If there is a current Eden,
It was modeled on Max Patch.
The trail winds secretly
Inside the line of trees,
Waiting for the right place
And moment to begin
Its long and winding climb.
It breaks into sunlight.
On cue the side ridge sways
And stands of daisies and yarrow
Bend whichever way the wind last blew.
The summit's soft in summer grass.
Green and golden waves wind lap
Against a lonesome rock.
Then subside into a meadow —
Green motion heaving sea-like
To the trees below.
And they in turn undulate gently in the sun,
And in the shadows of the passing clouds,
Until they meet the dark
And sometimes blue or purple hills,
Lying crumpled, misty in the cool distance.

CHAPTER 10

Hot Springs, North Carolina, to Erwin, Tennessee
Coming to Terms with the Trail

The climb up Mill Ridge was uncommonly steep with no easy grades or switchbacks. In many places, the Trail ascended straight up the rocky inclines, and I was forced to stop often to catch my breath and let my heart rate subside. It was a physically draining effort, much more difficult than I had anticipated; and it reduced the pleasure of the hike.

At the start, I had looked forward to the reputedly magnificent views from Lovers Leap, a large rock formation that overlooked the French Broad River valley and the mountains which surrounded it. But when I reached the promontory, I was disappointed. There really were no views. The day was very warm, and a thick haze had enveloped the valley.

Only the area directly below the rock could be seen with any clarity while the remainder of the valley and the panorama of mountains in the distance were engulfed in a gray shroud. I dismissed my negative feelings and focused my attention on Lovers Leap, which had received its name from a Cherokee Indian love tragedy legend.

According to the story, a maiden of the tribe, Mist-on-the-Mountain, had fallen in love with Magwa, an Indian warrior from a northern tribe. A rivalry for her affections developed between Magwa and another warrior, Lone Wolf, and a fight ensued. The fight ended in the death of Magwa, and Mist-on-the-Mountain became so overcome with grief on learning of her lover's death that she threw herself from the rock.

After Lovers Leap, the Trail ascended more gradually, and the walking became easier. Shortly before reaching Tanyard Gap, the Trail circumvented a quiet mountain pond nestled in a stand of mature hardwoods that opened at one end onto a large mountainside meadow. It would have been perfectly idyllic had it not been for the bottles, cans and food wrappers strewn along its banks. One of the most depressing sights I encountered in the southern Appalachians was the trash-filled gap. It seemed that every gap which could be reached by road had become a miniature landfill.

Just north of Hurricane Gap, I encountered a small rectangular, two- by one-foot, sand-colored, marble monument (or maybe it was granite). Engraved on it:

Rex R. Pulford, Sep 22 1920, April 21 1983

That was all it said.

I could find nothing in the guidebook about the monument and surmised that it must have been dedicated to a Trail adherent, a Trail club member or perhaps a hiker who had passed away at the spot on the date indicated. I later learned that Mr. Pulford was the father of Dorothy Hansen from Neels Gap; he was thru-hiking the Trail when he was stricken at that spot. Other Thru-Hikers that year, in a display of solidarity with the family and devotion to Mr. Pulford's ideal, carried his boots and hiking staff in relays to Mt. Katahdin.

I stopped for the night at primitive Spring Mountain shelter. The shelter, constructed in 1938 by the CCC (Civilian Conservation Corps) was little more than a run-down, bee-infested lean-to sitting in a small sag through which the Trail passed before making its final ascent up Spring Mountain. Thousands of bees crawled all over the shelter, the firepit, and a large tree that sat directly across the small clearing in front of the shelter.

I was sure the large tree was a hive tree. But try as I might, I couldn't find the hive entrance. The image of Melvin Wilson at the campfire in Birch Springs Gap describing how to find a wild honey tree came to mind, and I thought that if he were there, the opening would be found.

Here a small thunderstorm hit the ridge, bringing with it some amazingly strong wind gusts. just prior to the storm's arrival, the bees disappeared en masse; when the storm had passed, they returned. They performed the same disappearing act just after sunset, disappearing like a magician had waved a wand. Thousands of them had been flying all over the shelter and around the clearing. Now there were no lingerers. They were gone!

Each of those tiny creatures had built-in weather forecasting and communication or timing systems that informed them when to seek shelter. Later when I wrote my Trail notes, I reflected on the importance of the experience. Little things like the reaction of the bees were but a tiny manifestation of the intricate interdependencies of nature, and by the extension of logic, an indication of the power of the Being who could create and harmonize so vast a system.

When I entered the date, 12th of July, in my Trail journal, I realized that it was the one-month anniversary of my start on the Trail. I had been hiking for a whole month!

I calculated the distances I had traveled: 10.7 miles for the day and 280.7 miles overall which seemed like an astronomical number. "Imagine, I've walked 280 miles," I whispered in awe; but I still had more than 1700 to go. The deflation was instantaneous and complete.

I awoke at 6:00 a.m. the next morning to find the bees were already arriving at the shelter. But they didn't arrive en masse. They seemed to appear singly or in small groups over the course of about a 30-minute period.

Normally, I would have slept for another hour, but with the bees becoming a nuisance, crawling over me, my clothes and my gear, I decided to get out of their way as quickly as possible. Hurriedly, I packed my gear and walked for an hour before stopping to make breakfast and repack the disorganized mess I had made in my haste to escape the bees.

I stopped at Little Laurel shelter for lunch, then proceeded to hike some of the most difficult terrain I encountered on the Trail, Camp Creek Bald, Little Firescald Knob and Big Firescald Knob. I came to the conclusion then that there were no easy hikes on the Trail. I had thought with the Nantahalas and the Smokies out of the way, things would get easier. No way! Climbs were tough no matter where they were. In fact, some of the smaller mountains were more difficult than the larger ones. The changes of elevation on the smaller mountains were more frequent, and the cumulative effect of the constant ups and downs was as physically draining as the steady climbs up the big hills.

The approach to Camp Creek Bald was long and steep. The Trail from the mountains to the old jeep road, leading to Jerry Cabin shelter, went through a heavy undergrowth of rhododendron and blackberry bushes. It was difficult walking and slightly dangerous. Since it was so heavy with growth, I couldn't see where to step. Consequently, I stumbled frequently, trying to find footing along the rock-and-boulder-strewn pathway.

This was exhausting work. The long grass and limbs of the bushes tugged and clutched at my pack and body as I moved ahead. Then, too, the extended drought was having its effect. None of the springs mentioned in the *Trail Guide*, including the one at Jerry Cabin shelter, contained water. It was the first shelter I had encountered which had no water.

Although it had been a difficult day, it was not without its rewards. Views of the broad valleys and mountain vistas from the rock outcroppings north of Bearwallow Gap provided a welcome relief from the vision-limiting tangle of brush, trees and rocks in the forest. And the bright stands of wildflowers sprinkled along the Trail provided a happy contrast of color to the oppressive brown, greens and grays that dominated the color scale of the mountains.

I was surprised to again see large numbers of brilliant red fire pinks on the ridges. I also encountered large stands of bee balm in moist areas and deep violet Virginia spiderwort and blue Asiatic dayflowers that grew singly or in small bunches at Trail side. The brightest surprise awaited me on the west side of Big Firescald Knob where I observed two ruby-throated hummingbirds feeding on rhododendron blossoms.

When I arrived at a shelter, the first thing I normally did was look for a Trail register, and in the one at Jerry Cabin shelter I found an entry from Nick Sprague telling me to "hang in there." When I reflected on it, I realized I was doing just that — "hanging in there."

I was very proud of overcoming my negative feelings and of bouncing back mentally from the previous day. Even after a 15-mile day over very tough terrain with sore feet, I was in a positive frame of mind.

Meanwhile, my physical condition was excellent. I had lost about 15 pounds since departing Springer Mountain. In fact, my waist had shrunk about two inches. I entertained momentary thoughts of heading north for Katahdin about mid-August and hiking south as Dave Walp planned, thinking that I could complete all the really tough portions of the Trail in Maine and New Hampshire by the end of the summer while I was in such good shape. I could then complete the Trail in more leisurely fashion the following year. The idea had great appeal initially. But then I discarded the idea, deciding I didn't want the adventure of a lifetime to end at some nondescript road junction in New York or New Jersey. I wanted it to end in the sky on top of Katahdin where I could look across the ranks of purple mountains marching to the horizon, where I could feel an emotion suitable to my triumph.

I continued to be amazed by the range of emotions I experienced as I hiked. It was a day-to-day struggle against the elements and the negative versus the positive for control of my attitude toward the hike and the Trail. I was reminded that one battle does not make a war. It is the sum total of all the little battles that contributes to the mosaic of victory. There would be defeats as well as victories, and it was important to keep that in perspective — first, to keep from becoming overconfident from my victories, and secondly, to keep from becoming unduly pessimistic from my defeats.

I compared my experience on the Trail to a microcosm of the experience of life. At least, the Trail experience had life experience validation which was valuable to my transition. In a way, I had to endure on the Trail, just as I endured in life. I ultimately concluded that it was all basically one effort experienced in different settings.

Rain began shortly after I departed the shelter the next day and continued through the morning. The Trail differed from the description contained in the *Trail Guide* and confused me until I realized that I was following a relocation. After a few miles, however, the book and the Trail got together again. Because the descriptions in the *Trail Guides* were very accurate, I relied almost exclusively on them for navigation rather than the accompanying maps which, for the most part, were so broad in scale that they were useless. Those who wrote the descriptions in the *Trail Guides* deserve the gratitude of all who hike the Trail.

The climbs out of Devil Fork Gap and Sugar Loaf Gap were ridiculously steep, as steep as anything I had yet encountered, and there were no rewarding views. It seemed that graded trails and switchbacks could have eased some of the climbs. The construction and maintenance of the Trail depended on the volunteers of the various hiking clubs who devoted hours of time and gallons of sweat to the task; they were to be congratulated for their dedication and sacrifice.

Still, from a Thru-Hiker's perspective, it was difficult to continually "pay one's dues" for 2,000 miles. The longer I hiked the Trail, the more convinced I became that the Trail should be constructed within the physical capabilities of the 50-, 60- or 70-year-old weekend hiker and nature enthusiast and not be reserved solely for the 20-year-old, world-class power hikers.

Later in the day on Big Butt Mountain, the mist was so thick at times that I couldn't find the Trail markers. Mostly the markers were painted on trees at the edge of a tree line. If the pathway became obscured or diverged into multiple paths and I couldn't see across the fields to the tree line to orient my direction, I had no clue as to the direction I should take. I solved that by detouring along the tree line until I happily encountered a white marker. Occasionally, if the bald was small I relied on dead reckoning and hoped the Trail remained on the ridge crest.

Shortly before lunch, I passed the grave of William and David Shelton located in an area known as the Ball Ground. It was formerly a bald, but now a growth of 30-year-old white pines covered the former field.

The Shelton grave was a double grave with simple government tombstones at either end with the inscriptions:

"Wm. Shelton, Co. E, 2 N.C. Inf."
and
"David Shelton, Co. C, 3 N.C. Mtd. Inf."

According to the *Trail Guide*, the two men, an uncle and his nephew, both members of the Union Army during the Civil War, had been ambushed by Confederates as they were returning to the mountains on leave to visit their families. Their lookout, a young boy, was also killed, and all three were buried by their families in a common grave.

In 1915, two preachers acquired the two tombstones, hauled them to the site by ox sled, and erected them. Because the markers were Government Issue, the boy was not included in the deal. Obviously, the boy was not in the Army and did not fall within limits of the regulations providing for tombstones.

After a short respite feasting on blackberries in Devil Fork Gap, I crossed well-traveled Boones Cove Road, then followed an old gravel road for about 200 yards until it passed a large, invitingly dry barn that stood under a canopy of several tall oaks. The torrential rain sorely tempted me to ignore the "No Trespassing" signs that guarded the overgrown grass access road. I decided to abide by the desires of the owner, however, and continued on, eventually climbing a ridiculously steep, but thankfully short stretch up the ridge beside a stream bed.

One of the absolute musts in Trail etiquette is to respect the desires of the owners of property through which the Trail passes. A motto of the Trail which I found most appealing:

> "Take nothing but photographs and
> leave nothing but footprints."

This was cogent advice. The considerable good will toward hikers among the people who lived in the vicinity of the Trail could be attributed to those before me who had practiced the admonishments of that motto.

That evening I learned that not everyone had a high regard for the people along the Trail. A note in the shelter register on Hogback Ridge complained about the poor Trail conditions, the steep climbs and the "sullen locals." It compared them to the "sullen locals in the Nantahalas." I agreed with the comment about the steep climbs, but I thought the Trail was not that badly maintained. I couldn't agree with the comment about the "sullen locals," particularly in the Nantahalas. The folks in the Nantahalas were friendly, and I hadn't yet met anyone I could classify as sullen. Perhaps this was a case of the writer's negative energy finding that which it sought.

The shelter was a new structure as was the privy which boasted a first-class wooden toilet seat, not your run-of-the-mill cheap old wooden seat, but a smooth hand-rubbed dark wooden seat such as one might expect in an expensive hotel. I was amazed how such little niceties as a decent toilet seat could add so much to the quality of the day.

Before I turned in for the night, I told myself, Tomorrow I will have a great day! In fact, I was determined to make it a great day. I had to be positive and "keep on truckin'!" By programming my unconscious with positive thoughts, I almost always had a good next day.

The previous day's climbs had exhausted me, and the next morning it was nearly 9:00 a.m. when I awoke. As much as I desired to be on the Trail early, my body had simply taken charge.

The Trail was beautiful all day: strenuous, but beautiful. The six-mile stretch from Sams Gap to Big Bald seemed mostly an uphill climb, but since I was in good condition, refreshed and expected the Trail to be tough, I remained psychologically unaffected by the physical demands.

Shortly before Street Gap, The Trail broke out of the forest near the ridge crest and followed a long narrow meadow that swept down the ridge towards the gap. The presence of man's hand was apparent in the undulating hay fields that bordered the meadow, but man himself was nowhere to be seen, creating a somewhat mysterious atmosphere.

The meadow over which the Trail descended to Street Gap was a giant wildflower garden where dense colonies of oxeye daisies, black-eyed susans, Queen Anne's lace, and others swayed in family groupings, choreographed by the breezes that swept down and across the ridge. Patches of blackberries grew along the fence line down the hill, and I tasted their sweetness more than once.

In the far distance, the sky framed the green, sunbathed mountains with a light blue horizon that grew increasingly bluer the farther one looked up into the sky. Big Bald Mountain loomed, massively green, across the gap, and the life of summer hummed everywhere.

The trail from Street Gap to the summit of Big Bald crossed an extensive glacial deposit of steamer-trunk-sized boulders that stretched in a wide swath up the steepening ridge line. I picked my way carefully, hopping from boulder to boulder where possible, avoiding the narrow crevices, and maintaining my balance with my hiking stick as I negotiated the difficult vertical steps. The hiking club had arranged some of the rocks into a stair-step arrangement which was quite helpful in climbing the steeper inclines. But even so, climbing the two- to three-foot vertical steps with 40 pounds on my back was exhausting.

Big Bald reminded me of Max Patch. Like Max Patch, its size seemed awesome. The long, thick grass flowed easily with the upward sweep of the ridge line except where it was interrupted by occasional patches of wildflowers, scrub bushes or blackberry patches. Near the forest edge, a great number of scrub trees and bushes, looking as though they had spilled over from the forest, had taken over the field. I thought these were probably the forerunners of the forest's advance up the bald; unless checked by man, the bald would in time be completely covered.

Besides Max Patch, this was the only other true bald I had experienced. I had crossed other balds, but they were being maintained as balds by cutting back the encroaching forest. In the southern Appalachians, the mountains did not reach the heights required for a true timber line, and the origin of the balds had long been a source of debate. However they originated, the balds were

Author on summit of Big Bald after one month and two days on Trail.

almost certainly maintained, if not enlarged, by farmers who used the grassy summits for summer pasture land. But now, because they are no longer used for grazing, most were undergoing natural change into forest.

The major attraction all balds had in common were beautiful views of the valleys and the surrounding mountain panorama. Big Bald was no exception. Especially interesting was its view towards the south of an area developed for home sites. It was the only visual disturbance to the natural order. The road cuts didn't entirely disrupt the beauty of the ridge. In a way, they provided a contrast which made the whole scene rather pleasant.

There were far fewer scrub trees and blackberry bushes on the north side of the bald. Extensive stands of wildflowers dominated the meadows that swept to the forest edge. The only break in the grass was an access road that led to a parking area below the summit. After crossing the summit, I headed for Greer Farm where I hoped to find the outlines of a moat dug by "Old Hog" Greer over a century ago. The *Trail Guide* mentioned that Greer used the moat to keep his livestock penned. The usual practice of the time (early 1800s), was to let the livestock run wild until it was time to gather them for the winter or for slaughter. Unfortunately, I couldn't find any trace of Greer Farm.

According to the *Trail Guide*, Greer, a South Carolinian, became infatuated with a girl. But she rejected him, and he moved to Big Bald where he lived on and off for 30 years as a hermit. He dug a home under a rock, lined it with clay and used a rock for a front door. Greer lived much as his animals did, hence the name, "Old Hog." Reportedly, he had a terrible temper and is said to have killed a man during an argument. Later he, himself, was killed during an argument with another man. After reading about his rages, it occurred to me that his lady friend had probably made a wise decision when she decided against casting her fortunes with his.

It was late afternoon by the time I reached Big Bald shelter where I planned to spend the night. The shelter, a large wooden beam and log structure with upper and lower sleeping platforms, was another monument to the dedication and sacrifice of the members of the Carolina Mountain Club. There isn't enough money or gratitude to pay the volunteers who build the shelters and improve the trails. Those who hike the Trail owe a tremendous debt to those who dedicate their time and resources to keep the Trail functional.

Just after I settled in the shelter, a group of Boy Scouts struggled into the clearing and dropped their packs. There were 15 boys in all, counting the last, short-legged, overweight boy; he straggled in two hours later in the company of an equally overweight adult. I learned that they had tried to dissuade the overweight boy from going on the hike. But the kid had met all the requirements and earned the right to go.

As soon as the first Scout appeared, my mind conjured up bitter memories of the Boy Scouts at Cold Spring shelter. Fortunately, the evening was a surprisingly positive experience.

The Scoutmaster was a leader in every sense of the word. He had a gift for dealing with kids, and it was apparent that the kids liked him very much and would do anything for him.

The man treated each boy with respect, even when a kid was "screwin' up by the numbers." He did not coddle the boys, and his standards were demanding, though reasonable and understandable. He also exhibited pride in the boys and praised them when they did well. The boys reciprocated by showing pride in themselves and in the troop. He exhibited a "textbook" concern for the Scouts. He was always at the place where he was needed at the time he was needed, always in a position to take charge, while never intruding unnecessarily.

Each of the boys was charged to carry something that was common troop property or which contributed to the welfare of the group. It might be a cookpot or food, something other than what the Scout would expect to carry solely for his own use. Whatever it was, it was organized and labeled so that the boy knew he had a responsibility to the group for carrying and safeguarding the item. It was a perfect example of how to teach individual responsibility and discipline.

As soon as I climbed into my sleeping bag, which was quite early, the Scoutmaster admonished the boys to keep quiet since I was a "Thru-Hiker" and needed rest. That was a pretty tall order for the Scouts. This was their first night on the Trail, and it took a great amount of self-control to contain their natural exuberance. But, for the most part, the boys behaved; and I was able to sleep.

When I awoke the next morning, the troop was still asleep, but the Scoutmaster was already up and drinking coffee. He had made the rounds to ensure that everyone was accounted for and that everything was in order. I prepared breakfast, and we chatted in hushed tones while I ate. The Scouts were beginning to stir when I took my leave.

I stopped for lunch at No Business Knob shelter where I was joined about 15 minutes later by several summer camp boys I had met at the shelter spring the previous evening. The boys were in an unusual state of agitation caused by blundering into a yellowjacket's nest. Evidently, they had decided to take a break, using as a seat an inviting log laying beside the Trail. The log contained the nest. When the boys disturbed it, the insects attacked. Needless to say, they quickly vacated the area and skipped their break. A couple of the boys had been stung, and every time a bug of any type flew anywhere near them, they exploded in a panic of self-defense.

It was shortly after noon when I reached the ridge overlooking the Nolichucky River Valley. From the heights, it seemed only a short distance to the valley, but it took more than an hour to reach the valley floor, then another 30 minutes before I arrived at the Nolichucky Expeditions, a rafting company, that was temporarily closed because of low water.

The cost of primitive overnight accommodations with the rafting company was about as expensive as a motel in town. I opted for a motel, and from a pay phone on the porch of the administration building, I called a number listed on the bulletin board advertising rides into town. I quickly sealed the deal and went inside to drink a cold soda while waiting for my transportation to arrive. No luck. The soda was warm. A coffee machine sat conspicuously next to the refrigerator, and I poured myself a cup. The coffee was cold.

My chauffeur, a disreputable-looking 30-year-old, was so obese he had difficulty extracting himself from behind the steering wheel of his beat-up, old, Ford station wagon. His jeans rode very low on his hips, pushed down by his large girth; when he bent over or sat down, part of the cleavage between his ample buttocks became exposed and his T-shirt rode up exposing his large hairy belly.

Although the aesthetics were marginal, the price was right. For $10 he took me to the Tennessee Hills motel, ten miles away on the other side of Erwin. The nearest motel, the one where I wanted to stay, was much closer, only a couple of miles down the road toward town, but the owners refused to rent to hikers. Such was my introduction to Erwin, Tennessee.

CHAPTER 11

Erwin and the Episode
on Beauty Spot Mountain

The room in the Tennessee Hills Motel was plain, but it **was** air-conditioned, the bed had sheets, and the bathroom boasted a tub with a shower. (The hot water taps in the first room I was assigned did little more than leak water, and I was given another room after I complained.) The motel also had an adjoining restaurant, closed for renovation. That was an unpleasant surprise; it was three miles back to town. With no bus or taxi service available that meant either walking or hitchhiking, both of which were really unacceptable options. The motel clerk was very understanding of my predicament, though. She put me in contact with a man who, for five dollars, offered to drive me that evening to the local Pizza Hut.

I was starved for fresh food and made two trips to the salad bar, heaping my plate each time; then I ate a medium pizza supreme plus a spaghetti dinner and washed it all down with a pitcher of beer.

The waitress was astonished at my appetite. "You're too little to be eatin' so much," she said.

It was the first time in a long time anyone had said I was little.

My "chauffeur" appeared after supper, bringing with him a six-pack of beer as arranged and a friend (not arranged). The conversation on the way back to the motel was dominated by the driver's friend.

"Where you from?" he asked.

"Naples, Florida," I replied.

"Where's that?"

"Over on the west coast."

"You're walkin' the whole Trail, I hear. You a school teacher?"

"No, I'm retired military."

"Which branch?"

"Army."

"What rank was you?"

His questions and tone of voice irritated me. There was nothing subtle or any indication of the least bit of sensitivity in his style. I changed the subject. "My feet are about to kill me," I put in quickly. "Boots are wearin' out. Any place in town that sells boots?"

"What kind of boots you lookin' for?"

"Hikin' boots. Maybe HI-TEC or New Balance."

"No one in town sells anything like that," the driver allowed. "You'll probably have to go to Johnson City."

"How far is that?" I asked.

"'Bout 15 mile."

"Was you in Vietnam?" Another question from the friend.

"Yeah." Then, without waiting for another question, I asked the driver if he could give me a lift to Johnson City the next day.

"Long as it's not too early in the morning," he said. "Give me a call when you're ready to go."

"I got a cousin that was a sergeant major in the Army," the friend said proudly. "That's a damn good rate. He says the Army's full of niggers. You see many niggers in the Army?"

"I didn't see *any* niggers in the Army."

He stopped and thought a minute about what I said. I doubted he understood. "You don't see no niggers around here, do you? No sir! Any nigger comes into this town is in trouble. They know better than to come into Erwin!" he proclaimed authoritatively.

I bit my tongue as we drove into the motel driveway.

"What rank was you?" he persisted.

I looked him in the eye, put my face up to his like I was going to let him in on a big secret, then got out without a word.

I headed for town on foot the next morning, sticking my thumb out at the approach of every passing car, but no one stopped. I walked the entire three miles.

I stopped first at a neat, very clean laundromat where the charming woman custodian chatted with customers and helped incompetents like me who couldn't figure out how the machinery worked. (She gave me a cup of ammonia to put in my wash along with the soap, and it helped immensely in getting my clothes clean.)

After following the woman's instructions and starting the machine, I selected a seat from a row of waiting chairs and began a conversation with the only other customer, a middle-aged woman waiting for her clothes to dry. I mentioned that I was thru-hiking the AT and that caught her interest as well as that of the custodian who joined our conversation.

"You see many snakes?" asked the customer.

"A few garter snakes and black snakes but no rattlers. One copperhead — and one rattlesnake, but it was dead. Snakes don't bother me."

I was about to say that snakes are actually helpful because they have a niche in the food chain and help keep rodents and pests under control.

But the woman said, "I'm scared to death of 'em. The only snake I want to see is a dead snake. Ain't you scared bein' out there all alone all the time? What if somethin' happened?"

"I'm not really afraid to be alone. No animal is going to bother me. The only thing I worry about is running into some crazy who thinks he has a message from God to kill me."

"There are a few of those folks runnin' around, too," she said, nodding her head in sage agreement. "Wasn't too long back some man killed a girl on the Trail near here. He was a tree surgeon, near as I can recollect." She was knitting as we talked, and her hands fairly sped through the motions as she talked about the killing.

"Course, I carry a gun in the event I might run into a nut like that. The people in the ATC and the *Philosopher's Guide* say you shouldn't carry a gun, that if you think you need a gun, you don't understand the Trail. I agree with their philosophy. It's just that I want to be protected from someone else who doesn't understand that."

The custodian watched me intently and nodded in agreement.

The customer agreed. "I'd damn sure carry one, if I was you." The conversation stopped as her clothes dryer stopped.

After folding my clothes, I headed for the post office where a sign above the counter indicated that the place was closed on Wednesday afternoons. I looked at my watch: 12:30 p.m. "Dammit," I hissed. My remark startled another man who was sorting mail he had collected from his mail box. I apologized, saying, "I didn't mean to disturb you. I'm just venting my frustration at having walked over three miles to get to the post office — only to find it closed.

We talked for a minute, and I explained that I was thru-hiking the AT and that I was only in town for the day to rest and reprovision. I also mentioned that I intended to go to Johnson City to get a new pair of boots.

He said he was also going to Johnson City later in the day, but right then he had errands to do. If he saw me on the road later, he'd give me a lift back to the motel or to Johnson City.

I thanked him and went out to hitch a ride back to the motel. I got one almost immediately from an older man in a pickup truck. He told me he wouldn't have stopped if he hadn't mistaken me for someone else. However, since I was already in the truck, he'd take me as far as the road where he turned to go to his farm.

As he drove, he told me about an argument he had had with a man who challenged him about the way he drove. He said the other man had "come around to my side of the truck, saying he was goin' to 'kick my butt.' I always carry a gun under the seat and held it up so's he could see it and told him he better get away from me."

I glanced down to see if I could see the gun. It must have been under the seat. I wondered if all this was for my benefit in case I might have had any ideas of robbing him.

"Should'a seen how fast that bastard run back to his car!" The man became so involved in his story now that he passed the road to his house and carried me all the way to the motel.

After packing my food and clean clothes, I went to the motel office to ask the clerk where I could buy boots in Johnson City. She suggested a shoe store on the highway just outside of Johnson City. To eliminate a futile journey, I phoned ahead to inquire if the store carried hiking boots and to make sure they'd be open that afternoon.

I must have looked at 100 pairs of boots. Mostly, they were hunter's specials or regular, heavy-duty hiking boots that needed breaking-in. I tried on at least a dozen pairs before I found a pair of cushion-soled Georgia Giants that were comfortable. Unfortunately, the only color left in my size was bright blue; I felt conspicuously like a blue-footed booby as I walked down the Trail the next day. I visualized the exaggerated way in which the birds walked, lifting their colorful feet high for all the other birds to see, like dancers doing a cakewalk in slow motion.

Later at the motel, I threw the old boots in the trash. I did feel a fleeting twinge of sadness when I thought about how far we had come together, "these boots and me." But I disposed of them with the steely determination of the cowboy who is forced to shoot his wounded horse. The blisters, I suspect, saved me from becoming maudlin.

I returned to the Pizza Hut that evening for one last raid on the salad bar. The waitress who had waited on me the previous night saw me come in. Although I was led to a different section, she evidently said something to the kitchen staff. When I looked up, the eyes of the whole staff were riveted on me.

About halfway through my pizza, my "chauffeur," the one with the racist friend, appeared and came over to my table. He offered to take me back to the motel, making the offer sound like it was being made in friendship. Then, when I accepted, he said it would be three dollars.

I was tempted to tell him to forget it. But it was growing late and I was tired. Anyway, I didn't want to hitchhike or walk the road in the dark. I let it pass. At this point, he went over to a booth to join his friend and they waited until I was finished.

The friend, who had entered earlier, feigned surprise at seeing me, saying if he'd known I was there, he would have joined me. Of course, he was lying through his teeth. He was the sort that checked everything out before he sat down. He saw me before I saw him but chose to keep his distance. I suspected he had called the "chauffeur" to inform him that I was at the place. I didn't trust either man.

After dealing with all types of people in the Army, I had developed a gut instinct that told me when to be wary. It was a split-second thing that I came to rely on because I was right 95 percent of the time. It wasn't that they were overtly threatening or even rude. They were unnaturally deferential to a fault. That's what made me uneasy. They were not the type to be deferential to anyone.

The fact that they both just "happened" there when I was there also made me uneasy. They could be setting me up.

The "friend's" big black Lincoln was in the parking lot. He lamented the damage done to the front end of it when, in a drunken stupor the previous night, he had driven it off the road. Although his words contained a message of unhappiness, they also contained, by some strange twist of logic, a hint of braggadocio. The crumpled fender and bumper turned the headlight in such a way that it looked at me goo-goo eyed.

I climbed into the back seat of the "chauffeur's" car. I didn't want the "friend" to my rear and began thinking about what I could do should they try anything.

The "friend" again dominated the conversation. This time it was directed at my chauffeur — fine by me. We reached the motel five minutes later, and after paying my three dollars, I exited the car with a sense of relief.

The Trail the next day was fairly easy, though it was all uphill. Nicely graded, the path was almost rock free. Too, my new boots were a big improvement. They were soft and the cushion soles absorbed much of the impact of my steps. It was almost a pleasure to walk in them.

I was surprised not to be experiencing the negative feelings I usually had the first day on the Trail after a layover in town. Then I realized that this time I was happy to leave civilization.

The first mile led through a beautiful broad stream valley, and the Trail crisscrossed the stream several times over moss-covered rocks and ground that was soft and comfortable to hike. When the Trail reached the ridge proper, it resumed its narrow side-hill course, climbing gradually to the ridge top.

En route, I encountered a father and son I had met two days before on the road to the Nolichucky Expeditions; they had stopped to ask if I could recommend any easy places for a ten-year-old to begin his hiking experience.

After deciding where and how far they wanted to hike, they had hired my obese "chauffeur" to take them to their starting point at Indian Grave Gap. During the intervening period, they had hiked some five or six miles in the direction of the Nolichucky River and were surprised when I told them that it was only about three miles to the river. They had expected it to take much longer to hike the stretch they had just covered. Since they were ahead of schedule, the father decided to stop for the day when they reached the valley and camp overnight before finishing up the next day.

From the Curley Maple Gap shelter to Indian Grave Gap, the Trail ran along the ridge spine with little change in elevation. I reached Indian Grave Gap quickly. From there, the Trail became slightly more difficult as it climbed toward Beauty Spot and Unaka Mountain.

Beauty Spot was just as the name implied, a beautiful ridge-top bald with grand views of the mountains in all directions. A forest service road led to the open summit where a cul-de-sac loop provided easy reversal of direction. Next to the road was ample parking space.

The Trail crossed the forest service road several times on the way up the ridge. During one crossing, two vehicles rounded a bend in the road about 500 feet down the hill. I continued on into the forest and stopped about 25 yards inside the tree line to watch the cars.

One was a four-wheel drive wagon, perhaps a Ford Bronco or an International Scout; the other was a red, older model Ford sedan. Two men were in the front seat of each vehicle. Later, as I neared the open bald, I heard the sound of a vehicle on the summit; then it became quiet. I hurried up the hill hoping to meet the people on the summit. But the car had driven off well before I arrived.

The views of Roan Mountain, Big Bald, the Black Mountains and the Nolichucky River were spectacular. The *Trail Guide* indicated that a spring was located on the far side of the summit. Since I had used all my water during the climb, I headed for the spring. I couldn't find the blue-blazed trail that led to the spring. I reread the *Trail Guide* and realized I had made an error. I retraced my steps back to the Trail.

As I walked through a small patch of young forest just beyond the summit, I heard a vehicle driving very slowly up the forest service road towards the summit loop I had just passed. Then I heard another vehicle further away being driven very slowly along the same road in the opposite direction, as if the driver was searching for something. I didn't pay much attention, but my curiosity was aroused.

Eventually, the Trail climbed to within a few feet of the ridge-top road. I found the blue-blazed trail to the spring and stopped when I heard the car that had been on the summit approaching, again being driven at a very slow rate of speed. It was clear the driver was searching for something. Maybe looking to poach a deer, I thought. Then, it sunk in . . .

They were searching only that small area repeatedly. Must be after something else, I mused.

I was about to cross the road to the spring when the car that had been on the summit came around the bend. Instinctively, I stayed inside the wood line and crouched behind some tangled growth until it passed. I don't know why I did that except that my suspicions had been aroused. It appeared to be the same wagon I'd seen earlier while climbing the mountain. After it was out of sight, I crossed the road and headed down the mountainside for the spring. As I approached the spring, I again heard a car being driven very slowly along the road on the ridge directly above me.

I removed my pack and took a break, washing my face and gulping down as much of the clear spring water as I could hold. I was troubled by the activities of the people in the cars. They were certainly looking for something. Then it struck me. Maybe they were looking for me!

Visions of my two "chauffeurs" appeared in my mind. I had stupidly allowed them to see that I was carrying a number of travelers checks when I took money from my wallet to pay them for the rides.

Now my imagination took over. What will I do if I meet them? For the first time on the hike, I took my .38 calibre Smith and Wesson pistol from my pack and slipped it into my trouser pocket. I began to anticipate how I might react in different scenarios. The trick would be to determine their intentions. Since I couldn't be sure, I decided I had several options.

The first option was to evade them. The second was to react quickly at the first sign of hostile intent. The third was to show I was carrying a weapon.

Just stay out of sight! I told myself. That's the way to handle this one! Stay off the roads and trails!

After a few minutes, I headed back for the Trail. Just before I reached the road, the car that had passed above the spring on its way to the summit returned, again driving very slowly. I remained hidden behind the underbrush until it passed, then quickly crossed the road. Almost immediately after I crossed, I heard an automobile start up down the road to my left . . . But the car was moving in the other direction. After a few long minutes, the car returned from the summit, and I slipped well back into the forest and allowed it to pass before returning to the pathway.

Although separated from the road by only a few yards, the Trail was well concealed by thick vegetation for the next several hundred yards. I moved cautiously, staying keenly aware of sounds. After a time, I couldn't hear the cars. That worried me even more.

As long as I could hear the cars, I knew I was safe. Were the men now on foot? Then I arrived at a break in the woods at the same time the two cars departed in opposite directions.

They were definitely the same cars I had seen during my climb toward Beauty Spot. One car headed back up the hill toward the summit, and the other down the road toward Erwin, again driving very slowly. I waited until they were well out of sight before crossing the exposed area.

The clearing was several hundred yards long. The path was sited between a pasture fence and the road with almost no concealment available for 200 yards. After 100 yards, there was an access drive from the road to the pasture gate.

Several head of cattle watched as I walked along the fence. When I reached the pasture gate, about halfway across the open area, the car that had been headed in the direction of Erwin returned. I was fully exposed.

Just keep on going, I told myself. When it gets close, drop down in the Trail.

Fortunately, a slight dip in the path and a growth of bushes and tall grass came in sight. I slipped behind them and hunkered down until the car passed. Then I arose and headed quickly down the pathway. The car stopped. They'd seen me!

I glanced back up the road from where I had come and could see the men getting out of the car. It was the old red Ford. They had parked next to the pasture access and were looking in the other direction. I didn't wait around to see what they were doing. The Trail dipped out of sight from the pasture access; I moved out at double time until I began the climb up Unaka Mountain.

I was thrilled to see the road fall away behind me. Later, as I reflected on the episode, I became convinced the men in the cars were looking for me. If they had been looking for game, they would not have searched so intensely in one place. If they were looking for a lost animal, a dog or a cow, they would have searched beyond the narrow area where the Trail paralleled the road. Yes, they were literally combing the area where the road closely paralleled the Trail and no further. It was with a feeling of relief that I climbed toward Unaka.

I kept up a full head of steam as I hit the summit of Unaka Mountain and pushed on to Low Gap. I had originally intended to camp overnight at Low Gap. But I decided to put as much distance as possible between me and those men. I didn't slow down until I reached Cherry Gap where the shelter was far from any roads.

I'll never know for sure if the danger was real or imagined. But in light of subsequent events, I feel the danger was real.

The flora on Unaka Mountain was unique. Balsam and pine covered the broad ridges leading to the summit, giving the upper elevations of the mountain an appearance similar to the

Canadian north woods. The pathway was soft with a thick carpet of needles which made the walking easy on the legs and feet. The forest was open and reminded me of the higher elevations in the Smokies. Near the summit, I saw an animal which at first glance looked like a rabbit. It sat on a stump three feet off the ground watching a group of grouse. When I approached, it hopped down effortlessly and slipped out of sight behind some rocks. Its color was too tawny to be a rabbit and its behavior was completely different. I thought it might have been a bobcat. Unfortunately, I was unable to get close enough for a positive identification.

I also saw a bear on the summit of Unaka. At least, I thought it was a bear. I saw only the movement of a large, dark-colored animal through the forest shadow about 100 yards away. It moved with deliberate speed, but not the explosive acceleration I'd come to associate with deer. I was sure I would have seen a white tail waving had it been a deer.

I read in the Cherry Gap shelter register that Nick Sprague had passed through exactly ten days before on July 7th. He's really making good time, I thought; he must be in Virginia by now! God! I'd love to be in Virginia now. Why can't I walk fast? Then I paused in thought. I was exhausted and was becoming negative about the hike because of fatigue. After supper, I began to feel better. I concentrated on maintaining a positive attitude until I fell asleep.

CHAPTER 12

Roan Mountain
Challenge and Success

Beginning at Low Gap just to the east of Beauty Spot, the AT followed the ridge crest border between the states of Tennessee and North Carolina for about thirty miles. If one fell off the Trail to the left, he landed in Tennessee. If he fell to the right, he ended up in North Carolina.

When I reached Iron Mountain Gap the following morning, I fell off to the right and headed down a winding mountain road (N.C. 226) in the direction of Buladean, North Carolina, to a small general store about half a mile from the Trail.

The store was little more than a cabin next to a wide bend in the road. But, to my surprise, it was well-stocked with a variety of foods. I was able to reprovision and return to the Trail in less than an hour.

Traversing the ridge crest Trail was difficult. Yet, the scenery more than compensated for the effort. Particularly beautiful was the view from the cliffs below the summit of Little Rock Knob, an unspoiled high ridge west of Roan Mountain, that offered a marvelous panorama across the neat green fields of a sparsely populated farming valley to Ripshin Ridge, a large mountain mass about three miles to the north.

It was 2:30 p.m. when I arrived at the blue-blazed trail leading to the Clyde Smith shelter. I made certain of the time; I wanted to have plenty of daylight remaining to climb Roan Mountain, a 6,000-footer that promised a three-mile climb up some very steep terrain. I knew it was going to take three or more hours and figured that if it was later than 3:00 p.m. when I arrived at the shelter, I would remain there until the next day and tackle the mountain in the morning. I had no inclination to be stumbling around the mountain in the dark.

Still, I felt uneasy about my decision as I started down the Trail. Though it was well before 3:00 p.m. and I was pretty fresh, I questioned the wisdom of starting so long a climb so late in the day and debated with myself as to whether I should continue. I was only vaguely aware that with each step I took the likelihood of returning to Clyde Smith shelter became more remote. When I did realize it, it was too late to turn back. My feet had already made the decision final. I put the question out of my mind and concentrated solely on the task at hand.

The task at hand remained hidden for the most part by thick forest foliage. Occasionally, the tree canopy opened sufficiently to give me a tantalizing glimpse of the lower reaches of the giant across the gap. It looked intimidating; it was intimidating, but held an ominous attraction that drew me irresistibly on, an evil force that mesmerized its victim.

I was so intent on the mountain that I failed to notice an automobile parked in Hughes Gap until I was almost on top of it. Still spooked from my Beauty Spot experience, my first reaction, "Oh, no! Not again!"

A tall, shirtless, fat man, his hairy torso glistening with sweat, stood unsteadily beside the driver's car door. He supported himself by leaning against the top of the car with his elbows. The thinness of this arms on the car roof contrasted with his thick belly that hung in a roll over his trousers belt just above the groin. His faded jeans hung so low they barely covered his buttocks. He was talking or singing, then took a swig from a bottle wrapped in a brown paper bag. I was quite close to him before he became aware of my presence. Then he turned his head so quickly that the movement caused him to lose his equilibrium. His legs buckled momentarily and he lurched against the car.

He looked at me blankly for a second, then smiled and called out a welcome. "Hikin' the Trail?" he asked.

"Yeah, on my way to Roan Mountain."

"My name's Ralph." He smiled again, exposing gaps where his front teeth should have been. The roots were black. He badly needed a shave, and his black beard made him look darkly disreputable.

"Hi! I'm Jan Curran," I told him.

He held out the bottle. "Want a swig of 'shine?"

I shook my head. "No thanks!" I'd drunk some "white lightning" earlier in life and definitely knew it was not something I needed before a difficult climb.

"Got some bonded if you'd rather drink whiskey," he tried, still grinning happily.

Again I declined his offer. "No thanks. Can't be drinking hard liquor right now. Got to climb that monster." I pointed across the gap, "Last thing I need is to start off with a belly full of booze."

"Don't have any beer or wine," he apologized. "I can take you into town if you want some. All I had is gone."

"Thanks, anyway! That's generous of you. But it's getting late, and I need to get to the top of that thing by dark."

He took a crumpled piece of paper from his pocket. "I meet 'most all the hikers goin' through here. You know Nick Sprague?"

I nodded my head.

"Sonny Daze?"

I nodded again. He read several other names, none of which I recognized. He was having trouble deciphering the writing.

"What's yore name again?" He steadied the paper on the car roof as he prepared to write with a pencil stub he'd fished from his pocket.

"Jan Curran."

"How do you spell that?" he asked.

I spelled it for him.

"You got another name?" he queried.

"My middle name is Donald."

"No, I mean a Trail name," he replied.

"Old Soldier. Not many people know it. Maybe some late hikers behind me might have seen it in some of the Trail registers. No one ahead of me knows it except Nick Sprague." I turned toward the road, "Got to be going!"

"Sure I can't give you a lift anywhere? There's a pretty good motel in town. Sure I can't get you some beer?" he called after me.

"Thanks anyway," I called back. Old Ralph looked pathetic in a humorous way, hanging onto the roof of his old silver Mustang for support and trying to wave at the same time.

As concerned as I was about the time and the need to get started up the mountain, I was even more anxious to get away from Ralph and Hughes Gap. For a place that was basically very beautiful, the gap was an ecological disaster. In addition to the usual old tires, cans, bottles, food wrappers and six-pack cartons, there were parts from old mobile homes strewn about as well as dead washing machines and parts of cars. Looks almost as bad as Old Ralph, I thought, or his car . . .

I had looked inside his car as I passed. It was a gigantic litter container with paper, cardboard boxes, liquor bottles and beer and wine bottles in all shapes and descriptions on the floor and seats. The back seat floor was filled almost to the seat with bottles.

Bet Old Ralph probably helped fill the gap, too, I murmured under my breath as I began to climb the path across the road.

Initially, the Trail followed an old logging road, and climbing was not too difficult. Just about the time I became comfortable with the route, however, it turned to the left off the logging road and ascended steeply up Beartown Mountain. (Beartown Mountain was actually a shoulder of Roan Mountain.)

The Trail to the summit covered about 1,500 vertical feet in a mile and weaved through a series of barrier ledges and up steep rock outcroppings. After reaching the summit of Beartown Mountain, the Trail dropped slightly into Ash Gap, a fairly broad sag with mature beech trees and a thick growth of long grass. The walking was cool and the level ground offered a respite from the arduous climbing. I wanted to take a long break, but I didn't want to sacrifice the time. I pressed on.

The ascent out of Ash Gap was extremely steep. I scrambled over a seemingly never-ending succession of rocks and ledges interspersed with tree roots. Progress was very slow and the effort exhausting. It was the most difficult, most physically demanding section of the Trail I had hiked since the start.

After about an hour, I began to hear thunder and the sky became overcast. I worried again about being caught in an electrical storm. In fact, I had a slight panic attack as vivid scenes of the electrical storm on Cheoah Bald raced through my mind. Then I calmed down and tried to consider my options.

Basically, I had no options. There was no place to go for protection. I couldn't outrun the storm. So, I continued to climb, looking about for a ledge I could crawl beneath in case of lightning.

Now I became acutely aware of the air, nervously anticipating the arrival of the telltale calm and the charged air. Thankfully, my fears were for naught; the thunder passed high overhead and no rain fell. With the passing of the thunder, my mind again became preoccupied with the difficulty of the Trail.

By now, I was very tired. I slowed my pace, taking smaller steps and straightening out my leg after each step as a way of lifting my weight up to the next small level of elevation. I continually looked up the Trail, hoping against hope to see the telltale sign of light through the tree canopy that indicated an approach to the summit. Every time I saw a bright spot, it turned out to be only a ridge side, and the Trail turned upward again, seeming to ascend more steeply into the deepening forest shadows as if to punish me for hoping. I had the feeling I was on a mountain that had no top, that I was on an eternal climb.

My heart began to palpitate frequently, and I was forced to stop often to rest and allow my heart rate to subside. I leaned heavily on my hiking stick and envisioned myself hanging on my hiking stick like old Ralph hanging on his car. "Boy, don't I wish I had a car now!" I muttered.

The light continued to fade as I climbed. I began to worry that I might not make the summit before dark. I had no idea how much ground I had covered or where I was in relation to the top. I had been climbing well over four hours. I should have reached the top by now.

I was perplexed, stopping often to study my map and compare distances. I was too exhausted to think clearly. As if that wasn't bad enough, I was almost out of water.

Desperately, I wanted to stop, to set up camp, eat and sleep. I looked in vain for any halfway level ground on which to erect my tent. At one point, I even went off the Trail for several yards in both directions looking for level ground. For what seemed like hours, I stumbled upward mechanically. Finally, wallowing in a gloom that matched the deepening shadows, I stopped by a large log lying conveniently beside the Trail, removed my pack, slumped down and buried my face in my hands. I didn't care if I went on or not. I had no strength left.

My heart was skipping and beating irregularly at intervals. I felt alone, forlorn, forsaken. I sat for some time trying to determine how best to cope with my predicament. There seemed to be no escape. I couldn't make it to the top of the mountain; I couldn't leave the mountain. I was thirsty; I had no more water. I couldn't find a place to set up my tent; I couldn't go another step. The situation seemed beyond my ability to control or influence.

I thought about how I had coped during other periods of crisis on the Trail. I had done everything I could to influence my circumstances. But when developments had reduced my span of options to zero, I had had no alternative but to turn myself over to my Creator. Mentally, I compared my situation to that of a kid who was trying for the first time to build a model airplane, screwing up the directions and the material, then in a great burst of discouragement, handing the whole mess over to his father to fix. "When all else fails, read the directions! Lord! Hear my prayer!" Then, I prayed . . .

I prayed for the strength to continue and to endure, for greater awareness of the strength that derives from faith. I asked for spiritual awakening, for a better understanding of my relationship with God, for the peace that I hoped would come with the knowledge that God indeed cared for me.

I don't know how long I sat there trying to make contact with God, but I was aware of the impending darkness. I converted to my conscious reality, vowing to accept only positive thoughts.

I will succeed! I will not be defeated, I told myself over and over. Numbly, I got to my feet and continue I did!

The weight of the pack shifted as I tried to bounce it on my shoulders. It caused me to stumble to the side. I caught myself against the log to keep from falling. It seemed the pack was heavier than it had ever been. But I moved ahead, putting one foot in front of the other. I had no awareness of feeling or time, only the sense of motion.

First, I went around this tree, then that tree, and this rock, and that rock. Eventually, I came to an area where the Trail skirted a gigantic rock ledge and the ascent moderated. As I came around the rock, sunlight burst from the sky almost horizontally in front of me. It was blue sky! It was the first sky I had seen since leaving Hughes Gap. I pressed on and in a matter of seconds I was on the summit!

I was overwhelmed by the sense of freedom engendered by the enormous broad sweep of lush grassy meadows, clusters of spruce trees and extensive stands of rhododendron bushes waving gently from across the meadows. A tent pitched directly on the path blocked the Trail. I walked around it and as I did, a man grilling hamburgers over a small open fire called out, "You're just in time for supper." He said it in a matter-of-fact way, as if he had been waiting for me. That was all he said; then he turned back to the business of cooking. I was so stunned that initially I did not respond, and the man called out to me again. I could think only of what had transpired a half hour before on the log beside the Trail. Finally, I responded weakly, "I sure could use a home-cooked meal."

My host, George Baty of Weston, Ohio, was on vacation, along with seven members of his family. In addition to George and his wife, there were two daughters, a son-in-law, a niece, and a newly arrived grandchild only a few weeks old. It was a loving, closely knit family that impressed me by the concern they showed for one another.

After resting with the family for a few minutes to catch my wind and ease my aching muscles and feet, I headed for the shower and toilet facility to clean up and fill my canteens.

The bath facility sat some 200 yards away in a small cluster of spruce trees near the edge of the meadow. As I passed the Baty family motor home, I overheard the son-in-law telling Mrs. Baty about this "really neat guy hiking the whole Appalachian Trail."

After a four-hamburger supper, I explored the area to look for a suitable tent site and found one nestled in a small opening surrounded by young spruce trees. I returned to the picnic site to retrieve my pack, and while I did, someone drove up to the exact place I planned to set up my tent and unhooked a camper trailer. So much for that idea, I thought. I then decided to head for the shelter which was only some 15 minutes away. I wanted solitude. But out of politeness, I remained with the Baty family for another 30 minutes, talking about the Trail and my experiences — how tough the climb up Roan Mountain had been. Then I thanked them profusely for their hospitality and set out for the shelter.

I luxuriated in a glow of satisfaction as I walked down the quiet road through the twilight. The shadows lay darker across the road now, and the woods were dark. Only the path was open enough to admit light, and it was quickly fading there. I felt a strange sense of victory; this victory — it carried an aura of incomparable significance. I was euphoric. But I also felt a sense of humility that made me infinitely more sensitive to an awareness of God and an awareness of my spiritual strength.

How does one describe the wonder of walking on a beautiful mountain and inhaling the spruce-scented air?

I firmly believed God had answered my prayer, that I had experienced a spiritual phenomenon. I would never forget the moment when I came out of the forest and into the sunlight on the summit. It was like a rebirth!

I climbed a short gentle rise from the road to the very highest ground on the mountain and arrived at the shelter just in time to witness the final seconds of a sunset the color of glowing coals through a framework of spruce and rhododendron branches. The view reminded me of a scene from a stained-glass church window. I made myself a cup of coffee and relaxed in complete serenity. I had never in my life felt such peace.

The Roan Mountain shelter, the highest on the entire AT,

sat more than a mile in the sky at 6,200 feet elevation. It had served in the past as living quarters for forest ranger fire lookouts. It was fully enclosed with a second floor sleeping loft where a pair of old mattresses waited. As soon as the light faded, it became chilly. I climbed to the sleeping loft and slipped into my sleeping bag.

At around 2:30 a.m., I was awakened by the sound of a racing car coming from where the Batys were camped. The car's tires squealed like the driver was doing wheelies. Shortly afterward, I heard someone shouting. I was glad I had chosen not to stay at the campground. I opened the large boarded loft window to check the weather. The scene that greeted me would forever remain engraved in my memory.

The moon was full or nearly full, the sky above was an intense black, and the summit was bathed in the pale silver glow of moonlight. The wind gently ushered the mists of some wayward surface clouds through the spruce and rhododendron branches in gently swirling, sometimes undulating motions that contained a hint of mystery. I remained enraptured for almost an hour, drawing the beauty into my soul. When at long last I pulled the sleeping bag close around me for warmth, I said in awe, "God, what a day!"

I slept well and was fully refreshed when I departed the shelter in the morning. The walk down Roan Mountain to Carvers Gap followed an upgraded gravel road that I suspected remained from the time when the Cloudland Hotel occupied a part of the mountain's summit. From Carvers Gap, the view of Round Bald was impressive. The entire mountain from below the Gap to the summit was bald with only one or two small clumps of trees to break the monopoly of grass. The Trail followed a well-maintained pathway across a fragile stretch of eroding landscape and climbed directly up the side of the ridge to the summit. I climbed slowly, staying on the Trail as admonished by the signs.

The summit of Round Bald was several hundred yards wide. I walked off the pathway for about 50 yards through thick, coarse grass to a large rock which overlooked the mountains to the east. The vista was magnificent. The crests of the Black Mountains rose above the layers of low-lying clouds like purple islands rising above a misty sea.

After about 20 minutes, I rejoined the Trail, continued across the summit, and dropped down to Engine Gap which

View of Black Mountains from summit of Round Bald.

separated Round Bald from Jane Bald. Engine Gap was so named for a sawmill engine abandoned there after it was used to cut timber for the construction of the Cloudland Hotel. From the Gap, Jane Bald appeared higher than Round Bald, but according to the *Trail Guide*, it was slightly smaller (5826 feet to 5807 feet).

Jane Bald, although almost as large as Round Bald, was dwarfed by a massive, broad, ridge of high ground to the north known as Grassy Ridge. I enjoyed hiking up the balds. I could always see the summit and never had the feeling of being closed in on an endless hike uphill as I had felt on Roan Mountain. Shortly after I reached the summit, a man with a camera tripod joined me in admiring the view.

Michael Joslin, a free-lance writer from Bakersville, North Carolina, had come to gather information for a newspaper story about Grassy Ridge, the focal point of a heated controversy between the landowners on one side and the U.S. Department of Interior along with the Appalachian Trail Conference on the other. Grassy Ridge was an ecologically important, as well as aesthetically beautiful, piece of the Southern Appalachian Highlands which the AT Conference and conservation groups wanted to keep in its natural state. The original property owner also intended that Grassy Ridge remain in its natural state, but after he died, the Ridge passed to his heirs, and they wanted to develop the land into vacation homesites.

The owners had bulldozed a long trail diagonally across the face of the ridge to the summit, an ugly scar across the entire landscape. When the new owners' intentions became known, the government offered to buy the property, but the owners wouldn't sell, contending that the offered price was too low. The disagreement had become bitter and acrimonious. It appeared that no reasonable solution was in sight, and the government had, or was planning to, initiate condemnation proceedings.

A testament to the deteriorated state of affairs was a handpainted sign on the side trail leading to Grassy Ridge; it warned hikers not to trespass on the Ridge. There had been reports of the owners or their agents patrolling the Ridge with firearms, and supposedly more than one hiker had been invited to leave by someone carrying a gun. It made for messy relations throughout the region, and Michael was there to get a story. I learned later he had already written one newspaper story about the battle for Grassy Ridge, which itself had caused controversy.

Because he was wearing old, blue denim, bib overalls and a baseball-type cap over his long light-brown hair, I at first mistook Mike Joslin for a local hillbilly. That impression was dispelled when we began to talk. Mike was intelligent, well-educated and far more sophisticated than his dress indicated. He had attended the Military Academy at West Point for three years before resigning because of disillusionment over the Vietnam war. (It is unusual for a cadet to leave the academy after having survived the most difficult first and second years.) He subsequently finished his undergraduate work, then completed work on a master's degree in English and a Ph.D. in literature. For a time, he had taught creative writing at a small college until he decided to become a free-lance writer.

He expressed dissatisfaction with the petty institutional politics and the bureaucracy, and indicated they were the main reasons he had left to begin working as a free-lance writer. He said it had been difficult financially, but he was making more money all the time and was able to "make ends meet." He used the term "living on the edge" several times as he referred to his life-style, and it seemed to aptly describe how he viewed his life and how he wished to live. For him, security had an anesthetizing effect on the spirit which destroyed one's ability to live life to its fullest. He wanted a life where the thrill of the fight for survival was as important as the survival. The experiences of life were what made it worth living, not the successes or the comforts.

We talked at length about the Trail and the spiritual and psychological effects it had on the people who hiked it. I described my Roan Mountain experiences from the previous day and was surprised that he was not surprised.

He told me he had met many people hiking the Trail who had had similar experiences. "It's living life in its simplest terms," he said. "It's a reordering of individual priorities that brings people in closer contact with the Supreme Being. Have you ever read *Walden*? It's one of the things Thoreau talks about in *Walden*." He talked briefly about *Walden*, saying that what I was experiencing were some of the same things Thoreau experienced during his isolation at the pond.

He talked about having an unusual religious philosophy that was influenced by Eastern religions. To him, God was within man and man's neighbors, and getting to know ourselves in the way the Trail allowed us to get to know ourselves, was also a form of getting to know God. He also spoke of reincarnation. "I believe in it," he said simply, "but it's much too broad a subject to talk about in a short time."

I was glad he changed the subject. My mind was already beginning to suffer from spiritual overload. I was trying to digest what he had told me when he started off again.

He described how people need to get back to the basic religious tenets which made this nation strong. He felt we needed to turn away from materialism, from materialistic values.

In other words, we didn't need security in material terms. We needed to talk about quality of life, but only talked about it in material terms. We needed to return to spiritual values, to the spiritual quality of life. In a sense, we needed to go back to, as Michael said, "living life on the edge."

Michael accompanied me almost to Little Hump Mountain before turning back toward Grassy Ridge. I was sorry to see him go. I enjoyed his company, and with the fresh insights he provided, the time fairly flew as we crossed the lower shoulder of Grassy Ridge, dropped into Low Gap, then over Elk Hollow Ridge to Buckeye Gap and Yellow Mountain Gap.

I thought about what Michael had said long after he had

departed, reviewing it in light of my previous day's experiences and my prayer for spiritual understanding. Coincidence? I wondered. What about the climb to the summit of Roan Mountain and my encounter with the Baty family? Was that coincidence, too? I decided that only time could provide the means to sort it out.

CHAPTER 13

Hump Mountain to Braemer, Tennessee
At Peace with the Trail

Hump Mountain, a softly rounded giant with a blanket of scrub brush draped about its shoulders to the east and west, rose up in the hazy afternoon across the gap in front of me. The ridge line leading from the gap to the summit wore a swath of short ochre grass; from a distance, it looked as though it had been painted over the undulations. A pair of jagged rock formations interrupted the flow of grass, and the Trail snaked around them until it crossed behind one last small fold which hid it from view before it reached the summit.

I could feel the rapture building as I gazed at the mountain panorama that framed the horizon in every direction. The peaks in the far distance lay muffled in a blue haze that hinted of their timeless past. The closer mountains wore the verdant cover of the young summer. Below, to the east, a row of hay fields stretched down the valley in a shallow arc like gems in a necklace. Meanwhile, sounds of life pulsed in the air, a buzzing, whirring, chirping symphony of creation in action, each part existing in muted harmony with the rest.

In the Gap, I stopped for a moment to enjoy the magnificence of the scenery and to absorb the immensity and beauty of the mountain. Then I started up again.

At the summit, in the tall grass beside where the Trail joined an old road, a bearded man, lying on his back, his head propped on his pack, watched intently as I approached. He wore faded blue jeans with a gray cotton T-shirt and a blue baseball-type cap tilted at a jaunty angle. A long piece of grass protruded from his lips and a smile of contentment rested naturally across his features. A grown-up version of Huckleberry Finn, I thought.

I introduced myself, and we were soon engaged in conversation. The breathtaking view from the summit dominated our thoughts, and our talk naturally focused on the beauty we were experiencing. It seemed to lift us beyond mere observations of beauty; it gave another dimension of meaning to our words.

Dan Dunford mentioned that he took every opportunity possible to spend time in the mountains, often with his wife, but today he was alone. "She loves these mountains as much as I do," he confided. "Couldn't live anywhere else." He conveyed the impression that the mountains were beautiful, not only from a visual perspective, but also gave a sense of completeness to his life. He spoke with almost a religious fervor implying that the mountains added a spiritual dimension to his life. It was as if he was a part of the mountains and they were a part of him, and reminded me of similar feelings I detected in the young woman skipping rope at Neels Gap and the older couple I had met on the way to Albert Mountain. The mountains engendered the same spiritual quality in them that I sensed in Dan.

Dan taught horticulture at a local community college. He was a walking encyclopedia on wildflowers. It was from him that I learned that the spidery red flower I had seen by springs and moist areas in the woods was bee balm and that the pale purple and white flowers that grew abundantly in the upland meadows were plants from the mint family called Bergamot. (I had thought they were a wild chrysanthemum.)

As he talked, he warmed to the task of initiating a newcomer into the exciting world of wildflowers. He described the differences in leaf construction between Queen Anne's lace and yarrow which, at first glance, appeared to be the same. He identified two types of touch-me-nots called spotted and pale jewelweed, explaining that they were members of the impatiens family and that the fluid from the flowers and the leaves could be used to counteract the effects of poison ivy and bee stings by rubbing it over the affected skin. He showed me a plant called fringed loosestrife and another called angelica. Angelica made bees drunk, and scientists are studying the plant trying to identify its chemical properties. He told me the bees drank its narcotic substance until they lost their equilibrium and fell to the ground immobilized until the effects of the substance wore off; then they flew away. They reminded me of a higher order of beings, some of whom I knew intimately; they did the same thing with alcohol.

The afternoon was beginning its slide toward evening, and Dan suggested it was time to head down the mountain. We fell in naturally together, talking about the mountains and wildflowers as we descended toward Doll Flats, a level camping area set in a small open stand of mature hardwood trees at the forest's edge.

As we walked, two local men on all-terrain motorcycles came bouncing up the mountain toward us. The high-pitched shrieks of the engines shredded the serenity of the mountains with a ferocity that reminded me of the way chain saws shrieked as they tore at the bark of trees. The knobby treads of the tires ripped the fragile soil, spewing chunks of earth and grass behind them as they churned up the hill. We could hear the whines of the engines ascending or descending in volume and pitch long before we were able to see the bikers themselves.

"I'd like to stretch a rope about this high for those people," Dan said, pointing to his neck. I could see the anger in his eyes and feel the strain of it in his voice.

One of the men had difficulty with the motor on his machine, and it stopped several times, once directly in front of us. I was afraid that a confrontation might occur, but Dan only acknowledged their presence, and we continued on. About 100 yards down the Trail, we came across a helmet which had been lost by one of the riders. In a show of anger, Dan kicked it, sending it spinning off the pathway and out into the grass like a black soccer ball.

When we reached Doll Flats, we met Tim Evans, a botany major from Connecticut College, working for the Southern Appalachian Highlands Conservancy as a summer caretaker for the Roan Mountain Massif (Roan Mountain, Round Bald, Jane Bald, Grassy Ridge and Hump and Little Hump Mountains.) Tim didn't look like the stereotypical outdoorsman. He was slight of build with a peaches-and-cream complexion, smiling blue eyes, light blond eyebrows, and a generous tousle of reddish blond hair. A light blond moustache did not belie his youth.

After supper, Tim and Dan began discussing an unusual flower Tim had discovered during the day. Tim produced a specimen and began to study it at length, reviewing its structure in detail with a magnifying glass, referring periodically to a wildflower book and exclaiming that certain parts did not correspond to descriptions in the book. Dan responded occasionally with some botanical terminology which caused Tim to look elsewhere in the book or more closely at the flower.

Tim attempted to bring me into the conversation by asking if I had noticed a particular type of wildflower on the slopes of Little Hump Mountain. I was forced to admit to a complete ignorance of wildflowers. He said that hiking the Trail was a great opportunity to learn about wildflowers and suggested I get a basic wildflower book called, *Flower Finder*, to help me identify the more common species found along the way.

I had not previously considered carrying a book. My meager interest in wildflowers didn't justify carrying the extra weight. The fact that I was now very interested was an indication of the effect the Trail was having on me; my perspectives were changing. I thought I would get a book at the next opportunity, that is, if it wasn't too heavy. Tim assured me it was light.

Tim remarked about the abundance of false Solomon's seal and smooth Solomon's seal growing throughout the mountains. When I asked what they looked like, he pointed to a false Solomon's seal with a cluster of small bronze berries dangling from the end of its stem. Then he pointed out a smooth Solomon's seal which looked almost identical except that the berries hung suspended from the leaf axils along most of the length of the arching stem. There were other differences to be sure, but the location of the berries was the most striking.

While Dan and Tim discussed wildflowers, I walked the edge of the tree line in the fading light. I was aware only of the broad sweeping ridge of Hump Mountain to my front, the mountains in the distance to my left, and only vaguely of the connection between the beauty and my thoughts. Then I recognized how deeply my surroundings influenced my consciousness and how I was drawing the beauty into my spirit in the same way I took air into my lungs. It made me realize just how much the beauty of one affected the beauty of the other and how important that was to me spiritually. After a few minutes, I headed back to my pack and recorded my thoughts in my Trail notes.

The stretches from Roan Mountain over Round Bald, Jane Bald and Hump Mountain were certainly some of the most beautiful parts of the Trail I had hiked to date. They were not only beautiful, they were spiritually uplifting as had been my ascent up Roan Mountain. Each was a totally different experience, but each had its own reward. My Roan Mountain experience had significance that would reach far beyond my time on the Trail, lasting for the rest of my life as well. Today I had faith in myself and God reaffirmed. It was not so vivid as

Tim Evans (L) and Dan Dunford (R) at Doll Flats.

the previous day on Roan Mountain, but more like a reinforcement of that experience.

Clearly, my mind had been and still was digesting the content of my discussion with Michael Joslin. I was increasingly attracted to the concept that my spiritual awakening depended not in understanding something spiritually external to myself but rather in recognizing my own innate spirituality. I had never thought about my spirituality before in quite those terms. I had always looked at God as a supernatural or spiritual dictator who, if I displeased Him, would send me off to roast forever in Hell. I was nothing and God was everything. I had no worth; in fact, I was less than something of worth, because I was a sinner. I had come into this world already tainted by Original Sin, and everyone knew that God did not dwell in the presence of sin. That was the Devil's domain, and I, by virtue of being born, started off life unfit for the presence of God. I had a great deal of trouble reconciling any concept of self-worth with my status as a sinner.

Now I was coming to an awareness that I did have spiritual worth, that God could reside in me, that He was already in me and had been in me for as long as I existed. I was His creation totally. The very air that I breathed sustained God in me. I didn't need to look out into the sky, into the heavens, into the universe to find God. I had been looking in the wrong place all the time. I needed only to look inwardly. I needed only to experience life in its simplest form, to experience life as I was on the Trail, away from the distractions of daily existence. I needed to reflect on my inherent worth, to understand that my humanity did not disqualify me as a being of spiritual worth. In fact, I had the strange feeling that I really was a spiritual being, somehow embodied in human form. I couldn't completely understand the nature of my spirituality or, for that matter, my humanity or the relationship between the two. But I did understand that I was opening up completely new spiritual vistas.

In the past, my quest had been totally focused on material life. There had been no opportunity for my inner spirit to assert itself. There was no medium by which my spiritual self could be recognized as an essential force in my life. It was like I was talking to myself on a wave length different from the one I used for understanding. It was the same transmitter and receiver, but I was on two different frequencies.

Had it not been for the Trail, I doubt that I would ever have really understood how living life in its most basic terms inspired spiritual confidence. I was convinced it was absolutely essential to achieve an understanding beyond one's relationship with the external order of nature; to experience the vitality of inner spiritual awareness. I might have understood it from a reasoning process, but I could not have felt it emotionally or achieved it as an essential force in my nature. The Trail is one beautiful experience, I thought. I will leave the Trail when I am finished with my hike, but the Trail will never leave me. It is now and forevermore an essential part of Jan Curran, just like my heart and my brain. And it is also in my soul . . .

The night was deliciously cool, and the moon shone brightly through the trees, imparting a silver glow to the edge of the open forest. Beyond the tree line, a diaphanous veil formed by a mixture of moonlight and dew spread like a curtain across the meadow and the ridgeside. The nearby grass and trees fairly sparkled from its reflection, making the darkness of the shadows ominous by contrast. I laid out my sleeping bag on a soft patch of grass inside the tree line to take advantage of the thick tree canopy to protect me from the dew. I was excited. But I was also exhausted. It did not take long before sleep overwhelmed me.

The next morning Dan and Tim accompanied me down the Trail toward Route 9, pointing out different wildflowers as we walked. In the process, they introduced me to evening primrose, false fox glove and St. Johnswort, all three with bright yellow flowers. About halfway down the mountain, we encountered a group of Boy Scouts who had spent the preceding evening at the Apple House shelter, and I thought how wise I had been to stay at Doll Flats for the night rather than go on to the shelter. I was even more convinced after seeing the condition of the shelter.

We stopped by a giant patch of ripe blackberries and plucked the plump fruit by the handfuls, stuffing them in our mouths, and getting our hands and chins stained by the juice in the process. Just as we were about to leave the field where the berries grew, Dan found a patch of small yellow wildflowers. (I think they were Canadian dwarf cinquefoils.) Dan wanted to study them more closely, and he and Tim soon became engrossed in conversation and study. I would like very much to have stayed, but a long day's hike lay ahead. I said my goodbyes and hiked on.

Just before it reached Route 9, the Trail skirted a stand of small hardwood trees and opened onto a woods road that led directly to a long, narrow meadow blanketed by a dense growth of blue cornflowers or chicory. The flowers grew in such profusion that the meadow appeared as one great swath of ultramarine blue bordered by a cast of light gray from the dirt road which framed it. I stopped for several minutes to admire the colors and take pictures.

Later in the morning, after passing the summit of Big Pine Mountain, I encountered the remnants of two moonshine stills. They were rusted 55-gallon drums with the metal tops removed and replaced with wooden ones through which tubing and hoses passed. Both were located deep in the forest next to stream junctions. Black rubber hoses led from the drums to the streams, and pieces of glass and tin cans lay about on the rocks and in the leaves.

Shortly after crossing Walnut Road, I met a man about my age walking with his dogs. He wore faded blue jeans and a homespun gray shirt draped loosely on his spare frame. His shirt was a mass of patches and his left shoulder was exposed by a large tear where the material flapped loosely when he moved. He smiled frequently, exposing the dark roots of missing teeth. The nervous movement of his eyes and a timid, almost childlike quality in his voice made him appear ill at ease.

After a few moments, however, he became more comfortable and talked with credible authority, explaining that he had "lived in these hills" his whole life and that he had left only twice, both times to visit Roan Mountain. He said he wouldn't go back to Roan Mountain again; he hadn't seen anything different there from what he already had seen in life. He continued to speak softly, but his pale blue eyes, smiling as intently as before, now looked directly into mine as I asked questions. I was impressed by the unhurried manner in which he talked and the quaint expressions he used. When we parted, he said, "I hope you good luck."

Before going off, I asked about the Trail to Moreland Gap, and he told me it was all uphill for four miles from where we were standing. I figured anyone who had spent his whole life in the place would be a pretty reliable source of information about the terrain. Here I learned another lesson. His description was a casual approximation. It was at least five miles to the gap, and there were three or more miles of ups and downs before I came to the point where it became a steady uphill climb.

The Trail crossed many changes in elevation throughout the day. I felt like I was on a slow-motion roller coaster. It was a very demanding stretch. By the time I reached Moreland Gap at 7:00 p.m., I was exhausted. The shelter spring was about 500 yards down a steep ridge, and I grumbled all the way down and especially climbing back. When I returned to the ridge crest, I silently thanked Carl Friberg for suggesting I carry a collapsible water bag. It saved me many return trips to water sources throughout the hike.

The following day was tough with many steep little climbs and ledges. I was becoming irritated by pointless climbs — not a good sign. It was time to take a break from the Trail.

The probable catalysts for my displeasure were two absolutely pointless climbs up ridges of White Rock Mountain. Several deer bounding through the forest, their white tails flying like flags, cheered me up as did the descent along Coon Den Branch, a bright, refreshing, rock-strewn stream that bubbled and bounced its way down the mountainside, eventually feeding into Laurel Fork Creek.

The Trail descended steeply to Laurel Fork Creek on a rickety, narrow, wooden footbridge anchored to decrepit rock pilings on each bank. Here sunlight enriched the brown and gray colors of the canyon's earth and rock walls, contrasting them with the vivid greens and yellows of the trees and bushes that framed the horizon above, and deep blue and purple shadows of the stream below. After crossing the stream, the Trail followed an abandoned railroad bed, one of many spurs that remain from railroads constructed in the early 1900s to haul timber from the mountains to the saw mills in Hampton and Braemer, Tennessee.

I stopped to swim and bathe in the creek. I stripped and ventured gingerly into the cold water. Laurel Fork was only two or three feet deep at that point, flowing smoothly over the rib-thin rock ledges which lay lengthwise to the direction of flow.

As soon as I entered the stream, I could feel the tiny fish biting my feet. There was no pain, only the sensation of firm contact. I moved out into a stretch of bronze-colored water and basked in the sunlight, allowing the water to soothe my body and wash away the sweat and sand. After about 20 minutes and copious lathering, I emerged from the water fully refreshed and tingling from the effects of the peppermint soap. I read a section of the soap bottle label before replacing it in my pack:

> "All-One-God Faith started 1,000 acre Calif.
> rain-forest, with 1 trillion trees God's spaceship
> Earth can survive! Our 13 Essene Birth-Control
> Patents prevent overpopulation. Save life!
> So in your town, with 10 people start a chapter
> of astronomers Israel 6000 year great All-One-God Faith.
> Send $10 for 13 - $2 Moral ABC: 6 billion unite all free!
> Instead of bombs. 6 billion scrolls unite the Human race
> instantly in All-One-God Faith! P.O. Box 28, Escondido,
> 92025 CA (619) 743-2211 Soapmaker Dr. Emanuel H.
> Bronner, Rabbi."

It was only a short climb from the stream back to the Trail. But it was steep. I quickly became hot and sweaty again. The Trail now followed an abandoned railroad bed that paralleled Laurel Fork Creek for the next several miles until it reached Laurel Fork Falls.

Sometimes, the roadbed was routed uncomfortably close to the edges of deep chasms cut by Laurel Fork Creek. But mostly it stayed back on the mountain, passing through cuts in the solid stone ridges to provide for an even grade. In most cuts, rock walls rose almost vertically, sometimes for 25 or 30 feet, and often rock that had fallen from the walls filled or half filled the roadbed making walking precarious but infinitely easier than it would have been if I had had to climb the little ridges.

Laurel Fork Falls.

Laurel Fork Falls was a 30-foot-high, rock-framed cascade that poured into a broad, deep, quiet pool. The water actually fell over three distinct sections of rock before landing in the pool. Each upper section sat slightly back from the lower section in a stair-step configuration. Because of the prolonged drought, the volume of water flowing over the falls was meager. Even so, it was spectacular. I imagined what it might have been like in the early spring with snow run-off from the mountains. I wanted to go swimming again but resisted the temptation and headed downstream for Waycaster Spring where I planned to tent camp for the night.

While looking for a campsite, I met Terry Morrell and his five-year-old son walking up the Trail from U.S. Route 321. At that moment, I was having difficulty finding even a small piece of rock-free ground on which to erect my tent. We talked for a few minutes about the Trail, the drought and its effect on Laurel Fork Falls. In passing, I mentioned that there didn't appear to be any decent campsites in the vicinity.

Morrell suggested I head into Braemer for the night. "Just

stay on the blue-blazed trail 'til you hit 321, then turn left and its about a mile to Braemer. You can save yourself about five miles and the climb up Pond Mountain by hitching from Braemer to Watauga Dam. That's something to think about."

I thanked him for his advice and headed down the trail for U.S. Route 321 and Braemer — and hopefully a soft bed for the night.

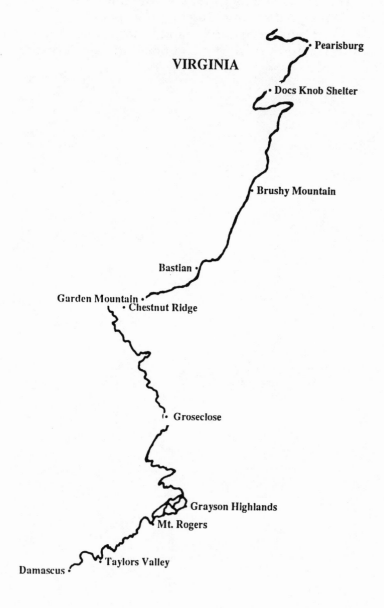

VIRGINIA

Pearisburg

Docs Knob Shelter

Brushy Mountain

Bastian

Garden Mountain
Chestnut Ridge

Groseclose

Grayson Highlands
Mt. Rogers

Taylors Valley
Damascus

Damascus, Virginia, to Pearisburg, Virginia

CHAPTER 14

Braemer, Tennessee, to Damascus, Virginia
The Battle Continues

When I had mentioned in my conversation with Terry Morrell that I'd "give my eye teeth" for a decent bed for the night, he had suggested I look up Sutton Brown at Brown's General Store in Braemer. "He's a real friend to hikers," Terry said. "He'll probably put you up at his place." With Terry's advice in mind, I headed directly for the store. Sutton was not in when I arrived, so I bought a pint of ice cream and looked about the store while I waited.

It was a typical general store with one-half of the building devoted to the food market and the other half housing a general merchandise, hardware section. The distinctive odors of leather, paint, metal, tools and seed blended with the meat and bakery smells from the market and excited a variety of long forgotten memories. It reminded me of the seed and hardware store in a town where I had grown up. Visions of the farmers, spare-framed, bronze-skinned men in denim coveralls, loading feed and fertilizer bags into the beds of their pickups flashed into my conscious. I could even smell again the aromas from that time.

I walked slowly down the aisles investigating the products on display. Items that conveyed a sense of strength and durability, of productive labor by proud men, of a closeness to the earth. I compared them with the merchandise contained in the chain stores of our modern day shopping centers, the antiseptic glass and metal behemoths of efficiency where the odors of life are sanitized into boring, cosmopolitan replicas of each other. It occurred to me that we had progressed in efficiency all right, but we had also lost personal touch with the origin of the products that affected our lives.

I was looking at rows of metal bins filled with nails of various sizes and purposes when I heard a voice behind me. The voice wasn't talking to me, but I suspected from the tone of confidence and the topic that it probably belonged to Sutton Brown. It did.

After he had finished talking with the customer, I introduced myself, told him I was a Thru-Hiker and asked if he could put me up for the night. Sutton said he would be glad to help and offered me "primitive accommodations" in his home for three dollars per night.

After I accepted his offer, Sutton gave me directions to his home and how to find my room, then, as an afterthought, warned me that were was a wolf named Cheyenne in the back yard. There wasn't anything to be afraid of, he assured me, but he wanted to let me know.

How do you get a wolf in the middle of Tennessee? I wondered. I was sure that wolves could only be found in zoos in the United States, except for Alaska, where I had heard they still ran wild. After dropping my pack in my room, I headed downstairs to see the wolf.

Cheyenne was lying in the shade of the kitchen porch along with a large male German Shepherd. As soon as Cheyenne detected my presence, she charged into the fenced yard to investigate. She was a beautiful animal, about two feet tall at the shoulders with a gray coat, heavily streaked with black, and white legs, feet and cheeks. The whiteness of her eyebrows accented her amber eyes, and the dark semicircles beneath her eyes gave a mask-like appearance to her face.

Later Sutton and I entered the yard so I could take photographs of Cheyenne. I felt a little apprehensive about being inside a penned enclosure with a wolf. But Sutton told me it was all right as long as he was there.

Immediately as we passed through the gate of the electrified fence, the wolf and the dog both came bounding over to Sutton and basically ignored me. Cheyenne dominated Sutton's attention from the outset while the German shepherd stayed on the fringe of the activity. The wolf reveled in the affection, and the petting and stroking that followed attested to the powerful bond between her and Sutton. Then it became the shepherd's turn for affection, and Cheyenne turned her attention to me.

Just before we had entered the enclosure, Sutton had warned me to keep Cheyenne to my front. She had a habit of sneaking up behind people and nipping them in the buttocks. He had indicated it was not a vicious trait, but I imagined it could have been disconcerting, to say the least. I mean, how many people could boast of having been bitten in the ass by a wolf? I thought. Nevertheless, I made sure she stayed to my front. She tried several times to get behind me, but I was just a bit quicker.

I mentioned that Cheyenne did not behave the way I had envisioned a wolf behaving, that she appeared to act very dog-like. I asked if Sutton ever felt apprehensive about being in an enclosure alone with her.

Sutton laughed and said she was very much like a dog, but every once in a while she would do something that reflected her primordial instincts. "I hate it when she kills birds," he said. "But that's nature, and you just have to accept that she's part of the natural process. You can't take it out of her." Sutton's home, a huge stone structure known widely as the "Braemer Castle," stood regally above the smaller wooden frame houses clustered for several blocks in all directions about it. It had seven or eight rooms on the second floor, and I was given one with a single bare bulb hanging from the ceiling and furnished with a chair, a packing crate table of sorts and a single mattress lying directly on the wooden floor. At the end of the creaky hall was a communal bathtub and toilet.

The building had originally been constructed as a commissary for the lumber company that first logged the area in the early 1900s. After lumbering operations ceased, it came under ownership of a couple who renovated the place into a residence, and later it came into the ownership of Sutton Brown.

During my second night there, Sutton invited me to his quarters on the ground floor for a bottle of home-brewed stout, and I had the opportunity to see the kitchen and the living room, both of which overflowed with old furniture, bachelor effects, and "treasures" of every description which he vowed someday to clean and fix up. The structure would take a "heap of fixin'," as he put it, because it had long been neglected. The stone shell appeared sound, but the woodwork, door and window frames, the eaves and roofing, were, in some cases, barely serviceable, and in most cases, needed to be replaced.

I enjoyed the conversation, the excellent stout, and the opportunity to get to know Sutton Brown better. He was about 6 feet tall and slender. His face was framed by reddish hair, and a moustache of the same color complemented the freckles that dotted his face. His eyes sparkled with intelligence and wit, imparting an impish quality — like a young boy who was testing the limits of behavior just to see where the barriers lay and if they could be moved a little further away. It was not an expression of foolishness, however; rather it was one of calculation mixed with humor. Even the speed and purpose with which he walked suggested that he clearly knew what he was about.

He was the quintessential free spirit acknowledging convention only so far as was necessary and deadly serious about his freedom. At the moment, he worked at his father's store. But I had the feeling that it was a sideline, that his real passion in life was outdoor adventures. He was an accomplished kayaker and skier, and worked at the Nolichucky Expeditions as an instructor and guide. It was only because the drought had caused a cessation of water sports that Sutton was devoting his attention to his father's store. If the water had been up, he would have been out on the river.

I decided to stay at the "Castle" for an extra day and day-hike the section from Waycaster Spring over Pond Mountain without pack, then have Sutton take me by car the following day to the point where the Trail crossed U.S. Route 321 to resume my hike. It worked to perfection, although I was a little late getting off the next morning; I had to wait for the bank across the street from the store to open to get a cash advance on my credit card. (I came to rely exclusively on my credit card as a source of cash during my hike, and I highly recommend the technique. It saves carrying too much cash or a wad of traveler's checks.)

At exactly the same time as I reached Waycaster Spring where the Trail turned to begin the ascent up Pond Mountain, I met another hiker going the same way. We fell in together. He was Bob Brewer from Dallas, Texas, owner of a small taxi business and a beginner in AMWAY. He had started from Dennis Cove that morning and was planning to hike to Pearisburg, Virginia.

We started off together chatting about ourselves and the Trail. But the climb soon became steep and difficult. Since I wasn't carrying a pack and he was, it was not long before I had pulled far ahead.

I examined many rocks as I traversed the mountain, hoping to find a "perspective rock." I had gotten the idea from Dr. Klaus Beyermann, President of Mainz University, who kept a billion-year-old rock on his desk as a reminder of the need to put things in perspective. He said that associating the age of the rock with the problem at hand helped him place a problem in perspective; that when one thinks in terms of a billion years, the awesome figure made other considerations seem insignificant by comparison.

When I thought about how impatient I had been in dealing with people and the bureaucracy, I realized I could've used such an aid to minimize the impact of events with only fleeting significance and no real importance in the great scheme of things.

I didn't find any likely looking rocks. If I had, I wouldn't have been sure if they were a billion years old. But the idea added interest to the hike. Then it dawned on me, I really didn't know what I was looking for. I remembered back to the zinger I'd received from Elmer Hall at Hot Springs. He could've had some fun with me on this one!

I finished the nine miles by 2:30 p.m. and 45 minutes later was back at Braemer, drinking beer. Oh, if only the rest of the hike could be so simple, I thought. I stopped by Brown's store to pick up some delicacies for the Trail and was introduced by Sutton to a hammer dulcimer-maker, a tall, strongly muscled young man with a thick dark beard and long dark brown hair. He wore a safari-type hat pulled low over serious brown eyes which judged the world. I learned that the hammer dulcimer was a Persian invention and the predecessor to our modern-day piano. It is reputed to be a superb musical instrument with outstanding clarity and purity of sound.

At the end of the day, while reviewing events for my Trail journal, it occurred to me that I had been very fortunate to meet Terry Morrell. The day previous to meeting him, I had been very concerned about finding water at Moreland Gap, about my heart holding up, and uptight about the hike in general. Now two days later, after an excellent meal and a great conversation with Sutton Brown, I felt on top of the world. It could all be attributed to my chance meeting with Terry Morrell.

It was about three miles from where Sutton dropped me off the next morning to Watauga Dam, a massive earthen structure that formed the waters of Lake Watauga. I followed the gravel road that spanned the dam, stopping beside a large boulder at midpoint to rest and admire the surrounding landscape.

The scenery in the gorge behind the dam and the mountains in the distance across the great expanse of lake were impressive, but not exciting like the huge stone faults visible at either end of the dam. During construction of the dam, sections of the mountain had been removed, and the result was a 500-million-year-old cross-section of the earth's geology. It clearly showed where the layers of the earth's crust had fractured, forcing older layers upward and over younger sedimentary layers during the collision of continental plates about 300 million years ago when Africa and North America were joined.

It was very lonely, and slightly eerie, sitting in the middle of the chasm with the wind streaming in noisy rushes towards me from across the lake. The wind pressed steadily against my face and body, then carried behind me, sometimes moaning loudly and sometimes shrieking as if in agony as it swept down the canyon. Here were the echoes of tortured spirits released from millions of years ago. They were being carried from their prison of rock and released to find peace in the valley.

The moment was like trying to comprehend an unknowable mystery. There was a surrealistic element to the scene which became incorporated in my feeling and begged for understanding. The scene and the mood of timelessness it engendered was so remarkable it stayed with me the entire day to Iron Mountain shelter, and it was still in my consciousness when I fell asleep that evening.

Shortly after starting on the Trail the next morning, I encountered a gravestone bearing the inscription:

Uncle Nick Grindstaff
born Dec. 26, 1851 - died July 22, 1932
Lived alone, suffered alone, died alone

I remembered having read something about Nick Grindstaff and the gravesite in the *Trail Guide*. I slipped the book from my pocket to refresh my memory.

Poor Nick Grindstaff was born the day after Christmas under an unlucky star. He was orphaned at three years of age, and at 26, during a trip to the West, he was beaten and robbed. The event so disillusioned him, he returned home and moved up on Iron Mountain where he lived as a hermit with only his dogs for companionship until he died 46 years later.

Perhaps the cruelest trick of all was the one nature played on him. Atop his grave monument rested a giant old tree that could have fallen anywhere in a 360-degree circle. But the old tree had chosen to come crashing down exactly on top of his monument.

The monument was a large brick edifice about seven or eight feet high, two feet wide and one foot deep at the top. The tree trunk rested squarely on top of the stone. The irony was inescapable. It looked as if fate was saying, "Damn you! Nick Grindstaff! I'm not finished with you. How dare you die on me!" It was the ultimate gesture of contempt.

At noon, I stopped at a roadside picnic table on U.S. Route 421 to eat lunch. I was joined by W. G. Steele, a retired professor of geology, who lived just up the ridge from the Trail. I had seen his house in the near distance before the Trail detoured to avoid his property. He lived alone with his dog, and I couldn't help making the comparison with Uncle Nick Grindstaff. However, that was shortlived. Mr. Steele was a very bright gentleman, slight of frame with wire-rimmed glasses and clear blue eyes that smiled as he talked. He spoke in a quiet, unhurried tone of voice that commanded my attention.

He told me that earlier in the spring he had "rescued" a pair of wet female hikers from the clutches of a raging rain storm. They were huddled in the downpour beside the road where we were sitting. "Took 'em up to the house and dried 'em out by the fire," he said. "Fed 'em and got 'em rested up again for the Trail." He said he enjoyed meeting the hikers that passed through. I was to learn later that many people like Mr. Steele rescued hikers in need or befriended people. I personally had already been the recipient of help from several like George Baty and Sutton Brown.

Mr. Steele asked if I had seen any bears or much wildlife and told me about a recent episode he had witnessed while walking in the forest with his dog. A family of black bears consisting of a mother bear and two cubs lived in the surrounding woods and were frequently observed as they foraged for food. The cubs were two-year-olds, and it was time for them to be on their own. But they didn't seem interested in independence. However, Mama Bear was interested in her independence and decided to get rid of the two freeloaders. She chased them up a tree, then ran off as fast as she could to get away from them. He laughed with gusto as he described how the young bears came scrambling down the tree, squealing and running after their mother.

I asked if he could tell the age of some rocks I had picked up from the rubble below the cliff on the north side of Watauga Dam. I wanted to know if I had any potential "perspective rocks."

He said they were both sedimentary rocks, not particularly

old in geologic terms. He laughed again when I told him why I wanted them, then said the green rocks in the Shenandoah National Park were really old; those were igneous rocks, but he couldn't say for sure if they were a billion years old.

We talked about hiking and how the equipment for backpacking had improved over the years. He had hiked parts of the Trail when he was younger — "back when hiking was a real challenge," he said. "Everything was World War II surplus. We didn't have stoves, and there was no such thing as freeze-dried food. You had to get up at 4:30 in the morning to get a fire going so's you could cook breakfast. By the time you had everything done, the food cooked, the pots cleaned and everything packed, it was eight o'clock. Then you had to stop early, like 4:30 or 5:00 p.m. to make camp and supper before it got dark."

I enjoyed talking with Mr. Steele and got the impression that he too enjoyed the conversation. I guessed that periodic contact with hikers gave him a welcome chance to meet people who shared some of his interests and attitudes.

I mentioned that occasionally he must have felt lonely living by himself so far from civilization. But he brushed my comment off with a wave of his hand, indicating that he was happy with his solitude.

After leaving Mr. Steele's place, the Trail dropped down the mountainside before regaining the ridge where the hiking was easy and conducive to meditation. Perhaps the serenity I saw in Mr. Steele also mellowed me. I thought about my spiritual development and my relationship with God and the impact the Trail was having on me. I was now at the point where I couldn't seem to progress any further — as if I had reached a spiritual plateau and couldn't find the route to the next level. I felt I had been touched by God, made aware of His presence and His strength but did not yet understand how to proceed to the next phase of my development. It was like a whole new world waited to be explored, a whole new universe to be probed, but I lacked the key to unlock the door that barred my way. Be patient! Remember your one-billion-year-old rock! reminded an inner voice. It will come. Just keep peeling the layers of the onion!

When I reached Abingdon shelter at the end of the day, I again met Bob Brewer who had stopped by the spring for water. Bob had a strange hiking schedule. He hiked from 7:00 a.m. to 8:00 p.m. every day. To conserve weight, he did not carry a stove but ate freeze-dried food by rehydrating it. He added water to the freeze-dried food at lunch, allowed the water to rehydrate the food, then ate it cold in the evening. He said his pack weighed only 35 pounds, even with a tent, a two-pounder made of Gortex.

I asked why he had decided to hike under such austere conditions, and he told me he decided to reduce his pack weight after suffering knee injuries while hiking the Maine wilderness during the previous year. "Started from Katahdin with 60 pounds on my back," he said. "Screwed up a knee and had to come off at the first logging road." That must have been a disconcerting experience, since the only links with civilization for the 100 miles between Katahdin and Monson, Maine, were three widely spaced logging roads.

Bob carried a miniature tape recorder to record his thoughts and observations of the hike. I liked the idea at first, until I thought about the batteries and replacement tapes, and wondered what would happened if it got wet. We did not talk for long; it was only 5:00 p.m., and Bob was anxious to return to the Trail. He mentioned something about possibly meeting again in Damascus, then disappeared into the forest.

Later, at midnight, I awoke with a start. My heart started to palpitate, and before I was alert enough to recognize what was happening, it converted into an arrhythmia. It happened so fast I didn't have time to react. Just as I had at Plum Orchard Gap shelter, I became extremely anxious. I had come to believe that my fibrillation problem was of psychological origin, born of anxiety which I thought I had traced to my lack of spiritual confidence. I had assumed that with my two recent spiritual episodes, I had gained control of that situation. Boy, was I wrong!

I tried, as I had at Plum Orchard Gap, to concentrate on gaining a positive attitude, to gain control of my heart. "Get back in line! Damn it!" I yelled at my heart, at myself. "Get control!" I said. I tried mentally to force my heart to regain its normal rhythm. I got out of the sleeping bag and walked around the shelter and then in front of the shelter.

The night was beautiful, the moon full or nearly so, the sky a star spattered blue-black. The clearing was bathed in moonlight. For some reason I had stripped naked before getting into my sleeping bag and didn't bother dressing when I arose. I was too angry. "Why in Hell's name do I have to go through this?" I screamed. The words rose from the recesses of my guts, my chest, and burst forth into the night in a rising crescendo. I stood naked in the moonlight in the middle of the clearing, shaking my fists at the moon, shrieking in anger, frustration and fear. "Why?" I demanded again and again. Only silence answered.

Soon I was drained. "What am I doing? How can I be angry with God? You want to end up in Hell? No one can be angry with God! Why shouldn't I be angry with God?"

I had made a deal with God. I had made a deal that I would build up my spiritual strength, and if I did that, then God would protect me from atrial fibrillation.

"Wasn't that the deal?" I demanded.

Now God had backed out on the deal.

Dejectedly, I walked back to the shelter.

God doesn't make deals. You can't deal with your soul like you were selling it to the highest bidder, I admonished myself, realizing how angry I was as I said: You don't control God! You better learn to accept what you can't control! The realizations hit me one after the other. Don't forget, the defeats are part of the mosaic! Get control of your emotions! You can do that! The thoughts raced through my mind with never a single thought remaining long enough to become dominant or to stand introspection.

The old demons pressed their attack — anger, anxiety, depression — all took turns boring in on my psyche. I vowed that I wouldn't let the demons gain control. I would master the situation. I might not have the power to control what was afflicting me, but I could surely control my emotional reaction. I took a Bufferin tablet and laid back down in my sleeping bag.

The arrhythmia became more severe. I sat up in a leaning position against the shelter wall and fell into a disturbed sleep. A short time later, I was awakened by a mouse that had crawled on my exposed shoulder and then onto my head. It leaped off as I swatted at it in a fit of anger. Then I fell back to sleep and dozed fitfully until daybreak.

Upon awakening, my arrhythmia had converted to a normal rhythm. But I was still exhausted from its effects. I barely managed a smile as I passed the Virginia state line marker. I referred to my *Trail Data Book*, the AT Conference publication that listed the various landmarks, shelters, road crossings, etc., giving the mileage of each, calculated both from the north and the south by section. For example, the Virginia state line was listed as 280.6 miles from the Little Tennessee River at Fontana Dam, and Fontana Dam was 166.1 miles from Springer Mountain. I had no reaction to the knowledge that I had traveled 446.7

miles to that point. I was interested only in doing another three and three-tenth miles to Damascus, civilization and sleep.

UNCLE NICK GRINDSTAFF

Beside the Trail in Tennessee
Is a monument of stone.
It looks much like a chimney
That stands some eight feet tall.
It marks the final resting place
Of Uncle Nick's old bones.
Inscribed it says:
    "Lived alone, suffered alone, died alone."

Now Nick was wont to travel;
And so, he went out west
To seek his fame and fortune
And show it to the rest.
But he was robbed and beaten,
And so, he came back home.
He moved up on the mountain
And lived a hermit's life
Away from thieves and scoundrels
And others of the like.
And thus the years did pass
'Till Uncle did so too,
And he was buried down
Below his monument of stone
That says:
    "Lived alone, suffered alone, died alone."

Now square atop the monument
There rests a great old tree.
It could have fallen anywhere,
But chose this hallowed spot
To come acrashing down,
Exactly on the resting place
Of poor old Uncle's bones.
Inscribed it says:
    "Lived alone, suffered alone, died alone."

CHAPTER 15

The Methodist Hostel

Damascus, (pop. 1500) traced its origins back to 1776 when the first settlers arrived. Fifty years later it became known as Mock's Mill, named after a man who built a grist mill on the banks of Laurel Creek. (Damascus sits at the junction of three large mountain streams.) Mock, the man, was responsible for a population "boomlet," fathering 33 children by three wives. He accounted for a substantial percentage of the population in the area.

After the Civil War, a retired Confederate General, John D. Imboden, excited by discovery of nearby iron, coal and manganese deposits, entertained dreams of developing a great industrial empire. He was instrumental in bringing a railroad into the region. In the process, he acquired the land on which the town was sited and renamed it Damascus, suggesting that it would, in time, rival that other Damascus as a producer of fine steel. The mineral resources proved to be insufficient to support Imboden's dream, but the surrounding hills provided a bonanza in hardwood timber. Beginning around 1900, a profitable lumbering boom began which lasted for a quarter of a century. The AT followed some of the abandoned railroad beds from that period.

People waved as I trudged wearily through the center of town, and it was clear that I was among friends. It was a good feeling. Although the *Trail Guide* and the *Philosopher's Guide* both mentioned that the Methodist Hostel was the place to stay in Damascus, I had reservations about it. My experience at the hostel in Wesser, North Carolina, still burned in my memory. I decided to check out the town for other sleeping accommodations. I really wanted a room to myself where no one would disturb me. (The *Trail Guide* also mentioned that Damascus offered a motel.)

I passed the Methodist Church and continued on for a short distance until a beige, compact car stopped and a tall gentleman unfolded himself from behind the steering wheel to tell me I had passed the hostel. "You've gone about 100 yards too far!" said the fellow who in time proved to be Pastor Bill Henson. "The hostel is the big yellow house directly behind the church." I started to say I wanted to check out the motel situation first and caught myself. If he's that proud of the place, I should go there, I thought. It was a good decision.

The Place, as the hostel was called, was a large, ochre, two-story wooden frame house that could comfortably accommodate 20 people. It boasted a bathroom with toilet and shower on each floor, a kitchen, a large living room with overaged, overstuffed furniture, a separate dining room with a long, rough, hand-built table, four large bedrooms upstairs, one bedroom downstairs, and a long screened porch off the kitchen which faced the rear of the church. Except for the living room furniture, it was equipped like a summer camp with basic but sturdy appliances (except stove) and furniture. In the corner of the dining room sat a large cardboard box full of free trail food which had been "donated" to the hostel by previous guests. Beds were six- inch thick foam rubber pads cut into mattress-size proportions and laid in rows directly on the floor.

When I arrived, a heavy-set young man with curly dark hair and a broad, heavy-browed face was removing a thick growth of bushes from beside the house. Rivulets of perspiration streaked his face, forming beads that dropped from his nose and chin as he worked.

He had already cut away the green upper portions of the plants and was attacking the root systems when he stirred up a nest of yellowjackets. We both ran inside the rear porch of the house where the screening protected us from the angry insects.

"Thru-hiking?" asked Mike Martin.

"Trying to thru-hike," I responded. "Think I'm a little late in the season to make it all the way to Katahdin. How about yourself?"

"I'm thru-hiking with John Fox. You've probably seen our names in the Trail registers: Gandalf and Strider. I'm Gandalf and John is Strider. John's working at a construction job right now, trying to pick up a little money. Both of us are low on cash. We've been here for about a week. I have a kidney infection that's put me out of action, but I expect I'll be okay in a couple more days."

I immediately recognized the names from entries in the

shelter registers. The names fit. Mike had solid, heavily muscled legs and thick ankles; he walked in a plodding manner which looked like he was laying claim to the ground on which he walked. Even the sound of the word "Gandalf" seemed appropriate. John was a tall, thin, strongly muscled young man who walked with an elasticity that fit the name "Strider."

I mentioned that I too had a "slight physical problem" with heart arrhythmia. Mike suggested I see the physician at the medical center about two blocks away. At first, I didn't think much about the idea, then, as I reflected more on it, I recognized the wisdom in his suggestion.

Dr. Luck asked about my medical history as he listened to my heart. "Taking any medication?" he asked.

"Some Digoxin," I replied.

"How much?"

"I don't know for sure. I take a white pill and a small yellow pill. I think it's .150 mg. The big pill is .25 mg. and the smaller one is .125 mg."

"That's .375 mg," corrected Dr. Luck.

"Last time I went to school, 125 plus 25 equaled 150," I replied smartly.

Dr. Luck started slightly. He wasn't used to being challenged. "Look where the decimal point is," he said evenly. "The zero is dropped from the .25."

Tired and slow as I was, I immediately recognized that I had outrun my supply line in that battle of wits. He was dead right. "You win!" I laughed.

He was gracious in victory, smiled without comment, and prescribed a medication, Norpace, which I was to take twice daily, 100 mg. each time. He also gave me some Inderal for use in the event I again suffered an onset of fibrillation. Meanwhile, he recommended I stay in Damascus for a couple of days to see if there would be any reaction to the new medication.

I readily accepted his suggestion. I was exhausted from the physical demands of the Trail and the fibrillation episode from the previous night. I welcomed an extra day or two respite and a chance to recover my strength. Besides, I thought, I'm tired of being alone. It would be a pleasant change to have company at the hostel, now that I knew I would have a room to myself. Mike and John were the only other guests at the hostel.

I spent the remainder of the day shopping and doing laundry. It was early evening when I finally returned to the hostel.

The noise from a loud conversation on the hostel rear porch greeted my return. Mike Martin introduced me to John Fox and Bob, an older man in rumpled clothes with uncombed hair and a day-old growth of gray beard stubble. I later learned that Bob often dropped by the hostel to visit with the hikers.

After observing Bob for a while, I suspected he probably wasn't welcome at other places in town and the constant change of faces at the hostel insured that no "institutional memory" remained to cloud his reputation among the hikers. It was apparent they all had been drinking for some time, and Bob mentioned that they made great "screwdrivers" at the local VFW. He was slobberingly friendly, and when he learned that I was a retired Army officer, he began to list his exploits from WWII. I listened to a rehash of nonsense he had concocted in the intervening 40 years and was greatly relieved when he excused himself and, I thought, headed for the bathroom.

In the meantime, a young woman drove up in a Ford compact and inquired if there was room to spend the night. She had a slim, but nicely rounded figure, long black hair and pretty blue eyes and, for some reason, was immediately welcomed into the group. Suddenly, somebody remembered Bob, I think it was John, and he went off to check. Bob had lost his bearings and had ended up on the front side of the house where he threw up on the front lawn, then passed out. John dragged him back into the house and laid him on the living room sofa to sleep it off.

Someone, probably a neighbor, had witnessed the incident and reported it to the church authorities. No sooner had John returned from attending to Bob, than Mr. Trivett, a local city official and hostel overseer, arrived on the scene. "Better hide the beer, here comes Mr. Trivett!" said Mike Martin.

"Someone must have called him." said John. They scurried into the kitchen carrying the beer with them but neglected to empty or cover a 32-gallon garbage can beside the porch door which was filled to the top with empty beer cans.

"Is it against the law to drink beer or against the hostel rules?" I asked.

"Not that we know of. It just doesn't look right to be sitting around with a lot of beer," said Mike. "We think Mr. Trivett doesn't approve."

Mr. Trivett entered and made a point of looking around and going through the house, then returned to the porch. He looked at the beer I was holding but said nothing. He tried to make small talk; it was forced and the atmosphere became tense. The others were psychologically immobilized by guilt and couldn't find anything to say.

After Mr. Trivett satisfied himself that an orgy was not occurring on church property, he departed, no doubt to report his findings to the pastor. Now the beer reappeared, and the conversation and atmosphere again became relaxed, albeit much more subdued.

About 30 minutes later, Bob came back to the porch. "Anyone seen my teeth?" he mumbled sheepishly.

Everyone remained silent, probably because Bob being drunk and without his teeth had not spoken clearly and no one had understood him. It took me several seconds to decipher what he meant and was about to translate it for the others when John bolted up from his chair. "Bet he lost 'em when he threw up," he said and went outside to look. He came back a minute later with the teeth, and Bob left for wherever he called home.

The conversation turned to the new arrival. She introduced herself as Leslie; no last name, only Leslie.

"We're Thru-Hikers, hiking the Appalachian Trail," said Mike. The tone of the sentence was more of a question than a statement. Everyone wanted to know what a pretty woman was doing alone on the road, looking to stay in a hiker's hostel.

"I'm on my way to Chicago," she said, "to go to school."

"What are you going to study?" I asked.

"It's a religious school run by the Mennonites. I'm a Mennonite and I hope to do missionary work when I'm finished."

"Why do you want to do missionary work?" asked John.

"I have a degree in marketing and advertising, but I really didn't like what I was doing, so I began a reappraisal of my life and decided I wanted to devote it to God."

"What made you come to that decision?" I asked.

"I've always been interested in the supernatural, always been looking for the 'light,' so to speak. At one time, I was into Eastern religions, you know, charismatic stuff. It just didn't work for me, and I decided to come back to Jesus."

"I know what you mean," said Mike. "I looked around like that, too." He recited a passage from the Bible that seemed appropriate to his life and what it had meant to him. Leslie responded with another passage which had significance for her. They then talked about various parts of the Bible, carrying on pretty much of a dialogue while John and I listened.

Earlier, I had learned that Mike had been active in church and at one time had worked in a church bookstore. He told a story about how he had gotten in trouble in the bookstore by dressing up a store mannequin in women's underclothing, panties and bra, I think it was. He laughed gleefully as he described the reactions of the people in the bookstore to the mannequin. I guessed the incident was one of the reasons for his departure, although he didn't exactly make the connection. He said only that it was by mutual agreement.

During the next couple of days, I had the opportunity to get to know the people and the town better. I didn't meet any more hikers, but several long-distance bicyclers came through. They were part of a transcontinental tour that had started in Seattle, Washington, and were headed for Washington, D.C. They stayed for only one night, then were on their way again in the morning.

In addition to the bicyclers, Bob appeared regularly at about 5:00 p.m., as though it were opening time at an English pub. Upon seeing me, he immediately launched into his repertoire of war stories. I guessed that I had become a stimulus that evoked a Pavlovian response in Old Bob.

In addition to Bob, another man by the name of Owen made a frequent appearance. He was always squeaky clean, his puffy face smoothly shaven and his longish gray/brown hair combed back in a pompadour a la 1950's style. He too was basically a beer-mooching barroom philosopher who usually disappeared at about the same time the beer ran out. He had an opinion on any subject and a unique knack for killing a conversation with the deft application of an inappropriate cliche at an appropriate time. It got to the point that as soon as he appeared, half the room left. As full of baloney as Bob was, he, at least, was occasionally funny.

Mike Martin was a very bright and interesting person with considerable talent who acknowledged that he was having difficulty sorting out his niche in life. He had spent several summers in his quest for personal identity, hiking sections of the Trail. One summer he had hiked by road, towing his pack behind him on a set of jury-rigged wheels which earned him publicity in the newspapers. He also was a pianist of some accomplishment and spent several afternoons of his recuperation period in the church's music room playing the piano.

He told me he had recently been struck by lightning while hiking the Trail. As he described it, he had been leaning against a tree during a thunderstorm when a lightning bolt hit a nearby tree. The lightning arced across the ground to the tree he was leaning against and jolted him in the process. He said he was still in a state of semishock when he rejoined John Fox at the shelter later that evening. Like many hikers, they did not hike together during the day but met at predesignated points for lunch or at the shelters for the night.

"Did your life flash before your eyes?" I asked.

"No," Mike laughed, "but I walked around cross-eyed for a while." He showed me a crayon drawing he had done of the incident and another drawing of a scene showing a figure hitting another figure with a stick. It was, he told me, a graphic depiction of another incident that occurred in the Indian town of Cherokee, North Carolina.

"What happened to you on that one?" I queried.

"When John and I got to Newfound Gap in the Smokies, we hitched into Cherokee. Both of us are interested in Indians and learning about their culture. Since we were so close to Cherokee, we thought we'd go for the experience. We met several Indians during the course of the evening and eventually became friendly with two men. We had an interesting conversation at first, but they were drinking hard liquor and started an argument. They became increasingly belligerent and then they got nasty. One of them hit John in the head with his (John's) hiking stick, causing a nasty gash. We both ran away but the Indians didn't follow us. Problem was we left our packs behind, and the Indians stole our food. We sneaked back to see if we could get our packs back, but the Indians were going through them. All we could do was watch from our hiding place until they left."

"Then you got your packs back?" I asked.

"Yeah, we got our packs back. But no food."

"What'd you do then? Go to the police?"

"No, we told another Indian we had met earlier about the incident, and he said he was sorry and that all Indians weren't like that."

"Sounds to me like you were lucky they didn't take all your stuff," I said. "You should have gone to the police."

Mike hung his head. "Yeah, we should have gone to the police, but we didn't want to hang around town any more."

"I can understand that," I sympathized.

After telling me about the incidents, Mike asked questions about my background and career in the Army. When I told him

I had spent the last six years in Germany, his eyes lit up. "How did you find the Germans?" he asked.

"I think the Germans are a great people," I replied. "They do a lot of things differently than we do in America."

"How do you mean?"

"For one thing, they take time to enjoy their lives. They recognize that life does not consist solely of work and making money. Another is their standard of excellence which I think we would do to emulate. They demand quality in their goods and services that we sometimes lack." I was about to say something about the cohesion of their families. But Mike broke in, saying, "I guess we could learn a lot from our neighbors if we would take the time to understand them."

"I think that's a good assessment," I replied. "We sometimes dismiss the accomplishments of others simply because they're not American. It sometimes seems that because we're a great nation we have developed this bias that Americans are somehow superior to the citizens of other countries. Of course, it is drummed into us from the time we start school that our system of government is the envy of the world, that no other nation has the freedom that we have, and that is continually amplified by our politicians."

"Do you think that causes the bias?"

"I suppose that's part of it. Some of it's a reflection of our history and past success in business and commerce. Perhaps it comes from having won all of our past wars, particularly World War II, except, of course, Vietnam."

I was about to say we need to understand that other nations and cultures have existed for far longer than ours and that they also produce things of beauty and quality when Mike interrupted again. "I keep hearing that we're headed for another Vietnam in Central America, in Nicaragua. What do you think?"

Just as I was about to open my mouth, Pastor Bill Henson arrived along with Mr. Trivett. John and Leslie disappeared. I think Mr. Trivett made them nervous, or perhaps it was because Leslie was staying there. The hostel was for the exclusive use of hikers. Since Leslie wasn't a hiker, she probably felt she needed to be unavailable before anyone asked her what she was doing there. Reverend Henson stood in the doorway and made small talk, asking how we were all doing, and if we needed anything; then he mentioned that he would be holding a service in the church the next morning and invited us to attend. Mike was also invited to sing in the choir and accepted. After this, Bill Henson and Mr. Trivett, who had been standing off to the side like a body guard, headed for the church rectory.

The next morning Mike and I dressed in our cleanest hiking clothes and headed for the church. I was disappointed that John and Leslie didn't come. Since Pastor Henson had taken the time to personally issue an invitation, we, as guests at the hostel, had an obligation of sorts to return the favor and go to the service. It was like a payment in kind for enjoying the church's hospitality. Pastor Henson introduced both Mike and me to the congregation during the part of the service where newcomers were welcomed, and we were acknowledged very cordially by the people as we left.

Leslie took her leave that afternoon to resume her journey, and the atmosphere lightened up. She and John appeared to have developed a mutual attraction which made Mike uneasy. I could sense a rift developing between Mike and John; Leslie's appearance had been the catalyst that brought it into focus. I had learned from Mike earlier that he felt he was still not fully recovered from his kidney infection and was planning to stay in Damascus a while longer. He had not told John, though, because John told me they were planning on leaving in the morning. I suggested he talk to Mike about that, and he looked at me with a quizzical expression. He had been sitting in Damascus for well over a week now and was anxious to get back to the Trail. I had the impression that Mike wanted to stay in Damascus and talk "Trail talk" with the new hikers and bicyclers who came through, that the lightning experience had made him reluctant to return to the Trail.

I was sipping my last beer before turning in for the night when John Fox came upstairs. He wanted to talk, and I think, in the back of his mind, wanted to test the water to see if I wanted company when I left in the morning.

"Mike and I aren't getting along," he confided. "He's a lot older than I am, and it bugs him when I know as much about certain subjects as he does and won't acknowledge him as the superior member in our relationship. It's too bad. We've been through a lot, but I'm not going to take a back seat and do what he wants all the time. I think Mike would be happy to just stay in Damascus. I want to get on the Trail. I'm going to put my stuff in order and leave in the morning."

"You're welcome to hike with me if you want. I don't go

very far or very fast, but I don't mind company."

John was unsure about how he wanted to proceed, and we left it at the point where he made no firm commitment to accompany me. But I had the impression that more than likely he would be hiking with me.

CHAPTER 16

Whitetop Laurel Gorge and
the Grayson Highlands

John Fox did not accompany me out of Damascus the next morning as he intended, but I didn't leave alone. (Evidently Mike persuaded John to wait for one more day.) Owen appeared as I started to leave and decided to walk with me to the edge of town. We walked together for about four or five minutes, until even with my pack my pace was too much for him. His breath became labored and he stopped talking. (He had been saying how he'd like to do some hiking again.)

When we reached the bridge across Laurel Creek, he stopped to catch his breath and at the same time waved me ahead without speaking. I felt a tinge of sadness as I watched him fighting to get air into his lungs. When he recovered sufficiently to look at me, we waved a last farewell, and I turned back up the Trail.

The AT followed the Virginia Creeper Trail for several hundred yards after leaving the edge of town, then, just as this hiker became comfortable with the route, it took an abrupt turn to the left and climbed the precipitous ascent up Feathercamp Ridge. The *Philosopher's Guide* indicated that the Virginia Creeper Trail continued straight ahead and rejoined the AT at the Luther Hassinger Memorial Bridge, a renovated railroad trestle that crossed high above the Whitetop Laurel Creek some 13 miles to the east.

I remembered Mike's enthusiastic description of the Virginia Creeper Trail and his assessment of its being not only more scenic than the AT but also much easier. The decision was easy, and I continued straight ahead. It was a good decision. Not only did I save myself the physical exertion of the climb up the mountain and the endless series of ascents and descents, I was rewarded with a journey through a magnificent mountain valley with cold rushing trout waters and spectacular boulder-strewn chasms cut from the mountains. I had the trail to myself except for occasional fishermen who stood in the foaming water trying to lure the trout with pieces of feathers dressed up as delectable insects, casting them repeatedly out into the current and allowing them to float downstream. The wary trout seldom responded and mostly their efforts were in vain.

The Virginia Creeper Trail followed an old railroad bed which carried the coal and timber train, named the Creeper, that had regularly labored through the mountains, "creeping" the long upgrade with its heavy load. The railroad itself had been dismantled long ago and only occasional railroad ties rotting alongside the cinder path reminded the hiker of its historical origins.

The scenery was spectacular. The Trail crossed Whitetop Laurel Creek many times on well-preserved trestles, giving the hiker a unique series of views of the stream. Once a deer crossed the creek about 50 yards downstream from the curving trestle where I stood, splashing as it bounded through the rock-strewn water, the sunlight gleaming from its rich tan coat and the spray it kicked up.

The hues of summer green were many and varied — from light, almost-yellow foliage reflecting the sunlight from the chasm walls at the highest tree levels to the almost- black greens of the bushes and small trees in the shadows beneath the overhang along the water's edge. The water rushed in torrents down its rock-strewn path, subsiding occasionally in pools glistening in the sunlight beside small sand bars and sand stream banks before tumbling again in a froth over more stones and rocks.

Just before coming to the small village of Taylors Valley, I passed an old gray railway section crew car with a rusty stove pipe protruding from its roof. It belonged to a gentleman from the community who in the past had rented it to hikers. It was now locked, however, and I had read in the *Philosopher's Guide* that it was no longer available for hiker use.

Taylors Valley reminded me of a Currier and Ives print with its rural flavor of simplicity and tranquillity. The lean, tidy homes and barns were freshly painted, although not so fresh that they had lost their character. The yards were neatly trimmed; brightly colored flowers grew in narrow rows along

Virginia Creeper Trail Trestle over Whitetop Laurel Creek.

the fences and in front of the porches and in small circular beds in the lawns. Red, blue, yellow and white flowers circled the houses like soldiers in protective ranks whose mission was to keep the imposing green at bay. A more subdued Whitetop Laurel Creek ran quietly through the settlement, and near the village center, a quaint, stone-supported, wooden beam bridge connected the few homes on the north side of the stream with their neighbors to the south.

The smooth steady incline of the railroad bed made the walking easy, and I made good time until I returned to the AT after crossing the Luther Hassinger Bridge. (A small commemorative plaque dedicated the bridge to Mr. Hassinger, a pioneer lumberman who had harvested vast quantities of wood from the region.)

The bridge itself was constructed high above a cut through which the creek curved in a wild figure "S" from north to south. The creek almost exploded into view from behind the north side of the ridge. It emerged in a froth from a run of boulders, then slid smoothly into the bend past small sand bars, occasional boulders and uprooted trees that lined the banks. Finally, it dashed through the boulder-strewn cut emerging from beneath the trestle, flowing swiftly like dark green silk streaming in the wind. It remained calmly fluid until it began to arc toward the south, then cascaded down a shallow path of rocks before disappearing behind the shoulder of the southern ridge.

Directly after leaving the east end of the bridge, the AT took an abrupt turn to the left and climbed a steep, rocky path to the crest of the ridge which angled toward the northeast away from Whitetop Laurel Creek. The Virginia Creeper Trail continued straight ahead, eventually arcing south into North Carolina.

The day was warm and I led a trail of gnats and flies as I sweated my way up the steep incline. As long as I remained in motion, the insects were not much of a problem, but when I finally stopped for the day, I was besieged by the devils. The flies were especially aggressive, biting through my exposed skin, sometimes drawing blood. I tried to discourage them with insect repellent, but today they went undeterred, and I resorted to swatting them with my hat or my *Trail Data Book*. (The book was an efficient flyswatter that served me well on several occasions.)

One especially irksome fly simply would not leave me alone, and I let it light long enough on my thigh before slapping it with my hat and knocking it to the ground where it lay stunned and motionless. Then I set to work erecting my tent and preparing for supper. When I next noticed the fly, it had revived, but was in the clutches of a tiny ant. The ant had the fly by the wing, and struggle as the fly might, it could not get away. Although the fly was many times larger than the ant, the ant succeeded in dragging the kicking and fighting fly toward the ant colony. I watched the drama for about five minutes until the ant decided he had had enough of the fly, attacked it with his mouth, and left.

A short time later, a group of small ants came for the fly, but they were intercepted by a group of larger ants, and a pitched battle ensued. With the attention of the ants focused on one another, the fly tried desperately to flee. But it couldn't summon the coordination necessary for locomotion. I started to make supper while I waited for the outcome of the battle to see who would succeed in getting the fly. I even thought once about rescuing the fly myself, then remembered the stinging bites I had been subjected to and decided to let the justice in nature prevail. Unfortunately, my attention was diverted for too long. When I returned to check on the progress of the battle, the small ants were gone and so was the fly. But the place was swarming with larger ants!

July 29th, my birthday, was a sunny, clear day, with fresh cooling breezes on the ridge crests. The Trail led through the Mt. Rogers Recreational Area and some of the most beautiful scenery in Virginia. The ascent up Whitetop Mountain crossed broad mountain meadows with dazzling displays of wildflowers, particularly asters. The views from Buzzard Rock and the ridge leading to Whitetop were extensive and as beautiful as any I had seen. The Trail passed below the summit of Whitetop and through a saddle before ascending Mt. Rogers, the highest mountain in Virginia at 5,729 feet. The AT did not go to the summit; instead a blue-blazed trail led half a mile to the left to the summit. The *Trail Guide* indicated that there were no views.

After leaving Mt. Rogers, I entered Grayson Highlands State Park, a magnificent high country region with sweeping vistas and exciting multicolored rock formations. The Trail wound around the rock formations, through canyons and evergreen tree-covered hillsides, and past herds of curious Black Angus cattle who watched quietly as I moved through their midst. The landscape resembled the scenery from western movies with sculptured rocks and cattle trails, and I half expected to see a cowboy come racing over the next rise.

I was so entranced by the scenery that I lost track of time. When I finally checked my watch at Massie Gap, it was already 5:00 p.m. I was exhausted, but I wanted to get to the Grayson Highlands Campground to call Anna. The campground was nearby, but I had no idea in which direction. I spied two people standing on the top of a gigantic rock formation about a hundred yards away and hurried toward them.

Carol Stielper said she and her daughter, Amy, were camped with the rest of the family at the Grayson Highlands Campground and that she knew the way to the campground, but it was easier to take me there than to explain directions. She offered me a ride. She didn't have to ask twice.

I had covered 16 miles for the day and wasn't sure I could handle another three or more miles, which is how far she thought it was from the gap to the campground. (I had thought in terms of one-half or three-fourths of a mile, but it was half a mile just to their car.)

Carol and Amy rounded up the remainder of the family, father Joe and daughter Laurel, and all five of us loaded into their subcompact car, the three women and my pack cramped together in back, Joe driving and me in the front passenger seat with my hiking stick poking out the window. I breathed a sigh of comfort as well as relief, thinking to myself as the distance increased, that it would have been at least another hour before I arrived had I been on foot.

The family collected copious amounts of huckleberries while they waited for me to complete my phone call to Germany (Anna was not at home), then took me to their campsite and invited me to join them for a supper of fresh barbecued chicken, rice, zucchini and yellow squash. I accepted without hesitation.

The fresh food was delicious, and I ate several helpings which I washed down with several glasses of excellent home-made white wine. Joe Stielper was an accomplished winemaker, and the quality of his wine was competitive with some of the best I had drunk anywhere. I complimented him on his wine-making, but he replied with the self-effacing comment that all he did was "follow the instructions." Because it was my birthday, Joe also offered me some red wine he had made as well as a couple of cans of beer, which I also gladly accepted.

The Stielpers were a close family with a strong bond between the daughters and the parents. Joe was the lone, "long-suffering" male in the group, and he loved it. It was refreshing to listen to the family banter and the girls talk about their friends and boyfriends, and the usual topics dear to teenage hearts. I related some of my adventures on the Trail, including my experience with the bear in the Smokies, and everyone laughed as I described the bear's reaction to my "attack." We talked until 11:00 p.m. when I stumbled off into the dark woods to put up my tent. After all that wine and beer, this chore proved to be quite a challenge. However, it did not take long for me to fall asleep. Except for the missed connection with Anna, it was a perfect birthday.

In the moments before sleep overwhelmed me, I thought about my intent to meditate for short periods during the morning and before going to sleep at night. The scenery along the Trail during the day had been so beautiful and the changes so exhilarating that I had had trouble maintaining sufficient concentration for meditation. I had kept at it, however, returning again and again when my mind wondered. Eventually, I established as my broad spiritual goal: "To become so confident spiritually that I could face death without fear."

That concept was nothing new. It was an accurate reflection of what I had envisioned as the ultimate state of spiritually. It was the point at which I had wanted to arrive, a point at which I thought I would be released from selfish temporal considerations, where I would be free to project beyond the limitations imposed by fear and human frailties. Now the question was to arrive at that condition. That would be more difficult. First, I had to establish who God was before I set about knowing Him. To identify my God was an essential step in the process. But how does one identify a spirit? I could not use my temporal powers to identify God; I needed something beyond my sensory and logical cognitive abilities. The word "faith" leapt into my consciousness. That's the key, I thought. Faith has got to be the answer.

The wind blew fiercely throughout the night. I was sure a front was moving in and fully expected to awake in the morning to a torrent of rain. Happily, I was wrong.

The deep blue sky which greeted me contained not even the hint of a cloud, and the wind had subsided. Carol cooked a superb camper's breakfast of sourdough pancakes with the fresh huckleberries picked the previous day and many slices of crisp bacon which I washed down with steaming fresh brewed coffee. It was by far the best breakfast I had eaten on the Trail.

It took half the morning just to climb the trail back to the AT. Again, I found myself admiring the natural splendor of the high country pine and spruce trees and sculptured rock formations. Shortly after reaching the Trail, I encountered a doe with her spotted fawn ambling lazily down the pathway directly in front of me. I followed them for some time, wondering why the deer was not spooked.

A gentle breeze was blowing from me towards them, and I was only about 50 yards away. After about five minutes, the doe jerked her head up and started. Looking around, she spied me and leaped off the Trail. Normally, when a mother deer runs, her fawn is right on her heels, but for some reason this fawn didn't follow its mother. Instead, it continued down the Trail for another 30 yards before sidling off into a stand of young hardwoods from where it watched as I passed. I could see the doe watching from deeper inside the woods.

On Pine Mountain, two more deer ran off the Trail for about 20 yards, then they too stopped and watched as I passed. Later, I encountered two more deer who also remained motionless as I passed by. The whole area was teeming with deer, a sharp contrast to North Carolina and Tennessee where I barely got a glimpse of a deer, then only a fleeting look at a bobbing white tail just before it disappeared in the forest.

On the way down the mountain, I met four people on horse-back coming from the other direction. The man in the lead was the guide from a dude ranch, and the three people behind him were guests. The guide's horse had a very nasty cut on its right front leg where it had been gashed by a boulder on the Trail. At that point, the trail crossed a several hundred-yard-long swath of three- and four-foot boulders strewn in a jumble down the forested mountain. I hopped from rock to rock to make head-way, but the poor horses were forced to stagger through, lurch-ing awkwardly when their iron shoes slipped on the rocks, wedging their hooves and legs between the gaps and cracks, and scraping hide in the process.

The guide said they had gotten lost and asked how far they were from the summit of the mountain. I replied that they were about 500 yards away, thinking that the guide probably knew exactly where they were. Horses were specifically prohibited from using the AT in that area, and I suspected the guide was telling me they were lost so as to excuse them for being there.

At noon, I stopped at the Old Orchard shelter, a rustic log lean-to, sited on the edge of the deep forest with its front open-ing onto a broad mountain meadow framed by a panorama of mountains. After lunch, I sat in the shade drinking in the beauty and reflecting on my adventure. My attitude toward the hike improved with the beauty of the mountains and the people I was meeting. I thought again about the "coincidence" in meet-ing the Batys and now the Stielpers, both coming at times when I was physically exhausted. I decided to stop worrying about the hike, to be reasonable in my planning and execution, and to leave the rest to God.

Although I was able to maintain my concentration for only short periods during my meditation in the morning, I did deter-mine that Christ had to be my God. I was slightly surprised by the remarkable clarity of my deliberation and the speed with which I resolved the issue. I had thought of the multitudes of divinities which formed the bases of the spiritual lives of people in other cultures: the Moslems, Buddhists, Hindus and others. My logic told me that we all had the same God, that the differ-ences among us arose from the religious traditions engendered by differing cultures. It just didn't make sense to me that the

God who sustained life in me was different from the God who sustained life in any of my neighbors.

It was also clear that I needed to devote effort to the learning process; just like in any learning process, I had to take the initiative. No bolt of understanding was going to descend on me from the heavens carrying Divine inspiration. It was also apparent that the quest for spiritual strength would be a lifelong endeavor, not something I would achieve only while I was on the Trail. I could lay out the directions and the milestones while I was on the Trail, but the journey would be for life.

I arrived at Hurricane Campground around 5:30 p.m. after a 16-mile day and camped next to a bathhouse with running water and hot showers. Taped to the bathhouse wall was a note from Mike Martin addressed to me and John Fox, telling us that he was waiting at the Trimpi shelter, which lay another six miles to the north. I was not surprised to see that he and John Fox had split up, at least temporarily. I wondered if Mike's kidney infection had cleared up enough to allow him to hike at a pace acceptable to John. I thought I'd learn about it in the morning and turned my attention to setting up camp.

The campground sat in a broad mountain valley through which flowed a shallow, quiet stream that passed alternately through sunshine and forest shadows. In the center of the valley lay a broad meadow covered with thick, lush grass interrupted occasionally by stands of trees where the campsites were located. The campsites were spaced widely apart to provide maximum privacy for campers, although at that time none was needed; there were no campers. I was alone.

On two or three occasions, a pickup with a camper shell or a motor home came by but left directly after surveying the area. I guessed they wanted to be around other people or that the four dollar fee had scared them off. Whatever it was, it was all right by me.

A little more than two hours into the hike the next morning, I arrived at the blue-blazed side trail which led about 50 yards to the Trimpi shelter and a subdued Mike Martin carving on a stick, apparently deep in contemplation. He told me he was trying to make a new hiking staff; that in his haste to leave the hostel he had forgotten his old one that had an elaborately carved cane-like handle end which formed a duck's head. Mike was trying to reproduce the duck's head handle from the piece of wood.

"Bob came by with a borrowed car," Mike said. "I was in such a hurry to load my things and get going, I forgot my hiking stick. Bob said he'd mail it to me at Atkins, but I doubt I'll ever see it again. The gas gauge was on empty all the way. I hope Old Bob got back okay. I wouldn't want him getting into trouble on my behalf."

"Where's John?" I asked.

"He left the day after you did. I told him I'd catch up to him on the Trail. I've already hiked this part of the Trail. We're not getting along too well right now. Maybe once we get back hiking together, things will work out. You see the note I left at Hurricane Campground?" he asked.

"Yeah, I saw it. I was really surprised. How are you feeling?"

"I'm okay. Still a little weak. The doctor said I could go on the Trail, but to take it easy for a few days."

We chatted for a few more minutes about the hostel and the Trail, and I told him about my experience with the Stielpers at the Grayson Highlands.

"The Grayson Highlands are probably my favorite part of the Trail. I've been through this stretch before; that's why I accepted the ride," he said. It was forced in the way it came out. In fact, the entire conversation was slightly awkward, not free-flowing as I would have expected, and I thought that Mike was preoccupied with John's arrival. He continued to whittle as we talked, not even bothering to stop when I said, "Goodbye."

About midafternoon, I reached the top of a ridge called Brushy Mountain where I found an arrowhead. It was a black flint stone, carefully chipped to a point in front and, in the rear, to shoulders for connecting it to a shaft. I wasn't paying much attention to the Trail at the time because I was meditating, but something about the texture of the thing caught my attention. At first, I thought it was a leaf, and I hit it with my stick. When I heard the ping, I knew immediately I had found an arrowhead. After carefully examining it, I put it in my pocket with two specimens of petrified wood I had found earlier in the day.

I was impressed with the number of wildflowers along the Trail, particularly false foxglove, evening primrose, and bergamot. I also encountered a bright orange flower comprised of clusters of small, wing-tipped blossoms that grew in small groups along the open areas of the trail. I learned later that they were called butterfly weed or pleurisy root. The name pleurisy root originated from its use by the Indians who chewed its tough root as a remedy for pleurisy.

It was late in the afternoon when I reached the visitors' center at the headquarters of the Mt. Rogers Recreation Area. Signs posted in the fields along the approaches to the headquarters informed hikers that camping was not permitted in the area. That was a major disappointment because there were no good campsites for some distance on either side of the headquarters, and it would have made a nice camping spot with access to fresh water and toilets with running water. I was sure that campers had used the area in the past and had probably made nuisances of themselves at the headquarters, and the bureaucrats reacted in their usual way, which was to close the place to all hikers. It was unfortunate. There were no shelters or facilities of any kind for hikers along that section of the Trail. With a little positive energy, the Forest Service could have constructed tent platforms or designated a small tenting area for hikers, and perhaps charged a small fee to cover the cost of maintenance.

A small museum-like display area in the lobby of the headquarters contained an impressive display of Indian artifacts, none of which were any nicer than the arrowhead I had found. The lobby also held a fairly extensive display of rocks from the region, including a specimen of igneous rock called cranberry granite which, a sign indicated, was a billion years old. I fixed the impression of its color and composition in my mind for future reference in my search for my "perspective rock."

After leaving the headquarters, I went across the highway which fronted the parking lot and began climbing the ridge hoping to find a level place where I could set up my tent. I wanted to be as close as possible to the headquarters; it was the only source of water for miles. I found a passable campsite about one-half mile up the ridge. I made camp and ate supper. It had been a long day. Although it was still light when I climbed into my sleeping bag, I was exhausted and fell immediately into a deep sleep.

ARROWHEAD

I found an arrowhead today.
Black stone, chipped and grooved.
Not your normal museum arrow —
This was real, lying on the trail
Where it was shot or lost
By someone long ago.

I wonder — was it on a hunt?
Or a battle between tribes?
Or perhaps he'd stopped to rest
And it fell unnoticed to his side.

What sort of man was this?
A proud and noble huntsman
After food for wife and child?
Or some mean savage
Set in ambush for a foe?
Perhaps a soldier of the tribe
Trying to hold the settler tide.

It is certain I will never know.
So it shall be a souvenir
Of whatever I decide.
I found an arrowhead today
Lost by a noble huntsman long ago.

CHAPTER 17

The Blessings on Garden Mountain

All told, the Trail probably traverses about 100 miles of Brushy Mountains. Although the *Trail Guide* and maps referred to each of the ridge spine segments as Brushy Mountain, it was impossible to distinguish specifically which Brushy Mountain, except to say it was the one north or south of such and such a valley or road or town. The Brushy Mountains were not particularly high (less than 4000 feet) nor particularly grandiose, but the distance for which they stretched was certainly impressive.

The Trail was more difficult than in the Grayson Highlands and around Mt. Rogers, but still much easier than in the rugged mountains of North Carolina and Tennessee. That knowledge provided scant solace, though. My "blue-footed booby" boots were beginning to break down. The soles were a little too soft, and my feet were sore at the end of the day. Walking over flat surfaces was not much of a problem, but the small, sharp, pointed rocks on the ridge spines could be clearly felt through the thin rubber. Not only that, there was almost no support in the boots. After walking for a time, the muscles in my feet ached from the strain of supporting the extra load they carried. Although I had traveled only a couple of hundred miles since buying the boots, I might soon have to replace them.

The change in the character of the Trail also had an impact on my meditation. In Georgia and North Carolina, I had been surrounded by almost total wilderness which was conducive to meditation. Now, with increased contact with people, I experienced increased difficulty in maintaining concentration and had to constantly refocus my thoughts.

The daily meditation routine that I had established in the Smokies was being disrupted. I just couldn't seem to remain focused in the morning, and in the evening my meditation was being cut short by sleep. This disruption led to a lack of progress toward my spiritual goals. Since I wasn't making spiritual progress, I was becoming semidisillusioned with the Trail. I also was becoming somewhat frustrated. It was as if all the ladders I needed to progress upward from my present level had been removed and I was stranded in a lonely predicament.

After some reflection on my circumstances, I reasoned that my unconscious probably needed time to sort out the implications of the new direction I was following. When it was ready to resume the effort, it would tell me. Remember your mosaic, I thought. There will be defeats and victories, and there will also be times when nothing is happening and that also contributes. Be patient!

It was shortly before noon when I reached Groseclose, a small cluster of filling stations and a motel with a restaurant beside busy U.S. Route 11. The *Trail Guide* mentioned that overnight accommodations were available, and I planned to spend the night there. I also needed to reprovision and wash clothes. My early arrival allowed me sufficient time to accomplish everything I planned as well as a little time for just plain relaxing.

I was finally able to contact Anna from the pay phone by the cash register in the motel restaurant later in the day, but it was a difficult conversation. She sounded distant and reserved, and the noise of the traffic from the road made hearing difficult. The customers entering and leaving the place also had an effect. It was difficult expressing private thoughts when the world seemed to be listening to every word I uttered. The message content I received was also a disappointment.

Anna had decided not to join me on the Trail. She wanted to use her vacation to rest and relax, not to engage in an arduous endeavor like hiking through mountains. Though surprised by her decision, it didn't make me unhappy. Unconsciously, I probably was prepared for the news. Nevertheless, I was slightly subdued in spirit that night as I prepared for bed and spent more time thinking about Anna than meditating as I had planned.

The Trail the next morning between Groseclose and Little Brushy Mountain crossed several farm pastures containing small herds of cattle, mainly cows and heifers, but occasionally very young bulls. Most of the time, the cows simply watched as I passed, but periodically, a younger cow, probably only intending to protect her territory from my intrusion, decided to play bull and conduct a limited charge. I had only to yell and brandish my hiking stick to dissuade the attacks. Still, it served to increase my apprehension about hiking through pastures where cattle were present. My greatest concern was that the Trail might lead through a pasture containing a mature bull.

At one point the Trail contoured the side of a small, dome-shaped, tree-covered esker that provided a miniature exercise in stile crossing. Cattle had worn several trails that wound around the hillside like contour lines on a raised relief map. Although the incline was steep, the Trail siting was reasonable and the walking not difficult. But for some reason, probably to discourage cattle from tearing up the esker, about a dozen wire and post fences had been constructed, one behind the other, for a distance of about 100 yards. The fences were no more than 20 or 30 feet long, about chest high to a normal-sized man, and were placed so they ran lengthwise up the hill.

The result was a series of obstacles placed directly on the Trail path. Stiles had been constructed at each point where the Trail encountered a fence, but it was unnecessary to always use the stiles to get to the other side. Some fences were so short that I had only to walk around the ends. At the shelter where I stayed that night, one of the wags questioned in the register if the ridge was a training site for "Olympic stile jumping."

The hike the following morning was relaxed. It was a quiet, lazy sunny day, and the valley hummed the soft strains of nature at its midsummer work. The tidy farmhouses looked cool in the shade of massive oaks and maples, the clean, fat cattle grazed contentedly in lush grass meadows, and the neatly fenced fields swayed heavily with ripening corn and grain. I saw only one person, an elderly farm woman, who came to her door to tell me which way to go when I was having trouble finding my way. The next blaze was on a fence stile barely visible in the distance across a very large pasture. (Evidently others had had the same problem.) After setting me right, she went back into the house.

About halfway across the field, I was challenged by a belligerent heifer who fled in panic after I feigned a charge in retaliation. I became so engrossed with the heifer attack that I failed to notice a small stream flowing through the pasture and got both feet wet. That abruptly stopped my heroics.

Shortly before leaving the valley, the Trail passed the ruins of a cluster of primitive farm buildings; and near the site of a collapsed animal shed, I found a stone axe head.

The axe head was lying in a broad cowpath, half covered by the powder-fine dirt that swept upward in small spirals whenever the heated wind swirled by. At first, I saw only the smooth blade edge and thought it was a steel axe head. I picked it up out of curiosity and was astounded to find that it was stone. It had been neatly beveled by grinding on one side, while the other side was already flat and had only to be slightly modified to make a cutting edge. The top part of the stone, where I assumed it had been attached to a handle, appeared to be broken. Even so, it was a beautifully crafted artifact and, after cleaning it up, I placed it in my pack pocket alongside my arrowhead.

As I climbed through the forest near the ridge crest of Little Brushy Mountain, a very large, fat squirrel, running along the tree branches above me, missed a jump and landed with a loud, startling thud directly on the Trail five yards in front of me. It seemed not to bother the squirrel — who immediately regained both its equilibrium and its feet; it scampered up the nearest tree without hesitation. It must have fallen from a distance of about 20 feet, and I was surprised that it wasn't stunned.

Further on, I encountered several ruffed grouse strutting about the forest floor flaring their neck feathers. They stretched their necks to surprising lengths in the process. I guessed it was a mating ritual; the grouse were so intent on their activity that they seemed not in the least concerned by my presence.

While eating lunch, I became a spectator at an ant parade. The ants were carrying white bundles that looked like miniature white dufflebags but which, I assumed, were larvae of some type. I inspected the log where the suspected larvae originated but couldn't tell if it was ant larvae or larvae from a different insect species that had become the booty of raiding ants. Whoever they had belonged to in the past really didn't matter; they now belonged to the ants.

The insects marched in a procession that came into view where their route crossed a cut made for an old logging road and disappeared after climbing over a small leaf-covered mound. It reminded me of a conveyor belt with ants going in both directions. Those going in one direction were carrying the larvae; those going in the opposite direction were unencumbered. By the time I finished eating, my curiosity had been so aroused I decided to follow the trail as it snaked through the forest.

Now and then, I became disoriented when a short break occurred in the line of ants, and I had to explore until I found the route of march again. It was a very long trek for the ants, at least 300 yards up and down embankments and over logs and rocks. Their strength and stamina were simply amazing. The ants carried loads three times their own size over obstacles, leaves, sticks and rocks that were gigantic in comparison. I followed the ant trail to a huge old log into which the ant columns disappeared. I stirred the leaves all around the log. Finding no more ants, I decided I had found their den and returned to my own Trail.

Because of the prolonged dry spell, the springs and streams along the Trail were bone dry, except for the spring at Knot Mole shelter, and it was almost dry. It became imperative that I find campsites with water. My selection of campsites or shelters became influenced as much by considerations of water as by distance.

I tried several times throughout the day to meditate. My progress seemed sporadic but certainly better than my feeble attempts of the previous few days. I remained stymied at the level I had been trying to leave. I just couldn't visualize the route to my next level of spirituality. My attempts to communicate with God seemed totally unsatisfactory. I was still having difficulty establishing something more than the usual "give me" bargains we humans invariably include in our communications with our gods. God knows, I needed strength and wisdom, and I needed to know God. I just didn't seem to know how to go about getting on with my goals. With perseverance and concentration, I thought things might fall into place.

After supper, I sat at the picnic table in front of the Knot Mole shelter in the early evening light, sipping coffee and enjoying the quiet and the solitude. My mind began to focus on the very questions I had been wrestling with during the past several days. I questioned the very basis of my relationship with God.

What did God expect from me? Had I really been tainted by the original sin of Adam and Eve? If I had been tainted, why? I hadn't done anything other than be born and He had control over that. Why should I be guilty of a sin?

The questions tumbled from my mind like they had been stored for a long time in a place too small, and when the opening came, they all tumbled out at once as if they couldn't wait to get free.

What was it God wanted from me? I knew what I wanted

from Him. God did not need Jan Curran. I needed God. Then I thought that if God didn't need me, why had I been created? It occurred to me that my very existence was proof that I was needed. I at least filled a part of the natural order of things, and if for no other reason than that, I was important.

This was a completely different perspective from which I had looked before. The focus was on my inherent worth as a creature God had created because it was important to God that I exist. What a wonderful approach to my understanding of self-worth and my spirituality! I thought. What a difference from the perpetual vision of self-abasement that had been drummed into my psyche during my youth!

My meditation was interrupted by a tiny gray hummingbird flying from behind the shelter and hovering momentarily over the table before disappearing behind a small stand of pines at the edge of the clearing. I continued to hear the humming periodically and hoped the bird would return. It didn't, and eventually the forest became quiet again. I tried to return to the level of concentration I had achieved before the bird arrived, but I was unable to get back on track.

I awoke to a wonderful 3rd of August. The weather was again sunny and the temperature pleasantly cool higher on the ridges. Initially, the Trail was easy but became increasingly steeper and more difficult the closer it came to Chestnut Ridge. It passed through a rock-strewn open forest, climbed a ledge-infested ridge, and crossed a giant ridgetop meadow that stretched for what seemed to be several miles, but in reality was probably only a couple of thousand yards.

Near the middle of the meadow, a spring-fed pond sat in a slight depression like a sparkling diamond in green velvet. Aquatic plants grew in abundance along it banks, and in the long grass to the high side of the pond, a boxed spring overflowed with pure cold water which ran into the pond. I stopped to fill my canteens and drank several draughts, letting the cold liquid soothe my heated throat while the timeless beauty of the ridge soothed my soul.

The ridgetop was awash in bright sunshine except for occasional clouds which drifted overhead, dragging with them the shadows that intermittently covered the ridge. The only sound was that of nature, a harmonious blend of the sounds of life about the pond that conjured thoughts of a supreme peace. Gusts of wind swept toward the summit, thatching the water's

Spring-fed pond on summit of Chestnut Ridge.

Shelter on Chestnut Ridge.

surface with broad patches of wavelets that sparkled with dancing points of sunlight. I followed the progress of the gusts after they left the pond by watching the tall grass bending in waves that seemed to roll across the undulations up the ridge.

In the distance lay the crumpled forms of mountains folded and bent, their shapes softened by vegetation and the blue haze that hid their lower elevations. Closer by, scattered old, gray logs and grotesque dead limbs lay in meager piles or singly like bleached skeletons in the lush young grass.

I stopped at the stone shelter on Chestnut Knob for lunch and relaxed in the breeze and the sunshine. I even napped for a few minutes after lunch. It was peaceful lying in the sun, listening to the wind and the hum of life in the summer field. Before leaving, I took a minute to admire one of the treasures of Chestnut Knob: a spectacular view of an isolated agricultural valley called Burkes Garden, which lay at the foot of Chestnut Ridge. It was quite large, about seven miles across, I guessed, and was completely surrounded by mountains, except for a narrow opening to the north.

I could imagine the scene being painted by some 18th century landscape artist from the old romantic school. The patchwork of colors from the roofs of the houses and barns and the coordinated shades of green from the various fields and the mountains, along with the symmetry of the roads inspired a feeling of nostalgia for a bygone era when I imagined man and nature existed in perfect harmony.

After Chestnut Knob, the Trail followed the crest of Garden Mountain for several miles along a spine of rock, actually a break in the earth's crust frozen in time since the age when the mountains were formed. The rock remained at a slanted level, presenting a knife-edge configuration to the hiker. It actually lay in a slant from south to north. Approaches to the spine from the south were somewhat less precipitous than the abrupt dropoffs to the north. The Trail traced the knife edge. Several times during the afternoon, I walked on the edge of cliffs 20 or more feet high. It was not scary, but it made for interesting and cautious hiking.

As I approached the point where Virginia Route 623 crossed the mountain, I thought I heard the sound of children in the distance. They were barely audible at first; then as I came closer to the road, the sounds grew louder. It was the sound of children at play.

Ridge-crest trail along Garden Mountain.

Their shrieks and excited laughter accompanied me as I picked my way down from the ridge crest to the saddle. When they saw me, they became quiet as did the adults with them.

John Blessing, who was working over a small barbecue grill, stopped and watched with curiosity as I approached. "Hi," he said. "Looks like you're just in time for supper." He was a slender man, a little taller than I, with dark hair and a soft smile that contained curiosity and the offer of friendship.

After looking into his eyes, it was clear the invitation was an open and spontaneous gesture which reminded me of the invitation from George Baty at Roan Mountain. It was 4:30 p.m., and I was bone-weary from walking 15 miles over some very difficult terrain. The decision to accept John's offer was an easy one to make.

Along with John and Jane Blessing and their two children, I also met Dick and Louise Rector from Romeoville, Illinois, who were visiting the Blessings. John Blessing was a truck driver by trade, and Dick Rector was a dispatcher for a trucking firm in Romeoville, so that was how they came to know each other. The Rectors had come to southern Virginia to see if they might like to relocate there. Although the connection had not been mentioned, I was sure John Blessing had probably been so convincing in his description of the beauty of Virginia that the Rectors felt they at least needed to visit.

John and Jane Blessing were uncomplicated, strongly religious, young country people, devoted to each other and to their children. A strong streak of independence showed through their hospitality and their relationship with the Rectors. John was clearly at home in the mountains. He was self-reliant but generous with his family and his guests. He made sure that I got enough to eat, that social politeness on my part didn't result in my leaving hungry. "I've done lots of hunting in these mountains," he said. "I know how hungry I got walkin' around these hills all day. Have another hamburger! Have some more potato chips!"

I ate three large deluxe hamburgers, drank two large Pepsi Colas and probably ate half a large bag of potato chips. When I finished, he offered me a very large piece of the best chocolate cake I could remember eating, and when I finished that, he shoved another equally large piece under my nose. I ate it, too. Then, as if that weren't enough, he stuck two Nestle's Chunky Chocolate Squares in my hand to "tide me over."

I talked with the Blessings and the Rectors for about an hour after eating, told them about my background, why I was on the Trail, and how it had become a spiritual experience for me. I related the incident with the bear at Doc's Knob shelter in the Smokies and other bits of my experiences on the Trail. They all listened attentively, asking questions now and again. After I ran out of stories, we exchanged addresses, and I departed.

I was on Cloud Nine all the way from Route 623 to Jenkins shelter. I was sure my meeting with the Blessings and Rectors had been another instance of Divine intercession. I climbed into my sleeping bag, after making a few notes in my journal, and tried to review the events of the day to put things into perspective. In trying to meditate, I laid my head down and that was the last thing I remembered. I had hiked 19.9 miles for the day, and to say I was exhausted was an understatement.

CHAPTER 18

Bastian, Virginia, to Pearisburg, Virginia

A card posted on the Jenkins shelter wall contained instructions on how to contact Ron Pauley (Dr. Frog) for a ride from the Trail into Bastian or Bland. After breakfast, I copied the information for use later in the day when I reached the point where the Trail crossed U.S. Routes 21 and 52.

The weather was warm and humid, but the Trail remained on the ridges and the hiking was not difficult. I made good time and arrived at U.S. Routes 21 and 52 by the middle of the afternoon. Following the instructions from the card, and fully expecting a sure ride into town, I marched up to a small wood frame house and rapped sharply on the door.

Mr. Morehouse answered the door and informed me that Mr. Pauley was out of town. (Mr. Pauley worked in the school superintendent's office and was busy making preparations for the new school year.) Clearly, there was to be no easy ride into town, and I headed down the road on foot. Although walking the one and eight-tenth miles of paved road down the mountain was easy, it seemed to take a long time to reach Bastian and the Long's Corner Diner.

Several people sitting on wooden benches in front of the diner watched intently as I approached. When I came to within about 20 yards of the entrance, the door burst open and a young boy about five or six years old raced out, looked me over, then ran back inside.

I stopped beside an old high-backed wooden bench and a soft drink machine and removed my pack. No sooner had it hit the floor, than the door burst open again, and I was loudly greeted by a little old lady smiling broadly in welcome and exclaiming gleefully, "You're a hiker!" The boy, his eyes wide with

82-year-old Kate Childress in front of Long's Corner Diner.

admiration, peeked at me from behind her dress. "We like hikers!" she exclaimed. "All hikers are good people. We ain't met a bad'n yet!"

I introduced myself and indicated that I didn't intend to change her opinion about hikers. Kate Childress, Jan Long's 82-year-old mother, fairly dragged me inside to show me the corner of the diner which served as a "hikers' shrine" with letters and mementos, cards and old Trail registers. "You can see we like hikers!" she said. "We ain't never met a bad'n yet."

Kate was a happy person. She exuded a joy and enthusiasm for life that one usually associates with children. It was most noticeable later that evening when she joined two other women on the front porch of the diner in front of three large brown paper shopping bags full of freshly picked green beans.

The women talked excitedly and laughed with vigor while snapping beans, making the work seem like entertainment.

As soon as I arrived, Kate took me under her wing to make sure I was properly cared for. Even while preparing supper, she came out of the kitchen periodically to check on me and to inquire if I needed anything, each time saying how happy they were to have a hiker staying for dinner "cause hikers is fine folks."

The food was really home cooking that demanded at least a second helping. It was a simple meal: hamburger steak, baked beans, coleslaw, potato salad and freshly baked corn bread. Jan Long knew from experience about hikers and their appetites and served me very generous portions. When I finished, she offered me more of everything. "Sure you won't have another hamburger steak? How about potato salad? Corn bread?"

Clearly, I was a guest more than a customer, and Jan was more interested in my welfare than the bill. When I finished a second helping of potato salad and corn bread, she suggested I try a pint of Meadowgold's Four Berry Ice Cream. "It's some of the best ice cream you can get," she said, nodding her head in authority.

Jan was clearly the person in charge of the diner. She carried the responsibility with poise and grace, exhibiting a lowkey leadership in running the operation, getting results by example and the common sense approach in dealing with others. Her demeanor was more reserved than her mother's, but there was the same sparkle in her eye, and she brought the same enthusiasm to her work.

Levi Long, Jan's husband, arrived in his pickup truck at about 6:30 p.m. after a long drive from a construction site where he worked. As soon as he drove up, Kate grabbed me by the hand and tugged me outside like a new toy or a prize she wanted to show off. I received the same warm reception from Levi that I had received from the others.

During the ensuing conversation, I learned that he had helped construct the Trail around Bastian. I asked about the condition and difficulty of the section north of Bastian.

"It's just like what you came over," he responded.

That was good news. I had visions of increasing my daily mileage. Although I had hiked 12 miles for the day, I had not really pushed myself and estimated that with a similar effort the next day, I could probably make the Wapiti shelter by nightfall. That was 23 miles, but I was in very good condition now, and the terrain was not too difficult. Then I remembered my old admonition, "Do what your body will allow!"

About 7:30, Kate came out of the kitchen carrying a walking cane and announced that it was time to "go home and go to bed." She started diagonally across the wide intersection in front of the diner toward an old frame house that I had passed on my way into town. A pig sty containing a huge hog was attached to the side of the house, and I suspected that at one time the house had probably stood by itself until the town grew up around it. A wide assortment of old, worn possessions and equipment cluttered the yard and the porch, and I wondered how many antique treasures might be hidden among the jumble.

I watched as Kate, in her faded blue striped cotton dress, her white-haired head bobbing, her beige stockinged legs battling the ravages of age, marched purposefully, if slowly, over the rough macadam and dirt and started tentatively up the steps of the porch. It occurred to me that I was seeing the first indication she had shown all afternoon of her advancing age.

The Longs owned a small cabin just out of town on a hillside overlooking the Bastian Valley, and after supper, Levi gave me a lift there to spend the night. Just before turning up the cabin driveway, we passed an old pickup truck parked beside the road where a small, wizened man was working on what appeared to be a driveway. "You might want to talk to that fellow," said Levi as we passed. "Irvan Shrader's his name. He's quite a story. You ought to see his house. The whole thing is built underground."

I quickly arranged my gear for the night and headed back down the hill to talk to Irvan Shrader. I stopped on the far side of the road for a minute to watch the small, thin, balding man, obviously wracked with pain, lifting and heaving 50-pound rocks into place. Jan later told me that he ate only soft food since it was all he could chew and digest, and I thought that may have been why he was so thin. She said that when he came to the diner, she barely cooked his hamburger, that it was basically heated raw meat. He walked in a stooped manner and a growth of some sort to the right groin area was covered by his trousers. His movements suggested constant pain, but his work continued, regardless, throughout the day and on into the evening.

Mr. Shrader noticed me when I started across the road. I stopped beside his pickup. He hobbled across the rocks to join me. "It looks like you're building a driveway. I imagine it's a mean bit of work trying to manhandle those rocks," I said, trying to initiate a conversation.

Mr. Shrader only nodded his head, but his eyes remained on me.

"How did you come by all those boulders?" I asked. "You must have ten tons at least!"

"I figure probably twice that," he corrected. "I get 'em from farmers who've cleared 'em from their fields. They're happy to be rid of 'em."

"You carry them in your truck?" I queried, wondering if the beat-up old truck could handle the load.

"Yep. Can't carry more'n three or four big 'uns at a time, though."

To my questions, Mr. Shrader responded warily at first, but the more we talked, the more relaxed he became, and the words flowed more easily. He didn't smile one time during our conversation, but his tone of voice was soft until he talked about the government and his family. Then it became somewhat harsh and the language of his responses was peppered with distrust and anger.

"Where did you get the plans for your house?" I asked.

He pointed to his head. "Right here. Ain't nothing on paper. This house can't be duplicated."

"What gave you the idea to build it?"

"To show everybody it could be done. To be an example to people what they can do, if they've a mind to."

"You've done it all yourself," I phrased it as a statement, but it was really a question.

"I done it all myself! Don't want no help! Just want people to leave me alone! I do just fine!" In a measured way, his answer was emphatic.

"How about your family? Do they help?"

"Kin folk!" he snorted. His voice lost its gentle quality. "They're all against me. Even my sons. They all know enough to stay away from me. They better stay away, if they know what's good for 'em," he said darkly.

"I'm absolutely flabbergasted at what you've done!" I exclaimed. "You have any idea how much money you have invested in the place or what it might be worth when you finish?" I sensed immediately that I had struck a raw nerve and regretted the awkward way I had asked the question.

Mr. Shrader's eyes narrowed, and he looked directly into my eyes like he wanted to be sure I understood. "Ain't interested in that," he said. "That's one of the problems! Everybody's out for money. One of the reasons I built this house is to show people that you don't need a lot of money to build a house. The government and big business want you to think you need 'em to get along, that you need 'em for money to build you a house. They ain't out there to help you. They're out there to skin the little feller. I got no use for any of 'em. All they want is to get rich by skinnin' the workin' man. They're in cahoots, government and business are, and I don't trust 'em for one minute."

We went inside the house, and he showed me how he had employed the split-level concept to realize his three-story vision. The walls and built-in furniture showed detailed and artful workmanship. He had crafted wood inlay patterns into the woodwork: stairs, door frames and wood paneling in various parts of the house. In addition to the wood inlays, he also had created patterns with colorful tile mosaics worked into some handmade furniture and walls. He pointed proudly to a small ceramic tile coffee table which he had donated to the local high school 4-H Club for a raffle prize to help raise money for a club outing. The legs and support members were polished wood as was the table top frame which contained the ceramic tile pattern. The tiles, mostly blue, red and orange, formed angular geometric figures.

I was still so astounded at what I was seeing that I didn't think to ask how it was that the table was still in his possession, if someone had already won it. "Where did you learn how to do this?" I asked. "You go to a school or take a course?"

"Just did it."

"You mean you just up and did it, no schooling or training?" I shook my head in amazement.

"Yep!"

"You must have worked at some of this when you were younger!" I said.

"You pick up things here and there, learn how to do certain things. I learned some of it in different jobs I've had. But I never had no formal schoolin'. Just odd jobs."

We went outside again, weaving through a jumble of tools and equipment on the bottom floor of his house and past a small steel cot with a dirty blanket and even dirtier pillow. "That's where I sleep. Stay here all the time. That way I don't waste time runnin' back and forth."

In the yard, he explained we were standing in the middle of the garage site. I thought his garage would have one of the most beautiful views in the world. It faced down the valley, overlooking a large meadow. To the rear of the meadow was a mountain stream and along it grew a line of bushes and pine trees; a picture of tranquillity in the fading twilight.

"You sure have some pretty country!" I observed, pointing out over the view.

"This is some of the prettiest land in God's creation," he nodded. "Don't see how people can spoil it like they have. It's a sin the way they've trashed the country here." He waved his arm across the expanse of hills in the background.

I knew what he was talking about. The forest service road that the AT followed high along the ridge above the town was a nightmare of trash and litter. For about half a mile along the road could be seen what looked like the village dump, spreading hundreds of yards down the mountainside. It was covered with every type of trash imaginable from old dead washing machines and refrigerators to old dead garbage cans and old dead everything in between. It would take a heroic effort to return it to its natural state.

I mentioned that he appeared to be in pain and asked how it affected his work.

"I been at this goin' on five years now," he told me. "I think of it as doin' the Lord's work. The Lord is keeping me alive to finish this work. When it's done, I'll be called."

Later, as I lay in my sleeping bag, I thought about Irvan Shrader and his dream. What a wonderful land America was, to make a place for a man like Irvan Shrader. In another land or another time, he would probably already be dead for lack of the opportunity to imagine possibilities or pursue dreams.

Pap Childress, Jan's 87-year-old father, was pressed into service the next morning to bring me back to the Trail. I didn't know who he was at first and only noticed him because he looked very thin in the way very old people do.

He was sitting at one of the dining room tables, drinking coffee and smoking a cigarette. A baseball cap with a Caterpillar logo was propped on the back of his white-haired head and too much trouser material draped from his rail-thin ankle.

After breakfast, when the time came to get me back to the Trail, Jan called to him to get his truck going, that he needed to take the hiker to the Trail. But Pap couldn't hear well; he didn't respond at first. Jan called out again.

Outside, Pap stopped in front of a pickup truck that appeared to be nearly as old as he was and motioned for me to throw my pack in the rear. It was a cool-starting machine, and Pap raced the motor to warm it up. Then before allowing it to return to its normal idle speed, he tried to engage the gear lever in reverse. The gears grated loudly until they meshed, and he let out the clutch pedal too quickly; the pickup lurched backwards, snapping both our heads forward. The motor coughed, sputtered and died, and we came up short against the back of the seats.

I looked over at Pap, expecting to see some reaction like laughter or irritation. Pap never blinked an eye. He was all business as he tried again to start the motor.

Unfortunately, he had neglected to shift the transmission out of reverse gear. As soon as he turned the ignition switch, the truck again bolted to the rear.

I looked over at him again. Still no response. I started to laugh, but with Pap so obviously serious, I held back.

Finally, he shifted into neutral and tried again to start the motor. All the time I watched, Pap's expression never changed.

The third time was a charm, and the motor roared to life. This time Pap waited until the engine slowed to an idle before engaging the gear in reverse, and we backed onto the road in short hops as he tried to coordinate the clutch and the gas pedal. After being jerked back and forth in the seat from the hops, I questioned if I should stay with Pap and his truck or whether I should just accept it as an act of fate and head up the mountain on foot. At least I knew I could make it on foot. I wasn't sure about the outcome if I rode with Pap.

I looked over at Pap again. This time he was looking at me. He smiled faintly, then turned his attention back to the truck with a steely-eyed determination. I decided to go along for the ride, mostly to see what happened.

The starting procedure was repeated, and we eventually made it about a 100 yards to the stop sign on Route 52. He approached the road junction with such speed that I was afraid he wasn't going to stop. Then at the very last moment, he slammed on the brakes, and we ground to a halt.

Pap never said a word during the entire episode and only nodded when I asked if the pickup belonged to him. He tried two times to get the thing in motion at the stop sign. The motor died both times, the truck rolling backwards down the slight incline. It occurred to me in a comical way that we were in a struggle and at that moment were losing ground. On the third try, we made it and hit the stop sign like they do at the Indy — with a running start. He didn't look right or left, and we shot out into the road. Luckily, no cars were coming and off we went.

I looked over at Pap periodically, when we weren't headed for a drop-off or an embankment, and watched the smoke from his cigarette curling up his face and into his eyes. At no time during the ride up the mountain did the cigarette leave his mouth.

After shifting into third gear near the ridge crest, however, he leaned back in the seat in a display of confidence and only then did he take the cigarette from his mouth, once to take a big puff and once to throw the finished butt out the window.

Pap coasted in neutral the three-fourths mile from the ridge crest to the Trail, using only the brake to control the speed. The acrid smell of burning brake linings filled the cab for the last few hundred yards as we neared the bottom of the gap. I thanked him very much for his help and his family's hospitality, then watched a rerun of the start of our drive up the hill. He raced the motor before engaging the clutch again, and it nearly jerked his head off when it took hold. He seemed incapable of coordinating the movements of the clutch with the accelerator, and the truck bolted forward in spurts as he eased up and pressed the gas to compensate for the reaction of the motor. Finally, it bolted forward one last time and headed smoothly up the hill with Pap still holding onto the steering wheel, as if it were the mane of a bucking bronc. After the battle between man and machine was over and Pap had disappeared, I signed Levi's Trail register and started up the mountain.

I thought about the ride with Pap as I climbed toward the crest of another Brushy Mountain. Levi had told me that Pap was a "real mountain man" who had spent his entire life in the mountains hunting, fishing and gathering what the forests offered. I guessed that accounted for his quiet way. Then I reconsidered. Maybe it was the result of being married to Kate. She was so full of life and vitality that she probably talked enough for both of them. Whatever it was, I admired the old man. He was clearly the product of a bygone era, probably one of the last survivors of a breed of men for whom survival was a challenge. Clearly, he was uncomfortable with the mechanization of modern man, but what was of even greater significance was that he refused to be dominated by it. At age 87, he could easily have decided to become an observer for the remainder of his life. But Pap was a different man. As long as there was life, there was challenge, and I think he relished that.

I could see again the steely determination in his face as he concentrated on mastering the machinery of an age that he probably understood little about. But he surely was not going to sit on the sideline, not while there was a challenge to be met!

Despite my initial intentions, it soon became clear that Wapiti shelter was just too far. I opted to stay at Jenny Knob shelter, ten miles closer. When I reached Jenny Knob shelter, however, I found the spring was dry. Since I was out of water, I decided to hike on to Lickskillet Hollow and walk Virginia Route 608 into Crandon, Virginia, which lay about a mile to the east. It was a good decision.

In Crandon, I set up camp on the lawn directly behind a church as advised in the *Philosopher's Guide*, then headed across the street to a small general store where I bought some beer to drink with my supper and filled my water bag from the tap at the rear of the store.

After supper, when I climbed into my sleeping bag, I was content. I was also glad I did not stay at the Wapiti shelter; it was the place where a thru-hiking couple from Maine had been murdered by an unemployed tree surgeon several summers before. Staying there would have felt spooky!

The next day I headed down Route 42 to Kimberling Creek where it was intersected by the AT five miles away. I didn't want to retrace the one and one-fourth miles back toward the AT and climb the mountain, only to reach a point which I could much more easily reach by roadwalking.

I excited every dog along the valley for miles, even those in farms up on the hillsides or valleys beyond the next rise. I "made their day." From houses beside the road came dogs of every size and breed, woofing and barking with varying degrees of intensity. Some, I was glad to see, were chained; others were big fakers, charging out of their yards or dog houses or wherever they had been sleeping, acting as though they intended to tear me to shreds. They would stop at the edge of the road and bark me off their territory or out of sight. Some, after rushing at me barking shrilly, simply stopped and watched me go; others reduced the volume of their barks and woofed only occasionally. Some seemed to go through the motions of being fierce guardians of their master's homes. They barked for short periods, then looked back towards the house, as if waiting for instructions on what to do next. All dogs invariably came up short when I raised my hiking stick which proved to be a formidable dog intimidator.

The only times I sensed any danger was when there were two dogs. A lone dog always backed off, but two dogs reinforced each other, appearing very much like people in that respect.

After crossing Kimberling Creek, the Trail turned north along Route 606 and paralleled the creek for about half a mile before turning into the forest to climb yet another ridge of Brushy Mountain. About 30 minutes later, I came to the blue-blazed trail to Dismal Creek Falls and went exploring.

Dismal Creek Falls was anything but what the name implied. It was a bright, cool stream that cascaded over a broad rock shelf and dropped into a sparkling clear pool at the base. Near the sides of the falls, the rocks were heaped in a jumble where they had been forced by the stream, but in the center the rock ledge had been worn smooth and, during times of low water, as was now the case, was easily traversable on foot.

An aura of ancient wilderness surrounded the falls. On the near bank, the forest consisted mainly of large pine and hemlock trees, and the forest floor was covered with a comfortable-looking carpet of pine and hemlock needles and moss. Traces of campfires seemed out of place, and I could imagine the pristine beauty of a former time. It had a garden-like atmosphere, a personal Eden, comfortable with time and worn smooth from tender Divine care. The rounded rocks, the soft-looking moss, and the slow speed of the stream gliding through the forest suggested tranquillity rather than splendor.

I drank in the solitude, the peace that pervaded the air. It was not impressive in terms of spectacular beauty, only in terms of its closeness with the spirit, a timeless haunting quality that made a person want to build a cabin on the banks and live an idyllic life surrounded by nature in its most appealing form. If I had been a boy, I would surely have gone for a swim in the pool at the base of the falls and rested on the banks or fished for trout. If I had been a boy, I might still be there. Oh, how I wish I was a boy again, I thought as I rose to continue back to the Trail.

After leaving the falls, the Trail followed Dismal Creek for several miles coming eventually to a small man-made pond. I left the Trail where it contoured the ridge below the pond's earthen retaining wall and climbed the slanting embankment for a look. Two deer, a doe and her fawn, were drinking from the water's edge about 30 yards away. The fawn was almost as large as its mother. Had it not been for the spots still clearly evident on its coat, I would have thought it was at least a yearling.

Both animals had their noses to the water as I popped over the edge of the retaining wall. As soon as I saw them, I froze; the doe jerked her head into the air. She looked right at me, then moved her head at different angles to get a better view. She lifted her nose further into the air, wiggling it as she tried to get a scent. Evidently satisfied that there as no danger, she returned to drinking from the pond. As soon as she put her head back down to the water a slight breeze carried my scent toward her.

Almost dry Dismal Creek Falls.

Immediately, she bolted from the pond with the fawn right behind her.

Shortly after beginning the climb out of Dismal Creek Valley, I heard thunder in the distance. It sounded ominous. When I realized it was coming closer, I began to get nervous. Remembering my experience in the Nantahalas, I became intensely alert to the possibilities of shelter along the Trail but none was in the offing. My premonition was accurate. About an hour later, just before I reached the ridge crest, the storm caught up with me. It began slowly with a quickening of the breeze and a slight rain sprinkle at first. Then the wind became stronger, followed by a series of lightning strikes and a torrent of water. With the first crack of lightning, I removed my ensolite sleeping pad from my pack and placed it about 20 yards away in an area devoid of any large trees and covered myself with the rainfly from my tent.

The lightning crashed all along the ridge, sometimes above me, sometimes below. Several times the explosions erupted so closely that I could feel the shock waves, and my ears ached afterward. The rainfly was almost useless. I got soaked immediately and cold a second later. I realized as I lay there, that I truly had gained some peace, or at least a measure of spiritual confidence. I was not nearly as concerned as I had been during the electrical storm I had experienced while climbing out of the Nantahala Gorge. I remained calm, and although I was aware of the danger, I was very detached and only the explosions of the nearby lightning strikes caused fleeting, involuntary surges of fear.

The storm lasted about 45 minutes, then left as quickly as it had come, with the rain diminishing as it moved away. A second storm hit the ridge almost as soon as the first storm passed. There was more thunder and more rain, but it was a high storm and presented no danger from lightning, only discomfort. I continued in the rain toward Docs Knob shelter.

Long before I reached the shelter, I had a premonition that people were there, and I wondered what they would be like. It was uncanny because I thought in terms of a couple. As I approached the side wall of the shelter, sure enough, I saw two walking sticks leaning against it and two red pack covers hanging from the main rafter beams in front.

Dr. Dan Cruse and Dr. Cathy Morris from Coral Gables, Florida, were spending part of their summer vacation hiking the AT. Dan, an Assistant Professor of Psychology at Miami University, was of medium height and build with a slight stomach paunch, fair complexion, thin reddish-blond hair and wire-rimmed glasses that framed his smiling blue eyes. Cathy, Director of Research at Miami-Dade Community College, had a very attractive figure and long curly brown hair, and appeared much younger than Dan.

We exchanged the usual Trail information, where we came from, how we came to be on the Trail, where we started, our planned destination, and so on. We talked about the thunderstorm and how scary it had been, and Cathy told me they had found shelter in a picnic ground privy where they waited until the lightning passed.

We laughed at how privies had all sorts of uses. We also talked a little about our backgrounds and jobs, and, of course, they were interested in how I found the time to be thru-hiking the Trail. Dan asked about my job in Germany which I explained as being basically that of a city manager for a small community. I tried to give Dan and Cathy a feel for the scope of the responsibilities it entailed.

"Now that you've tried to impress us, what did you really do," asked Dan.

His facial expression still retained the traces of smile, but the friendliness had disappeared from his eyes and the confrontational tone of his voice was discomforting. The remark caught me unprepared, and I replied that I had just told him what I did. I was very tired and not in a mood for ego games. To be impressed or unimpressed was his choice, and I couldn't have cared less. I thought about saying that in about those terms but decided to back off. I had to spend the night in the shelter with them and wanted only peace and quiet.

Dan then initiated a political discussion, "I assume you're a Reagan fan."

"Most of the time," I replied.

"I'm a Carter man," he said in a baiting way, as if he expected me to respond. "Carter was a great President."

I decided to keep the ball in his court. "How do you come to that conclusion?" I asked. "I've heard some people say just the opposite."

"Because he's truly a decent human being."

"I have no doubts that he's a decent human being, but that doesn't necessarily qualify one as a great President. I know a great many decent human beings who would make lousy Presidents." Score one for me, I thought, as I said it.

Dan "humphed" once but didn't reply, and the moment passed when Cathy changed the subject by asking if I planned to spend any time in Pearisburg. Cathy was a bright, happy person who appeared to be genuinely interested in me and what I was doing. That may have irritated Dan. She interjected herself into the conversation occasionally, asking questions about the hike, and guiding the discussion away from the emotional pitfalls toward which Dan seemed to be heading.

They had taken over the entire shelter to dry out their equipment after the rain storm, which left no room for me.

"Why don't you move that stuff outta there so he has a place to lay out his gear?" Cathy said to Dan. Dan didn't exactly grumble, but seemed displeased at the way she addressed him. Then she suggested he offer me a sip of whiskey or peppermint schnapps.

I opted for the schnapps, thinking that Dan might have had one sip too many from his whiskey flask. I realized that mentally I was much more serene now than when I had first come on the Trail. I felt much greater self-confidence which I attrib-

uted to the improvement of my spiritual confidence. At an earlier time, I would have argued with Dan Cruse and probably
become embroiled in a nasty confrontation. But now I remained
at an intellectual level, aloof, polite, detached, and refused to be
drawn into the wrench of an emotional confrontation. Nevertheless, I was disappointed at the turn of events, and I did not
sleep soundly despite having hiked 18.8 miles for the day.
Thankfully, it was only 7.7 miles from Docs Knob shelter to
Pearisburg. The next morning, I hiked slowly, taking time to
enjoy the views of the New River Valley from Angels Rest and
View Rock.

CHAPTER 19

The Holy Family Hospice

The Holy Family Hospice in Pearisburg is probably the best organized, best maintained hostel on the Trail. It was smaller and more compact than "The Place" in Damascus but was decorated with interesting and useful items like lanterns and farm implements and included a large, accurate scale. (I weighed 170 pounds, 20 pounds less than when I started my hike.) It also offered more amenities like a kitchen stove and an extensive collection of books that filled the shelves of a sunken brick-lined library by the front entrance.

The old gray, board building sat on a small, grassy knoll behind the church rectory in the shade of several massive oak trees. The ground fell off to either side of the hostel; on the left, to a large fallow field belonging to a nearby dairy farm, and on the right, about 100 yards down a gentle grass slope, to a small cemetery with a sparse collection of very old grave stones nestled in a stand of mature trees.

No one was at the hostel when I arrived; so I went exploring, looking to inform someone that I planned to spend the night. Initially, I went to the church, which was empty, then across a sheltered walkway to a large meeting hall, which also was empty, so I headed for the rectory. The long, dormitory-style building with individual rooms on either side of a central passageway seemed deserted, but I knocked on a couple of doors anyway. The sound of my knocking fractured the oppressive silence, and I felt uncomfortably like an intruder. No one answered, but as I turned to go back to the hostel, the barely audible sound of music came wafting down the corridor. I followed the sound until I identified the room from where it came and rapped on the door. "It's not locked," said a voice from inside.

Still unsure, I cautiously opened the door to a room in total teenage disarray. Pictures of rock stars were taped to the walls, and a pile of clothes on the floor beside a messy bed looked like someone had emptied a dirty clothes hamper on the floor. Personal items were strewn about; books cluttered the paper-stacked desk and in the corner a pile of cassettes sat in front of a cassette player that was wailing at something less than full blast but nonetheless made hearing difficult.

A boy, slouched in a chair with a book in his lap, looked up at me with a quizzical expression that conveyed some interest and a hint of annoyance. He didn't say anything, preferring to let me take the initiative.

"Hi! I'm Jan Curran," I said cheerily. "I'm hiking the AT, and I plan to stay for the night. Thought I'd come over and check in. How do I do that?"

"Jim's not here. He'll be back later this afternoon. You can come back then." He looked down at his book, intending to end the conversation.

"Who's Jim?" I inquired.

"The priest, Jim MacGee," he replied without bothering to look up from his book.

A teenager living in a Catholic Church was a rarity in my experience and twitched my curiosity. "You live here?" I asked clumsily.

"Yeah, me and four other guys. Jim's our father. I mean he's our foster father."

"When Father MacGee gets back, would you tell him I'm at the hostel and I'd like to stay for the night?"

The boy nodded his head and went back to his book.

While waiting for Father MacGee to return, I reviewed the *Trail Guide* and maps for the section of the Trail after Pearisburg and made an interesting discovery. The Trail headed north after crossing the bridge over New River, climbed for about two miles to the ridge crest of Peters Mountain which it followed for about ten miles to the northeast, then turned abruptly southeast toward Catawba, Virginia. The Trail made a giant arc around Pearisburg, which was ideally suited to day-hiking in sections, if I could get transportation to and from points where the Trail crossed the roads. That meant increased speed and mileage with a lot less exertion, because I would be returning to the hostel each night and didn't need to carry my sleeping gear, tent and food. It was an exciting prospect, and I couldn't wait to talk to

Father MacGee about it.

The Reverend Jim MacGee, a member of the order "Oblites of Mary," came to the hostel about an hour later and introduced himself. I had expected to see a cleric in a black suit or at least black trousers and a roman collar. Jim wore a casual short-sleeved shirt and khaki slacks, and at first I thought he might be the hostel caretaker, that is, until he began to talk, and it was clear that he was a man who liked to take charge.

Jim radiated energy. He was a dynamo and seemed to be constantly in motion. Even when sitting, he gave the impression of being in action. He appeared constantly pressed for time, since so much in the world needed to be tended and fixed. That isn't to say that Jim MacGee was short on conversation or curt. He wasn't. He was very considerate and open and exhibited an unusual concern for people which I was sure was the basis for adopting his five teenage sons. Still, it was clear that he had a mission in life that demanded constant attention.

I described my day-hiking plan and asked if he knew anyone who could provide transportation to and from the Trail. He gave me the names of a couple of men, then as an afterthought said his son Tony could do it. Tony, who was starting college in the fall, needed money and had a car. Jim thought it was a good opportunity for him to make a few extra dollars. "I'll send Tony over after he gets home from work tonight," Jim said. "Should be about 5 o'clock."

I waited until 5:15 p.m. for Tony to show. When he didn't appear, I went looking. A young man working under the hood of an old blue Plymouth parked in the rectory parking lot seemed like a good place to start my search. He looked up as I approached, then returned his attention to the car. He was a short, slender boy, about 18 or 19, I guessed, with a swarthy complexion and short, neatly trimmed hair. "Hi, I'm Jan Curran," I announced.

"Hello!" he replied, not bothering to look up.

"You're Tony. Right?"

He nodded.

"I talked with Jim MacGee today, and he suggested we might be able to work out a deal where you could take me to the Trail and . . . "

"Can't talk now! I'm supposed to pick up my date and some kids to go to a concert in Roanoke, and my car is broke." Actually, the generator mounting bracket was broken, and the generator could not be adjusted so the fan belt could turn the pulley. Tony had connected a wire coat hanger from the side of the engine compartment wall to the generator and was attempting to pull it sufficiently tight so that the fan belt would turn the generator pulley.

"You keep working," I said. "I'll talk." I explained my plan, saying I needed his services for only four days and that I would pay for the gas and also 20 cents per mile. I had calculated the mileage, and it appeared it would cost about 100 dollars, which was more than I wanted to pay, but considering I'd also be helping Tony pay for college, I accepted it as a contribution to a worthy cause.

"I already got a job." Tony looked up this time, shaking his head.

"This will only require a little bit of time at the beginning and the end of the day. What time do you have to be at work?"

"8:30."

"No sweat," I said. "Take me out at 6:30 or 7:00, and you'll have an hour at least to get to work. At night, just come from work to the pick-up point, and I'll be there, or if I'm not, I will be shortly. It shouldn't be more than half an hour by car to the pick-up points."

Tony looked down at the car again without speaking, shook his head like he wasn't sure it would work, and pulled a little harder on the coat hanger.

I pressed on. "Look, this is a chance to pick up an easy 100 bucks. You can use the money. Right? It'll cost you an hour in the morning and an hour in the evening for four days. That's equivalent, time-wise, to one eight-hour day, and you get 100 dollars. What're you makin' now? Maybe 50, maybe 75 bucks. You help me and I help you."

"Well, okay. But I can't take you out in the morning. You'll have to get Jim to do that."

I had the feeling he consented more to get rid of me than agreeing with the plan. "Can you pick me up in the evening?" I thought if I got him to work for me one time and he saw how easy it would work out that he would be convinced.

"Yeah, I can pick you up tomorrow night."

I showed him on the map where the Trail crossed Virginia Route 635, making sure he understood how to get there, then returned to the hostel. I was pleased with my efforts at having prevailed, but it was mixed with the disquieting feeling one gets from dealing with a key player who hasn't fully committed himself to the effort.

My plan was for Tony to pick me up at Route 635 the next night, then drop me off at the same place the following morning. From there, I would walk to Virginia Route 42, 18 miles away, where he would pick me up that night and drop me off again the following morning. We would repeat the process at Virginia Route 620 after 17.7 miles and Virginia Route 779 after 17.3 miles. He was to drop me off at Route 779 on the morning of the fifth day with full pack and that would end it. It seemed simple enough, but as I had learned from experience, the real test lay in the execution.

After supper, I sat in the kitchen sipping a cold beer that I had bought on the way to the hostel and reviewed the events of the day. I was pleased with my plan for day-hiking the Trail and of being able to enlist Tony's help.

As I basked in my alcoholic glow of self-satisfaction, the front door flew open with a bang and John Fox came hobbling in followed by a young woman. John was a mess. He was wearing only a pair of hiking shorts and boots, and his face, chest, arms and legs were streaked from sweat and dirt. He grimaced in pain as he limped across the room to sit on a bench across from me. The woman followed, attempting to support him as he tried to negotiate the short distance from the door to the bench and then sat beside him. She was a small woman and next to John seemed almost dwarf-like in comparison. It was comical, in a way, as she tried to keep up with him and support him at the same time.

John introduced Julie and explained that she had "saved his life" when she picked him up at Kimberling Creek where he was hitchhiking after injuring his knee on Brushy Mountain.

Julie wore a plaid blouse, jeans and jogging shoes. Short brown hair framed her pixie face. She smiled frequently, her blue eyes searching for affirmation. She was a volunteer van driver, supporting a group of people who were hiking sections of the AT in a charity effort to raise money to build homes for needy people. She took her job very seriously and indicated that she had a contact to make on the road at 8:00 a.m. the next morning.

I suspected she was carrying provisions, but later learned she was going to pick up some hikers who were leaving the Trail. She asked if she could spend the night at the hostel. I suggested she talk to the priest; I was only a guest.

Although John told me how he injured his knee and how he met Julie, he didn't once mention anything about Mike Martin.

That aroused my curiosity and I could hardly wait to learn what had happened between them. As soon as the opportunity presented itself, I brought up the subject. "Where's Mike?" I asked.

"We decided to split up. We were arguing all the time, and it was no fun anymore." John shook his head slowly, the regret and disappointment showing clearly on his face and in the tone of his voice. "Groseclose was where it really broke apart. Mike didn't want to hike the Trail anymore. He would have been just as happy to have stayed at Damascus. We hitched from Groseclose into Marion, supposedly to get food and stuff, and do laundry and come back to the Trail. At least that's what I thought, but Mike intended to spend the day there. I was really angry! I made Mike mad since I wouldn't recognize him as being my superior because he was older than I. I'd argue with him about different things because I had as much knowledge in the subject as he did. I wouldn't back down, and he couldn't handle that. He thought that because he was older I had to acknowledge that he was smarter."

Julie stayed at the hostel that night and offered to take me to the Trail in the morning which I gladly accepted. This meant that I wouldn't have to inconvenience Jim MacGee. It was 7:30 a.m. when she dropped me off on the north end of the Shumate bridge. The Trail paralleled the highway for about a mile, traversing mostly unattractive, overgrown and badly littered bottomland before beginning a tough little climb to Peters Mountain.

About eight miles into the hike, I caught up to and passed Dan and Cathy. They stopped for lunch at Symms Gap meadow where we exchanged final farewells, because each of us thought I was sure to outdistance them during my day-hiking period. Even with my heavy pack, I was much faster than they were, and now that I was hiking with a light pack, I was sure to pull even farther ahead.

The ridge crest of Peters Mountain was mostly level with only minor changes in elevation, and I made good time. At Pine Swamp Ridge, the Trail turned south and followed Pine Swamp Branch down to Stoney Creek. Right at the point where the Trail began its descent along Pine Swamp Branch, I found a beautiful white stone arrowhead.

Cathy had been impressed with my black arrowhead and told me she had been trying since she first came on the Trail to find an arrowhead. I decided to give it to her. When I reached the Pine Swamp shelter I put it in an envelope addressed to her and Dan with a note to Cathy to the effect that I was sure she would have found the arrowhead, but that I wanted to make sure no one got it before she did, and so, I picked it up for her. I left the envelope on the stone step base of the shelter where they wouldn't miss it. Cathy told me later that Dan opened the envelope, then immediately handed it to her saying, "Here, it's for you." That's all he said, and he never mentioned it to me later when I hiked with them.

After leaving Pine Swamp Branch shelter, the Trail turned northeast following Stoney Creek which paralleled Virginia Route 635. It was a difficult little stretch because it crossed the lower ridges and intermittent stream beds of Peters Mountain. Some of the ridge arms were very steep, and even with a light pack, the climbing was exhausting.

I followed the creek for several hundred yards and found myself approaching the impact area of a small rifle/pistol target-shooters range. The shooters had chosen to place their targets on the Trail side of the creek where the ridge provided a natural bullet catch. It was not a bad location at all, except for the small detail that the AT ran directly broadside to the line of fire.

As luck would have it, someone was target shooting when I arrived. I approached as close as possible, still within safety limits, and called out to the shooters to hold their fire long enough to allow me to pass. They complied and thoughtfully inquired if anyone was behind me before resuming their target practice.

I quickly reached the pick-up point, after passing a large field about 500 yards further upstream where a motorcycle club was holding a very loud party. I was apprehensive as I approached the pick-up point, fearing that Tony would not be there. But my fears quickly turned to feelings of elation when I saw the car and Tony sitting by the road. He had been waiting less than 15 minutes.

I loaded my pack and hiking stick in the trunk and hopped in the front seat, expecting a quick ride back to the hostel and supper. I was famished. Tony turned the key in the ignition. Nothing! He tried again. Nothing! Again, he tried, pressing harder as he turned the key. Again, nothing happened, not even a sound. "I don't believe it," I moaned. Tony was silent. He tried the ignition several more times, all with the same result, nothing. "You know anything about cars?" I asked.

"A little," he said, slumping back in his seat. "How about you?"

"Probably not more than you," I answered. "But it looks like an electrical problem, dead battery, blown fuse or broken ignition switch."

Tony nodded gravely, got out of the car and opened the hood. He reached into the engine compartment, wiggled some wires and announced that he had identified the problem. "Loose distributor cap," he said as he affixed the cap clamp properly. "That ought to fix it."

I couldn't help myself. "Distributor caps don't have anything to do with the starter motor."

Tony climbed back behind the steering wheel, convinced he had found the problem and turned the ignition. His face visibly sagged when nothing happened. "Jeeze!" was all he said.

"What are we going to do now? You know anyone to call?" I asked.

Tony shrugged his shoulders.

I continued. "Let's look at the fuses. You know where the fuse box is located?"

Tony pointed to a box under the dashboard on the driver's side, and I checked it out. All the fuses appeared to be in working condition. "Must be the battery," I said, "although I've never seen a battery this dead. It can't even kick the solenoid. Guess we'll have to hitch into town."

"I'm staying with the car. I don't want anyone ripping it off!" he responded emphatically.

"How do you expect to get back? You must know someone who could pick us up, or better yet, fix the battery. How about Jim?"

Tony thought for a moment, then said I should call Jim MacGee and have him bring a friend of Tony's who was mechanically inclined. "I don't trust any of those other guys. They'd only screw the car up. I'll stay with the car. You go make the phone call."

I wrote down the church number and headed along the road, cursing Tony and my rotten luck. I hurried toward the entrance to the place where the motorcycle club was having its party just as the party was breaking up and motorcycles began streaming onto the road. I was still a good 200 yards away as the last cyclist roared off. "Just my luck!" I muttered as I watched the motorcycle disappear around a curve in the distance. Then I thought that I wasn't all that anxious to get mixed up with a bunch of cyclists anyway.

I came to a small settlement of four houses grouped together, two of them standing side by side, not more than ten yards off the road. A middle-age woman with two dogs was standing beside the road watching the motorcyclists drive off. As soon as the dogs saw me, they began to bark. I waved at the woman as I got nearer, but she went into the house, leaving one dog outside.

I walked up to the front door and knocked, and I thought the dog would have apoplexy. The woman opened the door a crack, and I could see she had the security chain in place. From what I could see, she wore no make-up. Her lips were tightly pursed, and her unsmiling eyes contained the traces of fear and hostility. I told her my car had broken down and asked if I could use her phone. "Don't work. It's out of order," she replied.

"How about those people over there? Do they have a phone?" I pointed to the houses to the rear. I was having trouble hearing the woman because the dog was barking incessantly and she made no attempt to control the animal.

The woman shook her head. "Don't know."

"How far to the next house?"

She arched her eyebrows like she couldn't hear.

I turned and screamed at the dog. "Shut up, Dog!" Much to my surprise, the dog stopped barking, then began to woof intermittently.

The woman stayed behind the door and would not cooperate in any way. I was sure my appearance, my beard and dirty clothes worried her, and I tried to be reassuring as I talked. Nothing worked and I turned abruptly and headed down the road, kicking at the gravel in anger and frustration.

After walking a mile, I came to the house where the people had been shooting across Stoney Creek. Two men and a woman were sitting on the front porch, carrying on a loud conversation. They became quiet when they saw me, and I felt vaguely uncomfortable as I walked up the drive. They watched me closely. To relieve the suspicion, I called out from quite some distance. "Got a dead car, probably the battery. Can I use your phone? I need some help."

"George, I got some jumper cables somewhere!" said the younger of the two men. "No need to call anyone. If it's a dead battery, we can fix that. I just have to find my jumper cables." He called to the woman who had gone inside and asked where he'd put the jumper cables.

"You look in the shed? Last I seen 'em they was in the shed," she yelled back.

In five minutes, he had the cables and we loaded into his International Scout. We passed the house where the woman with the dog told me the phone was out of order, and I could see her through the window with the phone to her ear.

After a short time, the battery in Tony's Plymouth was sufficiently charged. It started on the first crank. Tony and I were both ecstatic and thanked our friend profusely. As we started to drive off, I told Tony to keep a heavy foot on the gas. "Don't let this sucker die!"

As soon as we pulled into the parking lot behind the rectory, Tony turned off the motor and went directly inside without apparent concern for the cause of the battery problem. "See you in the morning. 7:00 a.m., right?" he said.

"Sounds like a winner to me. If I'm not waiting here, just come to the hostel, and I'll be ready." We waved good night. I muttered under my breath that I bet the dumb car would be dead in the morning.

As soon as I entered the hostel, John informed me he had a date that night and would be leaving shortly. "Fine by me!" I said. "Just don't wake me if you return before morning." I was really exhausted after my 20-mile day and the frustration with the battery episode. I concocted a huge pot of noodles and franks and was busy slurping my way through the noodles and guzzling beer when Georgia Ann, John's date, appeared. She was a tall girl with light brown hair and a ready smile, and I enjoyed talking with her between mouthfuls while she waited for John to finish dressing. Now that's a new twist, I thought. Here the girl came calling and the boy was still getting ready.

Just as John and Georgia Ann reached the door to leave, it burst open with a bang and in stomped Mike Martin, exclaiming proudly and with great excitement that he had just done a 28-mile day, a personal best. He looked even worse than John had the previous night. His clothes were completely soaked with perspiration, and the sweat on his face ran in little rivulets, coursing through the layers of dust and grime to form streaks on his forehead and cheeks.

John had not expected to see Mike until the following day, and he was clearly surprised by Mike's arrival. Tension permeated the atmosphere, and the conversation between them was forced. After John left, Mike told me his side of the split, and I was astounded at the difference between John's and Mike's versions of the Marion incident.

Pearisburg, Virginia, to Turners Gap, Maryland

CHAPTER 20

Pearisburg to Cloverdale

As I suspected the previous evening, Tony's car would not start, and he appeared at the hostel in the morning to inform me that our deal was off. Subconsciously, I had been expecting the news and didn't try to change his mind. I had already tried unsuccessfully to secure a commitment from Tony and thought it was pointless to try further to influence him. In fact, I had already decided that if the deal with Tony fell through I would give up my day-hiking scheme and continue as I had with a full pack.

We drove in awkward silence in Jim's car to the drop-off point, the place where he had picked me up the previous evening. Tony was sheepish about reneging on the deal, and I was angry and frustrated by the turn of events and disappointed with him, so I kept my mouth shut rather than say something in anger.

Initially, the hike was tough, the terrain uninteresting, and my pack too heavy at 48 pounds. All that combined with my disappointment made for a bleak morning.

After reaching the ridge top, the Trail evened out and followed a grassy road through mature forests and wooded meadows, and my mood lightened. Big and Potts Mountains were not difficult climbs, and several overlooks afforded outstanding views of the valleys and the hills to the northwest.

Once again, I tried to meditate. I wanted to gain a positive attitude after the setback in my day-hiking plans, but it was difficult to achieve a proper frame of mind. Everything I thought was negative. I struggled to drive the negativity from my mind, to replace it with an attitude conducive to the formation of positive thoughts. I refused completely to accept negative thoughts and concentrated on identifying positive aspects of the Trail and the positive experiences I had enjoyed.

The more I sought to do that, the more my mood brightened, and my previously negative outlook was replaced by a sense of peace and strength. The Trail seemed to open up before me. I now saw beautiful forest where before I had seen only a trail cutting through the gloomy shadows of the woods. I slowed my pace and began to see the life that abounded in the forest: a flicker hanging upside down on a tree limb, pecking away for insects, and squirrels and chipmunks scampering around the deadfalls and stumps scattered throughout the forest. I wondered if they had been there all along or if I had just now noticed them.

It was about 5:00 p.m. when I reached the War Spur shelter. I sat on the sleeping platform for a few minutes to rest and review the day's events, trying to put everything into perspective. I was very pleased with how I had conquered the anger and the negativity with which I had begun the day. It showed that I really had achieved a sense of spiritual confidence and that confidence was continually building. It was a moment of considerable satisfaction.

I had just lit my stove when Dan and Cathy strode purposefully into the shelter clearing. They were totally surprised to see me and greeted me with the enthusiasm usually reserved for longtime friends, and I reciprocated. The spontaneity of emotion surprised me since we had known each other for so short a time. I later recognized it as a Trail phenomenon.

The shared experience of the Trail has a binding quality that makes fast friends of acquaintances. The special sharing of adversity as well as comfort creates a new reality and reduces our inhibitions toward the display of affection.

The atmosphere at supper was relaxed, and we joked and laughed about the day's activities and my failed plans for "slack-packing" (a Thru-Hiker's slang for day-hiking). We talked about the upcoming parts of the Trail and what we expected to do the next day and agreed to maintain contact while we were on the Trail. As soon as it was dark, we slept.

It started to rain immediately after I left the shelter the next morning. I spent the day slogging through the forest in a steady drizzle. Again, the hiking was fairly easy once I reached the grassy road which followed the ridge crest. That changed as I climbed the last few hundred yards up Kelly Knob to Big Pond shelter.

Big Pond shelter, as might be expected, sat just above Big Pond, which, according to the *Trail Guide*, was a stagnant pond and not recommended as a water source for those staying at the shelter. I learned that now, at least, Big Pond no longer held any water. I walked around the edge of what had once been its banks and watched the birds and chipmunks flit and frolic through the dense underbrush. Clearly, Big Pond had died and undergone a metamorphosis into a swamp which probably soon would become a damp spot on the top of a hill.

On the descent from Kelly Knob, I surprised two young raccoons playing in the leaves on the forest floor. When they saw me, they fled in opposite directions, one slipping into a mountain laurel thicket behind them, the other climbing up a large sapling directly to my front about 30 yards away in open forest. It was not a very good tree in which to hide; it had little leaf growth, and the raccoon remained visible as it climbed. It quickly reached a fork in the trunk about 15 feet from the ground where the tree split into two slender branches. The raccoon stopped and hung from the fork with its chin resting on its paws as though it were doing a chin-up. I was reminded of the cartoon with a cat hanging from a limb with the caption, "Hang in there, Friday's almost here," and started to laugh. I don't know what the poor animal thought as it watched me from its precarious perch.

I stopped for lunch at an abandoned farmhouse, sitting forlornly in the forest and almost hidden from the Trail by the dense underbrush which surrounded it. Knowing Cathy and Dan were not far behind me, I planted my hiking stick in the middle of the Trail with an arrow drawn in the dirt pointing in the direction of the house to let them know I was there. I then returned to the house to start lunch. When they arrived a short time later, they puzzled over my hiking stick, looking first at the stick, then each other and at the surrounding forest, but didn't see the house until I called out to them.

Time and elements had already wreaked considerable devastation on the house. Its warped and weathered frame barely supported a sagging shingle roof, the front porch had completely collapsed, and gaping openings, where the windows had once been, gave the place a haunted look. Inside, the wallpaper had separated from disintegrating walls with pieces of plaster still clinging to the paper, and several steps were missing from the stairs that led to the second floor.

I often thought about the people for whom buildings like this had once been home and wondered about their fate. What motives had led them to settle on remote ridgetops or in remote valleys, and why had they left? What dreams had brought them here? And what disasters had destroyed the dreams? I felt like an uninvited guest eating lunch in someone's home. Although clearly the place had been long abandoned, it was strangely disquieting.

After lunch, I again went ahead of Dan and Cathy and shortly encountered a small fawn, just beginning to lose its spots. I approached to within five to ten yards of it before it moved off the Trail. It meandered around the open forest to my front, seemingly unconcerned by my presence, stopping only occasionally to watch me. After a few minutes, it ran off, but not in panic, rather in a way that suggested it might be late for supper. My guess was that the animal was orphaned at a very young age and had not yet learned to fear man.

I reached Sarver Cabin one and a half hours ahead of Dan and Cathy. We planned to spend the night there.

The cabin was actually an old animal stall that had been "renovated" to accommodate hikers. The floor was hard packed dirt that still contained the odor of manure and urine. The walls consisted of sapling sections laid on top of one another like a miniature log cabin, but without the chinking to keep out the weather. Instead, someone had lined the inside with black plastic sheeting like that used to mulch vegetable gardens. A second stall containing decomposing hay also emitted a strong manure smell which added to the already unpleasant aura.

About 30 yards further down the hill lay the collapsed ruins of the old homestead. The large, hand-hewn, wooden beams stuck grotesquely out of the clutches of vegetation like the spars of a sinking sailing ship just before going under. A large, serviceable-looking, fieldstone fireplace and chimney rose incongruously from amid the destruction which surrounded it. Three deer browsing in the tall grass behind the chimney showed no great fear of me until I came uncomfortably close; then they bounded easily into the woods and out of sight.

After surveying the situation, I decided to start a fire and wait for Dan and Cathy before deciding where to spend the night. The whole area had been drenched from the rain, and finding acceptably dry wood proved to be time-consuming. After combing the area, I returned to the fire pit in front of the animal stall with a small bundle of damp twigs and built a fire.

I first heard Cathy as she and Dan descended along the cabin access trail. "I smell smoke," she called out. "He must have a fire going." Cathy's high-pitched voice carried even further in her excitement. If Dan said anything, I couldn't hear it. She was breathless from exertion and excitement when she arrived. "How did you get that thing going?" she said as she strung a clothes line between two trees adjacent to the fire.

"Easy — when you know how!" I lied. "The secret is to get lots of really small twigs for tinder to start with and don't start putting on big pieces too soon. You gotta build up a good base of coals first, then you add the bigger stuff. You gotta be patient, build it a little at a time." As I was talking, Dan got out his folding saw and went to gather more wood.

"We brought you a present," said Cathy. "Since you were nice enough to leave the arrowhead, we thought you deserved a present. But you can't have it until after dinner," she teased.

"What is it?" I asked.

"You'll just have to wait and see."

Here Dan returned, dragging two long pieces of wood, which he promptly started to saw into usable lengths.

Cathy went into the "cabin" and quickly backed out again. "You planning on sleeping in there?" she asked, holding her nose.

I shook my head. "Thought I'd find a place to put up my tent."

"Think we'll do that, too," she agreed.

"Matter of fact, think I'll look for a place now before it gets too late. There aren't many level spots for a tentsite here."

Dan stopped sawing, grabbed his tent, and accompanied me. Only one small area showed any promise as a tentsite, and Dan laid claim to it right away, throwing his tent smack in the middle of it.

"Hey, Bozo!" Cathy called out. "Move that thing over. Where's he goin' to put his tent?"

Dan agreed like it was unintentional on his part and moved his tent to one side of the clearing so there was room for me to put my tent up, too.

After supper Cathy proudly produced six ears of corn. "Your present!" she laughed. "Swiped 'em from a farmer's field we passed comin' through that last valley."

"You're going to give Trail-hikers a bad name," I said.

"They're a present and it's impolite to ask where presents come from. So don't ask where they come from, just enjoy 'em! Hope you have some salt," she said.

I passed my salt around, and Dan poured us each a swig of whiskey from the flask he was carrying. "Spend any time in Vietnam?" he asked of me.

"Two tours, 12 months each time," I replied.

"I was in the Marines during Korea. I was drafted," said Dan. The conversation then centered on Dan's experience in the Marines with a sadistic, alcoholic Drill Sergeant, and Cathy went to bed. I listened for a while, then excused myself; Dan stayed alone by the fire.

As I climbed back to the Trail the next morning, it dawned on me that it was the 12th of August and I had completed two months on the Trail. It was a jolt to realize that I had been on my odyssey for two whole months. It was not an unpleasant jolt, though, since it meant that I was winning my personal battle. I was going to succeed! I fairly flew up the ridge.

The weather was far from auspicious. The ridge crest was engulfed in a layer of low-hanging clouds, and the fog coated everything with a fine mist. There was no wind and the moisture-laden air lay in stationary pockets. The *Trail Guide* indicated that spectacular views could be enjoyed from the many open rock ledges that stretched across the mountainside, but I could see only the faint outline of some nearby tree tops.

The limited visibility and the wet ground allowed me to come very close to a flock of wild turkeys and a pair of grouse without being detected. If I had been hunting, I would certainly have had a turkey dinner that night. I saw the turkeys before they saw me. I counted seven birds nearing the ridge crest through open forest slightly to my right. We were both headed on a collision course on the Trail ahead, and I approached to within about 20 yards of them before they finally noticed.

I was surprised that I had gotten so close; turkeys are normally very sharp-eyed and wary. After they saw me, they scurried noiselessly into the underbrush. None of them flew away; they simply put their heads down and sneaked quickly in a crouch toward the nearest concealment.

Soon after reaching the ridge crest, the Trail followed a cliff line formed millions of years ago when the colliding earth plates thrust the earth's crust into a perpendicular slant. Much to my amusement, I found myself still crossing ridges of Brushy Mountain. I really didn't mind the hiking, and even crossing the little minigorges formed by the cross spurs running down from the main ridge was bearable. But I was annoyed to tears by the hordes of white-faced hornets that besieged me at every break. They crawled all over my skin, my clothes, my pack and even into my gorp bag when I snacked. I was afraid one might remain in my pack harness and sting me when I reshouldered my pack. I paid special attention to make sure my harness was clear.

I stopped for the day at Pickle Branch shelter after some 15 miles in wet clothes and boots.

When Cathy arrived, she was filled with wide-eyed excitement. "You see any rattlesnakes today?"

I shook my head.

"We did! Just after lunch! It was coiled on a rock right beside the Trail. Dan passed by and didn't see it, and it didn't react at all. Then, when I started to go by, it got all excited and started rattlin'. If it hadn't rattled, I would'a gone right by it, too!"

"Wonder why it waited until Dan passed by?"

"Must have been a male snake," Cathy said, laughing.

"That's sorta ripe for erotic interpretation . . ."

"Humph," replied Cathy. "I just called Dan'l, and he came back and flipped the snake off the rock into the bushes with his hiking stick. He was a big sucker!" Cathy was animated as she described the incident knowing that she had seen something I hadn't.

Normally, it was the other way around when I was describing something she hadn't seen. I wished I had seen it. I wondered if, like Dan, I had passed by and hadn't noticed it. I could have used something to brighten my day, I thought. All I got was wet and miserable. Some way to start my third month on the Trail!

I hiked with Dan and Cathy the next day. We started off at about 9:00 a.m., late by my standards, Dan leading the way. The weather was a repeat of the previous day's mist and fog, which depressed our morale. We climbed a torturous path through boulder-strewn hillsides, walked along knife-edged rock ridge crests, and dodged in and out of rhododendron thickets and scrub oak patches until we reached the highlight of the day, the magnificent stone monolith known as Dragons Tooth.

It was a massive stone slab that reached some 30 feet into the sky, depending from where it was measured. (There was about a ten-foot difference in the elevation of the earth on the north and south sides.) To either side along the ridge stood smaller monoliths to keep it eternal company. The bare earth and tree growth in the vicinity of the monolith tended to soften its stark image. It reminded me of a scene from a *Conan, The Barbarian*, painting. I could imagine a muscle-bound, animal-skin-clothed, Viking-capped giant, scowling in rage, crouched on the pinnacle, outlined by lightning from a storm-blackened sky. The wind blew eerily through the trees as we stood awestruck beside the monster.

Dragons Tooth.

After taking photographs of the monolith, we started down the mountain, carefully negotiating the treacherously wet soil and innumerable rock ledges and overhangs. This time I led the way. (I had become uncomfortable with Dan's slow pace.) The path was very steep, and the moisture made the soil and the rocks extremely slippery. Particularly dangerous were those rocks which had a certain algae or fungus growth; when wet they became as slippery as ice. I found that my long hiking stick was particularly well suited to climbing down the steep sections of the Trail because it helped me maintain my balance as I negotiated the ledges or stepped down from large rocks.

I soon reached Rawies Rest, another ridgetop ledge with views and some rock monoliths, which, although beautiful, were in no way as impressive as Dragons Tooth. From Rawies Rest, the Trail descended directly to the valley floor and the community of Catawba, a couple of scattered buildings and a small grocery store.

Dan, Cathy and I had talked with great anticipation earlier about eating soft white bread sandwiches the next time we hit civilization, so I bought a loaf of puffy, soft, white bread and a pound of bologna and cheese together with mayonnaise and tomatoes. I had barely finished with my purchases when Dan and Cathy arrived. (They had taken a short cut by omitting the trip to Rawies Rest.) I showed them the bologna and cheese, and Cathy immediately volunteered to make the sandwiches.

It had been tough hiking in the rain. We all needed a break. So, we decided to remain in Catawba for the remainder of the day.

That evening, while we were preparing supper, Dan started to open up. The more beer he drank, the more he talked. I was surprised to hear him say that he was an atheist. I had trouble believing that anyone who had hiked the Trail for any distance could be an atheist. We had a long discussion on the subject. At first, I thought he might be trying to provoke me for the sake of an argument, but later realized he was serious.

He told a story about a group of Boy Scouts in the Smokies who had taken refuge from an electrical storm in one of the shelters. The boys were all lying or sitting on the chain-link bunks when the shelter sustained a lightning strike and all but one of them were electrocuted. The boy who survived the lightning had gotten off his wire bunk to pray before the lightning hit. "Bet that made a believer outta that kid!" said Dan, laughing ironically.

The next day I didn't feel well. I had had too many beers with Dan. Thankfully, the weather was cool and the Trail only moderately difficult. Except for seeing a large buck with a huge set of antlers, the hike was uneventful.

My encounter with the buck took place on the ridge crest of North Mountain about two miles into the hike. He was standing crosswise in the middle of the Trail, munching on the leaves of a small bush. He saw me at the same moment I rounded a bend in the Trail, and in one majestic leap which covered about 30 yards, he catapulted straight out into the air off the mountainside at a horizontal angle and, with the velocity of his initial leap expended, arced downward, dropping far down the mountain. I was stunned by the speed, power and grace of the animal. Seemingly without effort, the deer just became airborne and soared down the mountainside.

Later, I saw another deer, this one a fawn. It appeared to be alone and, like the fawn I had seen earlier, appeared to have no fear of me. I guessed it not to be more than a few weeks old and that it also had become separated from its mother. I wondered if the magnificent buck I had seen earlier was its father. I was con-

Rawies Rest.

tinually impressed by the number of deer and other wildlife in Virginia, completely different from my experiences in Georgia and North Carolina, where I rarely saw them.

We stopped for the night at Lamberts Meadow shelter before pushing on the next day to Cloverdale where Dan and Cathy had reserved a room in a motel. I started off alone in the morning, passing through Lamberts Meadow which was no longer a meadow, but a fully grown forest with mature trees. The Trail was nicely graded along the ridge crests, and the weather was a delightful improvement from the previous day. With sunshine and clear skies, I was able to enjoy some of the vistas which had heretofore been hidden by clouds. Especially beautiful were the views from Tinker Mountain: Carvens Cove Reservoir gleaming in the sunlight to the south and the lush green Cloverdale valley to the north.

Shortly before Cloverdale, the Trail crossed a concrete bridge over Tinker Creek where a large copperhead snake was sunning itself on a log jam. I continued on across the bridge, then decided to come back for a second look. When I did, the wise snake glided effortlessly into the water and disappeared. It was 1:30 p.m. when I arrived at the Howard Johnson Motel in Cloverdale.

DRAGONS TOOTH

Tranquillity exists beside the monolith.
Trees soften harsh angles of stone.
Lovers' troths stand black on rock.
And coals of fires past
Blend grayly with the soft dark earth.
Who can imagine force so powerful
It drove this fractured slab
Into a skyward slant;
Or pressed the rocks that buckled into hills
To miss the torture?
Or contemplate the eons past,
Before we were around to think?

CHAPTER 21

To the Blue Ridge and Buena Vista

Entering the motel was such a drastic change of environment that I felt intimidated. The lobby with its glistening tile floors and polished wooden furniture appeared so civilized, and the receptionists so meticulously groomed and cosmetically elegant that I felt like a wild man fresh from the jungle. My hair and beard had grown long and shaggy, and my scalp and chin itched from an accumulation of dirt and vermin. The grime covering my arms and face was streaked with sweat, my fingernails were black with dirt, and my clothes, filthy and frayed, reeked of perspiration.

Based on my self-appraisal, I unconsciously expected the woman behind the counter to tell me all the rooms were taken. To my relief and delight, she didn't hesitate a heartbeat when I inquired about a room. Her only response was to ask for how many nights I wished to stay and if I wanted a single or double bed. I realized in that instant that the motel, sitting directly across the road where the AT crossed U.S. Highway 220, had probably already attracted its share of "scuzzy" hikers and, to the ladies, I was just one more customer.

After showering (three latherings to attain an acceptable level of cleanliness), I donned my blue nylon river shorts, my least dirty OD T-shirt, filled a plastic garbage bag with dirty clothes, and headed for the laundry room. (A sign in the motel lobby indicated one was available for guest use on the second floor.) I arrived to find a repairman trying vainly to coax a solitary washing machine back into operation. When I asked for his prognosis, the repairman shrugged his shoulders. "Have to order the parts, probably a week at least, most likely two," he said as he taped the coin slot shut.

No other washing machines were available in the motel,

and I learned that the next closest laundry facility was at the
laundromat in a truck stop beside the junction of U.S. Routes 220
and 11, about half a mile down the hill. I was not mentally prepared to walk another mile just to do laundry, and the inconvenience put me in a foul mood. I fussed all the way down the hill.

My clothes were so dirty I had to wash them twice, and to
do so cost more money than I anticipated. I had no coins and
asked a heavy, plain-looking woman in lilac-colored, polyester
pants at the cash register in the rear of the truck stop for change.
She gave me some, but in such a way as to let me know that I
was being a colossal pain for asking. Her face was set in a perpetual scowl that deepened when I approached the counter like
she expected to be insulted and mentally put herself into the *en
garde* position, prepared to do battle. She threw the change on
the counter without comment and turned away in much the
same manner as she might have done while feeding chickens
when she remembered she had another chore to do and turned
back before the last few kernels of corn had hit the ground.

I took my change and headed back to the laundry room feeling chastised and intimidated. When I went back a second time for
change, it was with considerable unconscious trepidation until I
realized what was happening. I became irritated with myself and
stormed to the cash register, loudly demanding change for a dollar. The woman's response was surprisingly meek.

I have always been a people-watcher, and the people in the
truck stop provided nonstop entertainment. I doubt that I had seen
as many different costumes at a carnival party as I saw that afternoon. In fact, the atmosphere of the place was very carnival-like.

One tall, well-built man wearing tight-fitting, knee-length
buckskin boots fringed at the top with rawhide lacing, skin-tight
denim short-shorts that bulged in the crotch, and a Budweiser
Beer T-shirt strutted back and forth among the aisles and
through the restaurant section. His hair was combed straight
back and fell in soft, curly brown cascades over his shoulders,
and a reddish-brown moustache flared from the sides of his
mouth, giving his face a permanent smile. He looked like someone who intended to dress in a certain costume, then changed
his mind in the process and assumed another costume without
bothering to remove the first one.

There were truck drivers of all shapes and descriptions:
burly, not so burly, fat and sloppy, some not so fat, but almost
always sloppy; some rail thin; and several sported Confederate

flag belt buckles the size of small pancakes. Many wore cowboy boots. Some were so short and slight of build that I wondered how they handled the huge rigs they were driving. Mostly, they went about their business with purpose and maturity. Of course, there was always one who swaggered about and chose to be loud and "on stage," acting out his fantasies of the country-western hero images sung about truckers.

Then there were the women. Some were wives of truckers; some were girlfriends along for the ride. Some worked in the truck stop. Some seemed to be just hanging around. Most wore skin-tight jeans and well-filled T-shirts. Many combed their hair straight back so it flowed down their necks and shoulders, sometimes reaching to the middle of their backs. Mostly, they went about their business pretending not to notice the lascivious stares of men who, without the hint of discretion, followed their every movement. One, who appeared to be on the truck stop staff, "performed" for the crowd, carrying on conversations with the men or other women, cracking racy comments, and almost prancing for the men like a stripper practicing her act.

Shortly before supper, I went to the motel pool. The water was deliciously cool, and the early evening air a refreshing change from the sultry midafternoon temperatures. After swimming a couple of laps, I paraded my new body around the pool, feeling smugly superior to the other males lying about like white walruses in their fat. It dawned on me that I was acting like an insufferable snob and felt privately embarrassed for strutting, even more so, when I realized that no damsels were swooning at the sight of me. In fact, it even occurred to me that no one really cared that I was a lean, mean hiking machine.

As agreed at supper, Dan and Cathy accompanied me on the Trail out of Cloverdale the next morning. After crossing under Interstate 81, we began climbing toward the Blue Ridge, crossing two lush hilltop pastures with outstanding views to the southwest of Tinker Mountain, which loomed behind Cloverdale and dominated the valley with its larger than life size.

Although the scenery was inspiring, with the Blue Ridge rising to our front and the hiking mostly easy, I felt slightly depressed. I guessed my short experience with civilization the previous day had probably had its effect. The episode that snapped me out of it occurred early in the afternoon at Curry Creek where Cathy persuaded me to stop and cool my feet in the water.

The cold mountain water not only caressed my feet, it

soothed my spirit, and I closed my eyes to enjoy the luxury, imagining the flowing water as fine silk brushing gently against my skin. Tiny fish and crawfish darted back and forth between the rocks and occasionally the braver fish nibbled on my toes.

Cathy threw crumbled soda crackers into the water, a few tiny bits at a time, and the fish attacked the floating crumbs with miniature ferocity. "Maybe these'll keep them away from your feet," she laughed, handing her last few crumbs to me.

I threw them out toward the middle of the stream where a gust of wind carried them toward some rocks with the fish darting after them. It was a pleasant interlude that impressed on me the wisdom in the quotation about "stopping to smell the flowers."

The Trail followed a long ridgeside relocation to Wilson Creek where the water rushed from a tangle of thick forest, cascaded down a small jumble of boulders, then flowed smoothly across a broad rock ledge. Several level, grassy areas beside the stream looked like ideal tentsites, but we continued for another half a mile to the ridge crest where the Roanoke Trail and Hiking Club construction crew was putting the finishing touches to their newest masterpiece. We were the first hikers to stay overnight in the shelter. It was so new the cement for the firepit had been poured only a few hours earlier, and we were asked not to use it until the next morning.

I was dead tired at the end of the day's hike, and the last thing I wanted was to walk another mile round-trip back to Wilson Creek for water. But that was exactly what Dan and I did. It was downhill all the way to the creek, and we made good time. But climbing back, carrying two gallons of water plus full canteens was exhausting, and we complained the whole way about the absurdity of building a shelter so far from water.

Afterward, as I reflected on my ill-considered remarks, I felt a sense of personal disappointment. The Trail crew had gone to great lengths to provide for our comfort and shelter. I knew that the club had originally intended to build the shelter near the creek, but a Forest Service official had disapproved the club's selected siting because of the danger of polluting the creek. Still, the irritation of having to go so far for water after an exhausting hike was not lightly overcome.

It appeared that a solution to the water problem might be solved for future hikers. There was a small stream about 200 yards from the shelter down a steep draw. The problem was that it contained only a trickle of water and would require consider-

Cathy Morris and Dan Cruse preparing to cool their feet in Curry Creek.

able improvement before it could supply sufficient water for camping. The trail crew indicated that improving the stream was one of their future projects.

Later that evening, a stray, black hound dog, attracted by the smell of cooking food, came bounding up to the shelter and collapsed in the leaves beside the firepit to watch with doleful eyes as we ate. We got the full treatment: sad eyes, doleful expression and just the slightest bit of whining. We all felt guilty for eating in front of him. If sympathy was what he was looking for, he was much more successful at finding it than he was at hunting.

Cathy had a soft place in her heart for animals, and it wasn't long before she caved in to the hound's supplications and gave him some tidbits. That was a mistake. This act induced the dog to remain at the shelter. Consequently, he spent the night in a bed of dry leaves beneath the sleeping platform, biting, gnawing and scratching and periodically dashing out into the forest through the dry leaves and branches chasing some animal which always escaped. The result: I didn't sleep well and awoke the next morning tired and in ill humor.

The views from the overlooks along the Blue Ridge Parkway the next day were spectacular with mountain panoramas rolling ceaselessly into the blue and purple distance. We admired again and again the vast sweep of forest from the mountaintops to the valleys, and the patchwork of rich green hues that formed giant mosaics across the ridges. We stopped for lunch at Bobblets Gap on a grassy mound beside a small island of trees from where we could experience the view, each of us savoring the beauty as well as the food.

At Cove Mountain we departed from the AT and headed for Jellystone Campground where we planned to spend the night. We followed the blue-blazed trail down the mountain, eventually coming to Jennings Creek where we interrupted a young couple lying on a blanket beside the stream bank. When we came into view, the couple quickly separated and watched silently as we passed, barely acknowledging our greetings. The blue-blazed trail ended in a parking lot, and we headed down a narrow, paved, country road toward Jellystone Campground. A rain shower arrived at the same time we started down the road, and I became so thoroughly soaked that even my blue-footed boobys squished in protest as I plodded along the puddled macadam.

After signing in at the campground store, we bought a few provisions and hurried to our cabin. The reason for our haste was that an inviting-looking swimming pool lay just uphill from our cabin, and we wanted to go for a swim before the rain started again. The rain beat us to the pool, but since we were already wet, it didn't deter us.

A couple engaged in animated conversation and laughter were splashing in the pool and did not immediately notice our arrival. They obviously hadn't anticipated company; the man's swimming trunks had been removed and thrown over the fence surrounding the pool. We didn't see the bathing suit lying on the ground until the embarrassed man asked if one of us would retrieve it for him. Dan retrieved the suit while Cathy and I remained a respectful distance away. The woman reacted to her companion's predicament with great amusement and peals of laughter. After some good-natured promises of vengeance, the man put on his bathing suit, which proved to be quite a trick under water, and he sputtered more than once during the effort. They continued to swim for a while, but it was clear our arrival had ruined the atmosphere. After a few minutes, they hurried off to their cabin.

We walked the entire next day in a driving rain and arrived at Thunder Hill shelter chilled, exhausted and again thoroughly soaked. As bad as the rain was, our greatest disappointment came when we found that, even after a full day of torrential rain, the shelter spring contained no water. Dan spread out a large, clear plastic sheet on the ground to capture rain run-off for cooking water, and we were able to fill our cookpots with acceptably clean water. (It still contained traces of dead grass, dirt and evergreen needles which we purified as we cooked supper.)

After supper, we amused ourselves by watching mice carry off pieces of soda crackers which Cathy crumbled and threw on the ground. The mice lived in small holes beneath the tree roots and rocks that lined the edge of the shelter clearing and took turns carrying the cracker pieces back to their nests. No sooner would one carry off a piece, when another mouse would appear and haul another piece of cracker to another hole. When it became too dark to see clearly, Cathy lit a candle, and we lay on our stomachs on the sleeping platform watching the mice come and go. They seemed to have no fear of us, often coming brazenly within arm's reach of the shelter to retrieve the crackers. Suddenly, they disappeared and no matter how enticing the morsels, they remained out of sight. I thought later that Cathy had hit on the ideal solution to the shelter mouse problem. Feed 'em early and they will be too stuffed to bother you during the night. I didn't hear a single mouse the whole night.

The rain was really with us now. It rained the whole night, and the sound of it beating on the roof kept me half awake, wondering if it would stop before morning or if we would be forced to hike another day in rain. My worst fears were confirmed, and we hiked the entire next day in the rain.

With each of us involved in our own thoughts and misery, there was little conversation, and because of the mist, there was very little to see. Eventually, we covered about 12 miles for the day, most of it along the Blue Ridge Parkway, until we came to Matts Creek shelter where we spent the night in the company of Chris and Paul Haessel, a father-and-son team we had met earlier on the Parkway when they stopped to inquire about hiking the AT.

Chris, the father, was a Professor of Shakespearean Literature at Vanderbilt University in Knoxville, Tennessee, and Paul was a high school student. Chris and Dan, both academicians, became involved in an interesting conversation about their various specialties, and I enjoyed listening to their banter, especially when Chris talked about doing research on Shakespeare in England. Cathy and I kept a low profile for most of the evening.

The Haessels accompanied us the next morning as far as the bridge which carried U.S. Route 501 over the James River and dropped off the Trail at that point to await pick-up by Mrs. Haessel. As we crossed the bridge, the rain, which had been a steady drizzle, became torrential.

Hiking the ridge above the river was miserable. The closer we approached the ridge crest, the stronger the winds and the cooler the temperatures. Near the summit, the wind-driven raindrops stung our exposed hands and faces, and the wind gusts chilled us to the bone with knife-like thrusts. The rain penetrated our windbreakers and ponchos, and in no time we were soaked completely through.

I was so miserable that, when we stopped for lunch, I preferred to eat standing up to avoid as much contact as possible with the cold, wet portions of my clothes. Because of my concern about hypothermia, I decided after lunch to move out on my own and increase my speed. (I had been hiking at a very slow pace behind Dan and Cathy.) I was not only concerned about hypothermia myself, but also for Dan and Cathy, and I told them they also should move faster.

Later in the afternoon, while crossing the summit of Bluff Mountain, I encountered a small monument to Ottie Cline Powell, age 4 years, 11 months and 25 days. The marker sat between a large rock and a massive oak tree almost directly on the summit. Later, I learned that Ottie was the son of the Rev. E. M. Powell who had lived on the eastern slope of the Blue Ridge Mountains in Amherst County, Virginia. Ottie had attended the Tower Hill School, and it was from there that he became lost on November 9, 1891, while looking for firewood for the schoolhouse.

A small book about the incident, written in 1925 by J. B. Huffman of Buena Vista, Virginia, describes a premonitory dream Mr. Powell experienced on the night of the 8th of November, the night before Ottie disappeared. In his dream, Mr. Powell saw a black wagon or a hearse, and sitting inside the back of the wagon beside a little, foot-long coffin without a top was an old man and a little flame suspended in the air above the coffin. The man beside the coffin said, "This is my house," and the dream ended. Mr. Powell awoke immediately and told his wife about the dream which so upset him that he was unable to sleep for the rest of the night.

When news of Ottie's disappearance spread, people from throughout the area came to participate in the search which continued without success well into the night and for several weeks thereafter. Eventually, the search was abandoned and nothing more was seen of Ottie until the 5th of April the following year when four young men crossing the mountain, alerted by their dog's barking, found Ottie's body lying on the ground at the exact location of the monument.

Ottie was fully clothed, his hat still on his head, and he appeared to be sleeping. His clothes had been torn and snagged by bushes and briars during his seven-mile ordeal, but except for that and his feet having been chewed, he looked to be in excellent condition. Ottie's ordeal probably ended fairly quickly; an autopsy showed that some chestnuts which he had eaten had not yet been digested, indicating that he had probably died of exposure during the night of the 9th. The family's ordeal lasted much longer, and Mrs. Powell was reputed to have died of heartbreak soon after Ottie disappeared.

It was only about a mile from Bluff Mountain to Punchbowl shelter where Cathy, Dan and I planned to spend the night. Because I was walking at a fast pace, I reached it early in the afternoon, some two hours ahead of Dan and Cathy. The shelter was set in an open mature forest about 100 yards from the bank of a grass-and-tree-rimmed mountain pond. Behind the shelter, the ground rose gently up a cleared ridgeside and to the left, a group of gigantic white pines, interspersed with equally massive oak trees, stood like sentinels guarding the serenity and beauty of the setting.

After getting water, I decided to start a fire. With absolutely no dry wood to be found, I gathered as many tiny twigs as I could. After assembling a mass large enough, I set them on top of my lighted Whisperlite stove. Eventually, as the fire dried the twigs sufficiently, they caught fire, and I patiently added slightly larger twigs until I had a roaring fire.

Cathy's voice rang with incredulity as she and Dan came down the hill. "I don't believe it! He's got a fire going! He's got a fire going in this rain!" Later she confided that Dan and she were conjecturing on what I would be doing when they arrived at the shelter, and the smart money was on finding me snuggled inside my sleeping bag. Cathy asked several times how I managed to get a fire going under such miserable conditions, but I said it was an old Indian secret that I was sworn not to divulge. I could see her imagination groping with all sorts of possibilities. I later "'fessed up" to the stove trick and destroyed a myth of fire-making invincibility with my candor.

We were able to partially dry our clothes over the fire, and Cathy used it to cook supper. Even though the rain continued unabated, our spirits were high. We celebrated the fire by finishing the last of Dan's peppermint schnapps. When we finally climbed into our sleeping bags, the hissing and cracking sounds of raindrops hitting the glowing embers made us feel snug and warm, and sleep came easily.

It rained throughout the night and continued on into the next morning, but it didn't bother Dan and Cathy because this was to be their last day on the Trail. They could look forward to a motel, wheels and civilization, but I couldn't envision any comfort beyond a motel for that night, and I was becoming irritated by rain to the point of exasperation.

About 30 minutes after leaving the shelter, we reached the Blue Ridge Parkway where we lightened our packs as much as possible by stashing our sleeping bags, tents and other articles in a big pile just inside the edge of the forest. (We intended to return for them by automobile after reaching Buena Vista.) We covered everything with leaves and brush, hiding our cache so well that it was impossible to detect from the road. We then continued down the Trail with such greatly lightened packs that the hiking was almost pleasurable despite the rain.

The Trail crossed Enchanted Creek near the base of Pedlar Dam where rocks and boulders strewn by retreating glaciers or powerful floods created a stark and barren landscape that reminded me of my childhood fantasies of lunar terrain. Pedlar Lake, despite the NO FISHING, NO SWIMMING, NO CAMPING signs scattered throughout the area, still retained the charm of a mountain tarn spreading through the valley, lapping gently at the ridgeside rocks which formed its boundaries. I would liked to have spent some time on lake shore had the sun been shining.

After Pedlar Lake, we entered a stand of virgin forest with some of the largest trees I've ever seen. The trunks of giant white pines, hemlocks and chestnut oaks, imitating massive cathedral columns, imparted a spiritual quality to the forest. As we wove our way among the trees, for some reason Dan began to talk about his problems with a department secretary at work which reminded me of a similar experience I had had during a time when I was assigned as an instructor at the Infantry School.

The spell broken, I unconsciously responded, and our conversation sank deeper and deeper into a negative, anger-filled discourse where previous frustrations rose up and again captured us. Cathy remained silent during the discussion until the negativity became too much to bear.

Suddenly, her voice rang out with irritation and frustration, "Hey, you guys, knock it off! Can't you find something else to talk about?"

Thoroughly cowed, Dan and I immediately shut up. I realized then that I had destroyed the mood of a beautiful setting. I wondered about Dan and myself. How could we be thinking about mundane trivia while walking through such inspiring scenery? It was totally out of sync with the beauty we were experiencing. I walked on in silence, trying to regain a positive outlook.

After reflecting on it for a while, I realized how deep-seated the negative influences had become in my unconscious. Here I was, passing through a rare, centuries-old forest where inspiring examples of God's Energy rose all about me, and I was not looking, preferring instead of focus on an unimportant ego-induced anger. I wondered how often I had made a similar mistake in the past. What a terrible waste of such a precious moment, I thought. I decided then to concentrate on eliminating or reducing the negative traffic in my psyche. Again, I thought ruefully, it would take much work.

Shortly after leaving the virgin forest, the Trail passed through the remains of an extensive mountain settlement along Brown Mountain Creek that had been abandoned about 200 years ago. Many of the stone foundations of the barns and houses still existed and provided clues to how the community might have looked. In several places, the AT followed the trace of the settlement's main street past stone walls built to protect the inhabitants from the ravages of floods from Brown Mountain Creek. In some places, the original timbers of the buildings still survived, but the wood was mostly green with moss and rot. Although parts of the settlement could still be identified, nature had reclaimed most of it, and I suspected that in another hundred years it would be impossible to recognize the place as having once been a settlement.

I felt strangely uneasy walking past the shells of homes and barns of people who a long time ago had called the place home. I again wondered why they had chosen this little piece of earth on which to live, and — after making the sacrifices they had and working as hard as they did to build their dreams — wondered why they had left.

Life along Brown Mountain Creek must have been extremely harsh. Arable land had to be reclaimed from the mountain at great effort and just getting to the place from the more hospitable environment in the lowlands was a major undertaking. As I thought about those questions, I came to the conclusion that God sometimes leads us to strange circumstances in our journeys.

We reached U.S. Route 60 after a leisurely lunch at Brown Mountain Creek shelter. No sooner had we arrived at the highway than Dan succeeded in getting us a ride into Buena Vista in the back of a pickup truck with a protective shell. The woman driving the truck stopped but would not open her door or let us inside the cab. She rolled down the window, just enough so that we could speak, and told us to climb in the back. We scrambled into the bed of the truck and relaxed while she swung the pickup through its paces on the curves and switchbacks toward town.

After retrieving his car, Dan and I drove back to the mountains to reclaim our equipment cache. The gunmetal gray skies began to break up during the return trip to Buena Vista. The sun slipped through the cracks with increasing frequency, and the patches of clear sky became correspondingly larger and bluer. The fresh smell of countryside after rain permeated the air. After a few minutes, sunlight bathed the mountains in verdant hues, dark and deep near the valleys, and light and airy at the summits. Suddenly, my rain-induced gloominess was replaced by exhilaration from seeing sun, sky, and the magnificent scenery. Suddenly, everything seemed bright.

After showering, I went outside to relax on the porch and was joined a minute later by Cathy. "Well, Old Soldier," she said, "looks like you're going to have to go on alone. How far you figure on making it?"

"Maybe to Pennsylvania. I don't know. Maybe I won't even get that far. I'll get to the Maryland border for sure. Then it depends on the weather, the Trail and how I feel. I may come off the Trail at that point. Come September 12, I'll have three months on the Trail. I have a lot to do back in Naples, and I still have to visit my children and grandchildren and all the friends I've promised to visit when I got out of the Army. Yeah, the 12th would be the time to come off. Come to think of it, that's only a few days away. Well, 22 days — to be exact — three weeks." I was hunting through my shirt pocket for a pen so we could exchange addresses when the sound of someone speaking German caught my attention. "What's that language?" asked Cathy.

"German." Two women were walking toward us.

"Say something to 'em in German," Cathy prodded.

Right after we had met the first night, when I had mentioned that I had spent the last six years in Germany, Dan asked if I could speak German. I had replied that I was fluent. I was sure Cathy was testing me.

"Go on, talk to 'em."

It was not said with a tone of voice that indicated she doubted I could speak German, but from natural curiosity.

"*Schoen Guten Tag!*" I started.

The women's heads both jerked around towards me at the same time, their eyes widening with surprise.

They stopped. "*Guten Tag*," they replied slowly, waiting for me to continue.

We engaged in a short conversation which included the weather, questions about where they were from in Germany, their jobs, and details of their visit to America. One woman was a dental assistant; the other, an older woman, her sister, was the owner of a garden and florist shop in Freiburg in the Schwarzwald. They had come to the United States to visit their relatives who lived in Illinois and were now touring the country.

"*Sind Sie Deutsch?*" asked the younger woman.

I was flattered that she was impressed enough to ask if I were German. I replied that I was American.

They then told me that the relatives they were visiting in Illinois were descendants of Germans who had immigrated to the U.S. over 250 years ago and that the family branch in the U.S. had maintained their German language proficiency through the centuries, although it now appeared that the current generation might be breaking the chain. If that were to happen, it would end a rich family heritage. I told them I hoped that wouldn't happen. It is so seldom that the children of immigrants to America speak the language of their parents.

Later, on my way to the restaurant, I passed the ladies' VW van and saw a little sign with crossed German and American flags displayed from the rear window along with a notation that they were from Freiburg and greeted America. The family was standing in the parking lot as I passed, and I stopped to talk with them. They asked many questions about my hike and experiences with wildlife. (They were particularly interested when I described my bear encounters.) When we parted, they gave me a miniature doll dressed in a *Schwarzwalder trachten* (costume) as a remembrance of our visit. It still adorns my tree at Christmas.

PUNCHBOWL SHELTER IN THE RAIN

We came from Matt's Creek shelter,
Cathy, Dan and I
And walked the whole rain day,
The third such in a row.
We climbed up several ridges
Through sheets of biting rain.
We all were chilled and soaked
As only mountain hikers get.

Each of us endured
The wind, the rain, the cold;
Continued on without complaint;
Accepted what we got.
We sang, we talked, we laughed;
Saw beauty in the hills and mist —
In rivulets along the Trail
And flowers bowed across the lane.

And when the day was over,
In the comfort of the fire,
In the beauty of the pond,
Amid the graceful oaks and pines,
We felt the special glow
That comes to those who dare,
To those who share in hardship
To be amid a beauty
That only they can know.

CHAPTER 22

The Blue Ridge to Rockfish Gap

It was nearly noon by the time I loaded my pack into Dan's car for the return ride to the Trail. It was a quiet trip, each of us trying to make happy conversation to cover the awkwardness of parting. In a reluctant goodbye speech, I thanked both Dan and Cathy for their help and especially Dan for the generous use of his time to chauffeur me into town and for loaning me his maps from the most recent *Trail Guide* for Virginia. The three of us had developed a fairly close relationship over the past several days, sharing hardship and pain as well as the excitement and enjoyment, and I knew that I would miss the camaraderie, especially Cathy's bubbly enthusiasm. She had a way of keeping everyone's spirits high even under the most trying circumstances.

It was a struggle to return alone to the Trail, to again be without the human companionship which helped ease the ardors of the Trail. I had developed a certain dependence on Dan and Cathy, a psychological comfort from their physical presence. I could share my thoughts or troubles, joys or misery with them.

I wondered what effect their leaving would have on me, on my commitment to the Trail. Visions of our experiences together, feeding crackers to the shelter mice, the fish in Curry Creek, the fire at Sarver Cabin and the sandwiches at Catawba pond, flashed through my mind as we drove. They were but memories now, and there would be no more of them, at least with Dan and Cathy.

When we finally parted, Cathy ignored my handshake, preferring to give me a big kiss and a hug instead. I moved off to the side of the road and watched as they drove off. I felt much like I had when my son had driven off the first day at Nimblewill Gap. It was an overwhelming sense of aloneness, but now it was tempered by the confidence of knowing that I had the physical and mental strength to succeed and that I would continue. After the car was out of sight, I sat beside my pack and drank a bottle of beer I had carried along for the occasion and contemplated what I had accomplished and where I needed to go.

While hiking with Dan and Cathy, I had neglected my commitment to meditation and spiritual development which had characterized my periods of solo hiking. I found it impossible to retain the concentration needed for meditation while in the presence of other people. I wanted to return to that effort and reaffirmed my vow to pursue my goal of spiritual development. I became more comfortable with my aloneness when I thought about it in those terms; I almost welcomed the solitude where I could again devote my total efforts toward my goals without having to consider someone else's feelings or desires. In a way, it was a strange feeling of "coming home." I felt content as I began to climb away from the highway toward the summit of Bald Knob.

Unfortunately, Bald Knob was no longer bald, which was a disappointment. There were no panoramas or sweeping vistas as I had imagined during my climb, only trees, rocks and roots along with a generous sprinkling of colorful wildflowers that helped compensate for the lack of views.

On the north side of Bald Knob, I met eight teenage hikers led by a tall, slender, young man with wire-rimmed glasses and a very thick black beard, dressed in worn jeans and a plain blue T-shirt. The hikers were separated into three groups: first came the hike leader along with four black boys, then about half a mile behind them, came two white boys, and about 15 minutes behind the two boys came two girls. The group was from Newport News, Virginia, and gathering from their behavior and the fact that one girl was wearing a USNA (United States Naval Academy) sweatshirt and knowing that Newport News was a large naval base, I concluded that they were "Navy brats." The girl with the USNA sweatshirt told me it belonged to her father which further strengthened my suspicions.

I stopped to talk with the hike leader and the four black boys. The boys were incredulous when I told them I had spent over two months on the Trail. They looked at me suspiciously trying to decide if I was pulling their leg or simply deranged. Then one of them spoke up, shaking his head emphatically: "No way, man! Ain't no way no one could get me to live like this for two weeks let alone two months."

"You get used to it after a while," I countered. "It depends on your perspective."

"You been alone for two months?" asked another boy.

I nodded. "Mostly."

"No way! Ain't no way you'd catch me out here by myself with all the bears and wolves and snakes. Ain't you scared?" said the first boy, rolling his eyes and lifting his head skyward in disbelief.

I tried to put things into perspective for them by explaining that no animals in the mountains would hurt humans, that animals were afraid of man and tried to keep out of our way. I told them that the wolves had been driven from the mountains long ago, and if there were any, they wouldn't hurt hikers because wolves don't attack humans. I also told them that the only bears that lived in the Appalachians or anywhere in the eastern United States were black bears and they were timid animals, that they wouldn't even see a bear unless they went to one of the national parks where bears are protected.

"What about grizzly bears? They eat people."

"There are no grizzly bears here. Grizzlies exist only in the extreme western U.S. in Yellowstone National Park and Montana, up in Glacier National Park."

"How much your pack weigh?" asked another boy.

"About 45 pounds."

"You carry that for two months, too? Where'd you start?"

"I started at Springer Mountain, just north of Atlanta."

The four boys became silent, and I looked over at the group leader who was enjoying the conversation immensely, smiling broadly at the reaction of the boys. Suddenly, one boy, not trusting what he had just heard, repeated to me, "You started in Georgia? You been steady walkin' for two months up to here?"

I nodded my head.

"A man's got to be crazy to do that," he scowled. "You sleep in the woods every night? When do you take a shower or a bath?"

I looked directly at the boy who had just spoken. "I'm not crazy. I sleep in a shelter when one is available and in a tent otherwise. I shower and wash whenever I can find water. Sometimes when I come to a town, I pull off for a day and clean up and rest."

"Only thing I want is to get back home, get away from all these bugs, get back to walking on streets instead of stumbling all over the place over rocks and climbin' these dumb mountains."

"You can learn a lot about yourself in these 'dumb mountains'," I replied. "You have a great opportunity to experience nature and a different way of life and to learn from it. All it requires is that you approach it with an open mind and look at the experience as a learning opportunity. You should look at it from a positive perspective. If you allow a little physical discomfort to negate the benefits of the experience, you might as well have stayed home in the first place. It's all in how you approach it. It's a wonderful opportunity. I hope you won't let a little discomfort spoil it."

The one boy continued to spout negative rhetoric, but the others were quiet. I don't know if anything I said had any effect on them. I could still hear the loud one of the group as I rounded a switchback in the Trail below them: "Ain't no way you ever gonna catch me out here again. Man's crazy!"

I had originally intended to stay overnight at Wiggins Spring shelter. However, I had heard that locals used it frequently for parties, and since it was a Saturday night, I figured the odds on meeting a party at the shelter had increased to an unacceptable ratio. Instead, I chose to stay at the Cow Camp Gap shelter which was two miles closer. Although it was early in the afternoon when I reached the shelter, I had been climbing for four miles and the shelter was a welcome sight.

As I had vowed earlier, I tried to meditate but found it difficult to focus my concentration for any length of time. Eventually, however, I decided that my spiritual questions had basically been answered during my fibrillation attacks, the episode on Beauty Spot, and my encounters with the Batys, Blessings, Stielpers and Mike Joslin. I recognized I was just beginning the process and much effort would be required to develop a comprehensive spirituality as a guide for life. I needed to reach another level in my meditation and much time would be required to work through the transition. There was no way I could accelerate the process; that would take its own good time. Meanwhile, I needed to develop patience and the serenity that comes with patience. All in all, I was confident and quite pleased with my conclusions when I turned in.

I awoke the next morning to find the mountaintop completely enveloped by clouds. The meadows of Grassy Ridge and Cole Mountain were soaked from cloud mist. After about five minutes, my feet were as wet as if I had walked through a stream. It was not bad hiking, though. It was deliciously cool on the balds, and occasionally the mist cleared enough to let some partial sunshine through and provide some tantalizing views of the valley and mountains in the distance.

Even with the dampness, the beauty of the balds was exciting and at the same time mysterious, since the mist allowed only partial glimpses of reality, as if it were afraid to show too much and wanted to tantalize the hiker into continuing. Even familiar objects assumed strange and unfamiliar shapes which continually challenged and excited me, and I thoroughly enjoyed experiencing a "safe" unknown. I also enjoyed the extensive stands of butter-and-eggs flowers that bloomed profusely across the meadows creating their own little slices of sunlight through the mist.

As I descended the north side of Cole Mountain, I encountered a dog like none I had ever seen. It had a boxer's body but was longer, taller and less compact. Its head was broad and flat across the face, but its nose had a distinct point with powerful jaws that reminded me of the jaws of a pit bull. It stopped in the Trail a few feet ahead of me and I also stopped. Its master called with a tinge of urgency in his voice for it to come back, but the animal didn't move. He hurried forward to grab it by the collar. I asked what kind of a dog it was, and he told me it was a cross between a pit bull and a Doberman Pinscher. I immediately recognized the traits of the Doberman's slender body and the powerful neck and chest of the pit bull. I was glad he had control of the dog. I imagined it could have been a formidable adversary had it decided to attack.

After descending the north end of Grassy Ridge into Hog Camp Gap, I decided to follow a jeep trail shown on the old AT Guide Map and bypass the climb up Tar Jacket Ridge. I walked down the road looking for the jeep trail. Somehow I missed it and went another 500 yards before I realized my mistake and retraced my steps. This time I was much more attentive and found the rather ill-defined path leading from a place where dirt had been heaped at the roadside.

The path led across a broad ridgeside field through brown, waist-high grass and a deserted apple orchard full of beautiful-looking, but terrible-tasting, apples. After about a mile, the trail split, one side of the fork leading through some even taller grass to the bank of a beautiful stream that flowed noiselessly through a small patch of sunlight.

The mist had cleared at this point, and I could see the summit of Tar Jacket Ridge looming above me as I walked through the fields. I wanted to stop and enjoy the beauty of the stream, but I had already spent too much time and decided to push on. I returned uphill to the other trail branch. But it, too, ended in a tangle of thick bushes and tall grass, and I was forced to return to the road and eventually go back to Hog Camp Gap and the Trail. I was not very happy at the turn of events as I started up Tar Jacket Ridge. I had walked about three useless miles and wasted about an hour and a half in the process.

After a short period of self-chastisement, I recognized the destructiveness of my negative conditioning and tried to put a positive slant to the experience. I thought about the beautiful little stream gliding through the woods at the forest's edge and saw again the patch of sunlight. Had I not made the excursion I would not have experienced the moment or the beauty. It was another example of how I could broaden my perspective. It became a foundation on which to build a positive attitude. When I thought about it in those terms, the whole episode turned into a positive experience.

It was late afternoon when I reached Spy Rock Overlook, a massive rock deposit on a ridge arm of Maintop Mountain, that overlooked a vast panorama of mountains and valleys to the east and south. The site had been used by both sides during the Civil War for signal purposes and, I suspect, for intelligence gathering because of its commanding view of the terrain. I tried to make the mountain masses in the distance correspond to the names of the mountains indicated in the *Trail Guide* as being visible from that point. I knew I could see Priest Mountain, Little Priest, the Friar, Porters Ridge, the Cardinal, and Pompey Mountain, but I couldn't tell which mountain belonged to which name. I abandoned the identification effort and allowed myself to simply admire the splendor, then left my perch only when it began to thunder. I became concerned that a storm might be approaching.

My heart engaged in a couple of short arrhythmias as I headed back towards my pack, and I thought it might be time to rest from the ardors of the Trail. Not only did my heart begin acting up, the wind also began acting up, and I sensed rain in the offing. Although it was fairly early, I decided it would be provident to erect my tent and stay for the night.

This was a good decision. The rain started as soon as I erected my tent, and except for a short break during which I cooked supper, it continued for much of the night. Despite the torrent, the tent remained completely dry inside, and I snuggled a little deeper into my sleeping bag and savored the protection and comfort. About 2:00 a.m. the rain ceased, but the wind increased in intensity. It screamed through tree tops and tore unmercifully at the rainfly, and, even as I slept, visions of trees crashing down on top of me flashed intermittently into my consciousness. Despite the shrieking and moaning and the visions of violence, the calm morning found me in one piece with the tent still intact.

I awoke before dawn to a crystal clear, dark blue, almost black sky with the suggestion of a pale pink glow toward the east. I climbed from my sleeping bag and stumbled to Spy Rock to watch the sunrise. The beauty I saw and the feelings I experienced during those few moments will forever remain engraved in the images of my mind. I was reminded once again of how provident events became for me. If I had not had the heart arrhythmia and if it had not rained the previous evening, I would have continued on the Trail and probably never experienced the beauty.

The deep and foreboding shadows of the collective mountain mass stretching before me contrasted with a blazing thin line of red-orange light that traced the silhouette of the horizon looking like a crinkled bolt of red lightning frozen in time. The lightening hues then faded imperceptibly skyward as the sun crept above the mountains. When it finally cleared the horizon, the sun's rays reflected brilliantly from the mists that layered in the distant valleys. It was a feast of color: the layers of mist looking like a sea of gold from which rose dense purple mountain islands, stabbing into the pale sky. It was so intense, so silent, so awesome that I was consumed by the emotion of pure beauty that swept through me. I remained long after the sun rose, hoping somehow to experience another comparable beauty, but it was in vain and after about 45 minutes, I climbed back down, struck my tent and headed for the Priest.

The Priest was slightly over 4,000 feet high, but the Trail followed an old logging road and the climb was not difficult. Cold, clear spring water flowed from a pipe near the shelter, and I stopped to wash my cookpot and spoon as well as my face. (There had been no water at Maintop or Spy Rock.)

Just before I left the shelter, I found a white quartz arrowhead lying in the dirt in front of the shelter. I cleaned it off and stuck it in my pack along with a spear point I had found earlier lying in the Trail amid a jumble of other rocks and stones. At the summit, I stopped at a rock outcropping with a magnificent view of the valley to the north, but coming on the same day that I had witnessed the sunrise from Spy Rock, it seemed strangely inadequate by comparison.

Shortly before beginning its precipitous drop down Priest Mountain, the Trail crossed an open rock face which sloped gradually to the northeast. I stopped to eat lunch and admire the valley stretching like a living miniature model thousands of feet below me. Tiny cars barely crawled along black ribbon roads. A farmer on a tractor cutting hay was creating a geometric figure like others that had been created in adjacent fields, their gold and amber hues contrasting with the bright Kelly green pastures and the deeper greens of the other fields that surrounded them. Cattle drinking from a pond almost directly below me looked more like insects than cattle. The sun was glorious and there was little wind. I closed my eyes to bask in peace, letting my mind recreate the scenes I had just witnessed below.

Near Harpers Creek shelter, I detoured over the Mau-Har Trail to view a 40-foot waterfall mentioned in the *Trail Guide*. The word Mau-Har comes from an abbreviation using the first three letters of the shelters at the termini of the trail: MAUpin Field shelter to the north and HARpers Creek shelter to the south.

The pathway was well maintained, and the walking was easy in the beginning; but the Trail soon deteriorated to the point that crossing some of the make-shift little bridges across steep drop-offs was dangerous. The elevations which the Trail traversed were much more difficult than they appeared to be on the map.

The waterfall, although beautiful, was not a true 40-footer like other falls I had seen. This was more of a steep rapids where the water tumbled over a series of rocks ending with a straight fall of about ten feet at the bottom. The climb back to the AT and Maupin Field shelter, where I planned to spend the night, was difficult and exhausting. The Trail paralleled Campbell Creek up the ridge to its source, and I spent the remainder of the afternoon shinnying over gigantic boulders, negotiating very steep banks with often slippery roots and moss-covered rocks, and climbing giant drop-offs.

Campbell Creek was large enough that, in places, large rock deposits captured the swirling water into inviting pools. I was tempted to go for a swim. Unfortunately, the temperature had dropped. Although pleasant for hiking, it was too cold for bathing. It was after 5:00 p.m. when I reached the more hospitable upper levels of the ridge where the Trail evened out.

Despite the difficulty of the climb back, the trip was worth it. I had experienced a pristine wilderness. The forest was very rocky and the vegetation thick and tangled giving the landscape the appearance of being untamed. I doubted that many people took the effort to visit the falls, at least from the AT.

The next day was basically uneventful despite a promising start. I awoke in the morning to the sight of a large deer watching me from about 20 yards away in the shelter clearing. As soon as I moved, it bounded gracefully into the forest and disappeared.

My feet hurt when I put my boots on. The big toes of both my feet had developed ingrown toenails. After walking a while, however, the pain either subsided, or I became used to it.

I found, throughout the trip, that in the mornings I almost always faced physical discomfort of one sort or another: sore muscles, stiff neck, sore ankle, pulled groin, blistered heel or ingrown toenail. Although all were irritating, they probably had more significance mentally than physically. It usually took only a short time on the Trail for the aches to disappear. I guessed they were a reminder of my age and a joke told by one of the members of my tennis team in Germany. The punch line: If a senior player awoke in the morning without a pain somewhere in his body, then he knew he was dead.

The hiking was boring now. There were almost no views, and throughout the day all I saw were trees and rocks, more trees and rocks, and an occasional rabbit, squirrel or bird of some type. The Trail was not conducive to maintaining a positive attitude. I had to constantly rescue myself from the clutches of a negative mindset. All in all, I was ready to call it a day when I arrived at Rockfish Gap.

I intended to stay at the Howard Johnson motel, but the place was deserted. However, on the ridge directly above the Howard Johnson restaurant was a new Holiday Inn, so new in fact, that workers were still completing various parts of the building. Many of the rooms being rented had not been completely finished. Although they lacked certain basic items like bulbs or lamps and shower curtains, management still charged the full price.

The reservation clerks were busy attending to some businessmen when I arrived. I stood back in the lobby until their transactions were completed before approaching the counter. Much to my surprise, the clerks completely ignored me. They disappeared into a rear room, and I had to call them back. They acted surprised to see me, though they had been looking at me while I waited in the lobby for them to finish with the previous customers. I thought once about leaving, but there seemed to be no other operational motel in the immediate area. I stuffed my anger and took a room.

After showering, I set out to do my laundry. I followed the signs to the laundry room where there was no soap powder. I asked one of the passing maids where I could get some soap. She shrugged her shoulders saying, "Front desk maybe." I returned to the front desk and again had to call someone from the room behind the counter.

A young woman with blond hair swept meticulously back on both sides of her face like folded wings came from behind the door. She looked very businesslike in her blue uniform suit with brass nameplate. "Kin I hep yew?" she asked.

"By any chance, do you have any soap powder for the washing machine?" I asked.

She shook her head.

I tried again. "Know where I can get any?"

This time she thought a minute before she shook her head.

"Where's the nearest place I could get some?" I asked. The woman had yet to respond to me orally, and I was becoming angry. A vacuous expression accompanied the shrug of her shoulders.

"Waynesboro?" she replied like it was a question.

"How far?" I dug. I was really getting angry.

"'Bout five miles."

"No place closer?"

She shook her head and started back toward the room behind the counter from where I heard several peals of laughter.

I was within a heartbeat of calling her back and telling her just how lousy I thought she was in dealing with customers, but I was afraid that I would say something I shouldn't and I didn't want to destroy what tranquillity I thought I had achieved. I was surprised at how angry I had become and realized that I had not yet put past frustrations behind me, that I hadn't yet learned to cope properly with current manifestations of incompetence that reminded me of my military past.

I headed back to a laundry room I had passed earlier where the motel linens were washed. An elderly, black woman, sitting beside a gigantic commercial-type washing machine, looked up as I entered. "Don't by any chance have some washing powder I could buy from you?" I called out, trying to get my volume above the din of running washers and dryers.

"Jes' a minute," she replied and disappeared behind the machine. She returned about 30 seconds later with a styrofoam cup full of blue, liquid wash detergent. "If you needs more, jes' holler!" she yelled.

"Thanks a million, you're a lifesaver!" I yelled back as I pressed a dollar into her hand.

She handed it back. "Don't cost nothing."

I gave it back to her again. "I may not look it, but I can afford it. Thanks again!"

After washing my clothes, I headed to the motel restaurant where I ate a poorly prepared meal under the haughty eye of the restaurant manager, a gaunt-looking man with a pencil-thin villain's moustache. It was not a pleasant experience. The whole scene: the overly ornate furnishings, the snobbish motel clerks and the pompous restaurant staff seemed totally out of character with the Virginia mountains. I was so irritated by the phoniness of the place that I became angry again. It was useless, destructive anger. It was for me, an unhealthy anger, and I recognized it. But I seemed powerless to control it. I was definitely not in a good frame of mind when I went to bed.

BROWN MOUNTAIN CREEK RUINS

Across the creek, half hidden in trees
Lies a rock wall that doesn't belong.
It leads up the valley
Past ruins of stone,
Past corners of homes
And ends as abruptly as time.
There are traces of buildings,
Of chimneys and walls,
Of sheds and barns and animal stalls,
Of places for gardens
And roads through the woods.
All remnants of lives
That 'til now have withstood
The press of the land to its past.

It is sad to consider
The people who dreamed,
And the struggle
They fought with the land —
For the gardens they lost
And the ruins of hope
That lie buried a-deep in the moss —
To the dreams they let go
To the valleys beyond.
Where new gardens awaited the seed.
And to finally know
The forest has won,
And that time is a tyrant in green.

CHAPTER 23

The Struggle Continues
The Shenandoah National Park

I stopped at the southern entrance to the Shenandoah National Park the next morning and registered for backpack tran-
sit through the Park by filling out a two-part registration tag,
one part of which I tied to the back of my pack, so that authorities could see at a glance that I was registered with the Park Service; the other part I deposited in a slot at the sign-in point. (I
assumed the second part served recording and statistical purposes and wondered why the form had not been designed with
a carbon duplicate rather than making the hiker fill out the
same information twice.) I was visually checked once by a Park
Ranger who slowed his patrol car as I walked along the Skyline
Drive, but that was the only time anyone in authority paid any
attention to me.

I hiked the Skyline Drive for much of the time, stopping at
overlooks to rest and admire the vistas through the haze of the
sultry midsummer day. I also enjoyed the colorful displays of
wildflowers: sunflowers, oxeye daisies, black-eyed susans and
others that grew in profusion along the road and from the crevices of the rock walls that were formed when the road had been
cut into ridges. Now and then, a cardinal or a robin added its
color to the forest, and sometimes small yellow birds with black
wings, which I thought were probably goldfinches, flitted between the trees.

The Trail to the summit of Bear Den Mountain wound
through an extensive deposit of shale-like rocks that looked like
snake den territory, so I proceeded with caution. Evidently my
concern had some justification.

A short distance from the top was a large boulder with the

word SNAKES painted in bold white letters. But that was the closest thing to a snake that I saw. I had been warned and asked about snakes so often that I had developed some perverted sense of herpetological curiosity. Not only that, I wanted to appear credible as a hiker by being able to boast of having seen a giant timber rattler or at least a pygmy rattler. Unfortunately, the only snakes that could have mesmerized me with their beady eyes had slithered off the Trail well in advance of my coming. In fact, the only live snakes I encountered in the Park were small, night-crawler size, black snakes with a single thin yellow band directly behind the head. I did run across occasional dead timber rattlesnakes and copperheads lying flattened on the Skyline Drive where they had been run over by cars. But they were a poor substitute for the living reptiles with which I wanted to populate the imaginations of my listeners.

It was late afternoon when I reached Blackrock Gap and headed up the mountain toward Blackrock Hut, the shelter where I would spend the night. I had climbed about 300 yards when movement about 75 yards up the Trail caught my attention. A small, black bear cub was rooting through the leaves and twigs alongside the Trail.

My first reaction was to look around to be sure Mother Bear wasn't to my rear. Much to my relief, she materialized from the forest background about 30 yards behind the cub. I remained motionless as the bears ambled down the Trail. They didn't walk directly on the Trail itself but rather used it as a guide for direction, going off to the side for a few yards, nosing through the leaves on the forest floor, then coming back to it. They were completely focused on their search for food and unaware of my presence, even though I was close enough to see the fur rippling across their shoulder muscles and could discern their facial features. The cub's face was coal black, but its mother had a brownish muzzle. The cub had not yet fully learned to control its muscles and moved in the clumsy way young animals do until they master their motor skills.

The bears continued down the hill towards me. When they got too close, I retreated, grudgingly giving up the yardage I had so laboriously gained during my climb. I enjoyed watching them and wanted to be nearer to them. But that was tempered by the discretion of not wanting them to get so close that the mother bear felt her cub was threatened.

After I had retreated about 50 yards, I decided to let the

bears know I was present. I rapped my hiking stick on a stone. The sound reverberated like an explosion in the forest silence.

Both bears jerked their heads up simultaneously and looked directly at me. I remained motionless, hoping the sound would convince them to leave the Trail. I wanted to remain as inconspicuous as possible. No luck!

Although I was less than 20 yards away in open forest with no obstructions between us, the bears could not see me. The mother bear sniffed the air several times from different directions, then, apparently satisfied there was no danger, put her head down to the path and resumed her progress down the hill.

I rapped the rock again. This time, when the bears looked up, I waved my arms. The mother bear saw me and immediately went crashing down the hill through the forest to my right with the cub galloping hobbyhorse-style behind her.

I was both slightly relieved and slightly disappointed — relieved that an occasion of possible danger had passed but disappointed that I could no longer watch such beautiful animals in a natural setting without fences or zoo-like barriers between us. After the bears had disappeared, I continued climbing toward Blackrock Hut, but my mind was still absorbed with the scene I had just witnessed. I again pictured the cub, a miniature of its mother, ambling slowly down the trail, swinging its head, investigating all the strange and exciting things that take place daily in the forest.

After a few minutes of climbing, I reached the shelter access trail which veered obliquely back down the mountain for a couple of hundred yards in the same direction as the bears had run. I surveyed the forest ahead of me as I descended, peering intently down the ridge, hoping to again see the bears. My attention was so focused on looking for the bears that I was surprised when I came to the shelter.

Jim Goode, a tall, strongly muscled young man in his early 20s, had already laid claim to half the sleeping platform. We struck up an easy conversation, and it was immediately apparent that Jim was very knowledgeable about the Trail. He informed me he had thru-hiked the entire Trail the previous year. He became increasingly animated as he talked, saying he enjoyed the experience so much that he was considering hiking the whole thing again.

Jim Goode was not unique in that respect; almost everyone I met who had thru-hiked the Trail was enthusiastic about the experience. We talked for about 30 minutes after supper until the shadows began to gather and fatigue overwhelmed me, and I climbed into my sleeping bag. Jim took a candle and a book from his pack and began to read.

I slept very well and awakened fully refreshed and enthusiastic about the hike the next morning. The weather was beautiful when I started, but by afternoon it had deteriorated into a humid, cloudy day with intermittent showers. Despite the weather, I enjoyed the hiking and especially the wildlife.

At Simmons Gap Ranger Station, I encountered two does and two spotted fawns feeding on the lush vegetation beside the road. One of the fawns ran off in a minor panic as I approached but stopped in confusion when its mother didn't follow. She merely continued feeding, paying scant attention to me as did the other doe and her fawn. I stopped to watch and eventually the first fawn ambled back to the group and began feeding again. I was a little surprised that the deer did not react when I stopped to watch them. I was not more than 10 or 15 yards away and had expected them to move further into the forest or at least further away from me. It was good to see animals that were not terrified of man, yet I was uneasy. Their lack of fear put them in some danger from people like the two poachers who had killed the buck at Birch Springs Gap in the Smokies.

At Loft Mountain, I stopped at the campstore concession and bought a sack full of goodies; candy (I had developed an insatiable sweet tooth.), bologna, cheese, mayonnaise, a couple cans of beer, and two Dixie cups of ice cream that I devoured as soon as I stepped outside the door. I then followed the Trail downhill through an extensive stand of black locust trees until it crossed the Skyline Drive beside a small service center containing a filling station, burger bar and gift shop. The temptation of a hamburger with french fries and a milk shake was too powerful to resist. I stopped for lunch.

I ignored a large NO PACKS sign in front of the entrance, placed my pack just inside the front door, where I could keep an eye on it, and headed for the counter. A six-inch wide black line painted on the floor wound through the dining area to a narrow counter across the room where customers placed their orders a la McDonalds. A sign placed conspicuously near the entrance ordered all who entered to follow the black line.

I ignored the line and deliberately cut across the room, coming to the order counter from the side opposite where I would have come had I followed the line. I expected someone to challenge me, but no one said anything.

A teenage boy took my order, going through the motions with mechanical indifference as he jotted check marks beside my choices on the order form. He never once smiled.

When he was finished, he handed me the stub and gestured toward the dining area, saying, "They'll call your number when it's ready." He turned away with hardly a glance in my direction.

I sat near the window by the front entrance where I could watch my pack. After about 15 minutes, my number was called. I wolfed down a surprisingly good hamburger along with a creamy thick milk shake.

After eating, I went to the men's room. Although it was only shortly after noon, there was no soap in the soap dispenser and no towels or hand-drying machines. I thought I'd use toilet paper to soak the excess water from my hands. No toilet paper. I went to the burger bar and informed a young women that the men's room needed towels and toilet paper.

"The rest rooms don't belong to us," she snapped. "They belong to the gift shop."

I could feel the familiar surge of irritation as I turned towards the gift shop. I got the same type of response from the woman at the gift shop who turned away from me without the courtesy of a reply. It was apparent that the maintenance of the rest rooms had become a "turf dispute" with no one wanting the responsibility and the result was obvious.

I thought about the incident later in the afternoon, and the more I thought about it the more irritated I became. I was still in a snit when I arrived at Hightop Mountain to spend the night. The shelter was a beautifully constructed wood and fieldstone lean-to set in a small opening carved from the hardwood forest. Off to the side of the clearing stood a stout, 12- or 13-foot tall steel pole with several tines at the top. At first, I was puzzled by the pole until I deduced its purpose. It was for pack protection. Another shorter, six-foot steel pole with a U-shaped hook at one end was attached to the taller pole by a length of chain. It was used to lift packs and place them on the tines of the taller pole.

Here was a great idea but difficult to execute. When a 40-pound pack was added to the hook end of the small pole, great strength was required to overcome the leverage of so much weight at the end of the pole. Just getting the pack into the air was difficult enough, but tying to balance and control the pole movement so that the pack frame or straps could be seated on the tines, required patience and coordination as well as strength. After several close misses, during which I nearly lost control of the pole, I succeeded in slipping the pack onto a tine and stepped back to admire my efforts. The pack looked funny hanging in the air, but it was perfectly safe from bears. When I thought about it, I preferred that arrangement to the chain-link fencing solution in the Smokies.

Supper that evening consisted of bologna and cheese sandwiches made from the fixings I had bought at the Loft Mountain Campground store. My thoughts slid automatically from the store to the Service center and the burger bar bathroom incident and I reviewed again, with some disappointment, my reaction to the inefficiency and indifference I had experienced.

I was unhappy with myself for allowing anger to dominate my disposition and outlook. I had allowed anger to again control my consciousness when I was hiking through a place of magnificent beauty. I had focused on the source of my anger and ignored the positive experience of the spectacular natural setting and my part in it. I had lost a significant opportunity to experience something I might never see or feel again. I had seen with my eyes the beauty of the day, but I had not taken the beauty into my soul because the avenue of awareness was blocked by a blinding shroud of negative messages.

Despite the seeming progress I thought I had seen earlier, I seemed not to have mellowed at all. I had let anger dominate me at the Holiday Inn the previous day, and now I had allowed anger to again assume the upper hand. I was, in a sense, still "spring loaded in the pissed-off position," prepared at the slightest provocation to unleash the fury of my wrath on the "miscreant" who displeased me.

I needed to create a response pattern different from the one I had created in the Army. The "kick ass, take names" mentality, the guilt-fixing, the ego-building anger binges were inappropriate now. I had to find another way to react to the stimuli which caused anger. I had to get back to the source of my destructive urges and recreate an entirely different response pattern.

I had been conditioned by my profession to obtain results by demand and fear more than by proactive means. I laid down what I expected and if I didn't get what I demanded, if my standard was not met, then my response was to savage the party who was at "fault." It occurred to me that I never appealed to the

God in myself and, by way of implication, the God in others in my dealing with them. I simply didn't think about God residing in me, let alone His presence in others. In fact, I had ignored everything which was remotely connected with spirituality. I could find no positive direction in my limited concept of spirituality. It simply did not exist for me.

I again became aware that a very integral part of me had never been developed. There was no tradition of spirituality in my family or among those with whom I grew up. When I thought of things spiritual, I automatically relegated them to the care of "religion." I didn't realize at the time that there was a difference between religion and spirituality.

Suddenly, I understood for the first time that my life was out of balance. I had never before perceived life as an entity that required balance for fulfillment or meaning. Rather I had viewed life as a quest for pleasure. It was, for me, a series of experiences guided by a desire for material gain, increased sensual satisfaction and increased physical comfort. My next promotion assumed more and more importance. The accumulation of possessions: houses, cars, appliances and wealth in general became the driving forces which shaped my existence. Now, I realized there was another aspect to my life which I had completely neglected. I had so totally focused my attention on the material aspects of life that I had no concept of the other dimensions in my life. In short, I was out of balance. But I was not alone.

Almost everyone I knew was out of balance. I ventured that most Americans were out of balance, that our attention was so intensely focused on our material well-being that we had no time or inclination to look around us. We seemed never able to get enough. When I was a teenager, I thought perfect happiness was a secondhand 1934 Ford convertible coupe with a rumble seat and a spare tire on the back. It was coal-black with red wire wheels and white-wall tires, and I was the envy of kids for miles around. After about a week, I realized my little dream car was not the source of perfect contentment. I saw a 1936 Ford that made me forget all about my little coupe.

I became more aware of the vital importance balance played in our lives. Balance affected us in almost every way, from diet to work patterns to our recreational endeavors. I included the lack of exercise, overuse of alcohol and drugs, and overindulgence in pleasures of all kinds as examples of our lack of balance.

Clearly, we were paying the price of a drug-riddled society because of the lack of a moral or spiritual counterbalance to the materialist or hedonistic nature of our culture. Our children had no spiritual navigational system on which to rely in their journey to adulthood. They understood only the materialist passions of life because we had not provided the counterbalancing spiritual values that teach them to become whole people. And the reason we did not provide them those values was because we ourselves had not received them from our parents.

The more I analyzed it, the more convinced I became of the need for balance that only spiritual understanding could provide. I especially needed it to eliminate the vestiges of stress which remained like a lamprey sucking the life from my creative psyche. It appeared that the key to countering stress would be to develop a counterbalancing spiritual accommodation with God, one wherein I could place the responsibility for control with Him who really was in control. Just pass it to Him, I told myself firmly.

Now the question arose of how to achieve balance. The fact that I recognized my lack of spiritual power was a serious deficiency was an absolute necessary first step toward attainment of balance. The second step was to develop a harmonious life-style reflective of the balance which spirituality would bring. With that harmony would also come serenity and understanding and acceptance of life, at least that was what I intended it to do. The more I looked at the problem, the clearer became the solution. I alone could not achieve spiritual balance, but if I allowed myself to give control to God, He would help me in my struggle. I was basically back to the concept of faith, to belief in the possibilities represented by God.

As the daylight dimmed, my eyes closed, and I perceived that I had again made some very important personal discoveries and decisions. It also seemed to me that I had reached that next level in my search for spirituality. I snuggled a little deeper in my sleeping bag. But I did not sleep well at all.

A squirrel had set up housekeeping somewhere in the shelter, and it and the shelter mice gnawed and scratched wood the entire night. Not only did the animals keep me from sleeping soundly, I also experienced several episodes of prolonged heart palpitations which added anxiety.

When I awoke the next morning, I had no desire to hike 20 miles to Big Meadows Lodge. My disinclination was bolstered by several severe heart palpitations and dizziness as I climbed Hightop Mountain. When I reached U.S. Highway 33, two miles further on, I came off the Trail and hitched a ride into Elkton, Virginia, where I took a room at the Misty Hills Motel, a run-down but seemingly adequate place to rest.

After settling into my room, I went to the motel office and called the Big Meadows Lodge to make a reservation for the following night. I learned that the Lodge would not honor the reservation if I arrived after 4:00 p.m. I explained that I was hiking the AT, that I was on foot and that I couldn't guarantee I'd arrive by 4:00 p.m. But it was to no avail.

"I'm sorry, sir. The policy is quite ironclad. We can hold the reservation until 4:00 p.m. only."

I was about to ask for her supervisor. I could feel the familiar surge of anger as I mumbled about the "stupid bureaucracy in the middle of the stupid woods." Then something told me to cool it. "I'll surely make the place by 4:00 p.m." I said. After all, it was only 18 miles and if I walked the road, I'd get there in six hours. And so what if they let it go? I had a tent on my back or I could go to a shelter. What's the big deal? My anger subsided and I returned to my room.

A number of highway construction workers had booked several rooms in the motel and spent the evening drinking and conversing in loud voices that carried their profanity-laden thoughts to everyone in the motel.

The motel manager, a young man with the same mentality as the construction workers, did nothing to control the situation. In fact, he was intimidated into currying favor with the workers and became part of the problem. Eventually they all passed out or fell asleep, and I was able to get some rest. Fortunately, I had napped for a couple of hours earlier in the afternoon so I was in pretty good shape.

At 5:00 a.m. I was awakened by the sound of racing truck motors and banging on doors and shouts from the straw boss trying to rouse the workers from their drunken stupors. The commotion lasted for about an hour. More than once I thought about telling the noisemakers to be quiet. But I realized that I was unlikely to get any satisfaction. More than likely, my complaining would have resulted in a confrontation which I certainly didn't need. I kept quiet.

After they left, I dozed intermittently for about an hour and then got up. I was on the road by 7:00 a.m. trying to hitch a ride back to the Trail. But two hours passed before a man with a fully loaded station wagon picked me up. I was concerned that my late start would cause me to miss the 4:00 p.m. reservation deadline at Big Meadows Lodge, and I maintained a three-plus-mile an hour pace. I stopped only twice, once to watch a skunk that had become trapped beneath one of the low fieldstone walls that acted as a traffic guardrail and once to take a short break immediately afterwards. The skunk had either dug under the wall or attempted to wriggle through an existing hole and had become wedged in place in the process. It tried frantically to extricate itself as I approached, clawing at the air and twisting at the same time so as to keep me in sight as I passed. It was stuck in such a way that its rear end, the dangerous end, was under the wall. Despite its humorous gyrations, it was unable to free itself.

I took some photographs of the skunk, then climbed to a small parking lot where I met two young women returning from a day-hike. I told them about the skunk, and they hurried off to see the sight for themselves. The skunk had extricated itself by the time they reached the "skunk tunnel" and when they returned, they accused me of sending them off on a "wild skunk chase."

I arrived at Big Meadows with about 30 minutes to spare and checked into a small but comfortable attic room in the wood and fieldstone lodge. After cleaning up and washing my clothes, I headed for the lodge dining hall where I sat directly behind an older German couple who were conversing loudly in German with a female dinner companion. I couldn't help myself and intruded on their conversation, much to the delight of the couple, but evidently not to their companion who began translating for me. It appeared that she was of German descent but had been in America for so long that her German ethnicity seemed stereotyped.

The man, a school teacher from Kassel, West Germany, informed me he had recently suffered a heart attack and retired early. He was basically a very pleasant gentleman but exhibited a certain pedantic mentality by being an authority on every topic we discussed. As we talked, I was reminded of a 1950 vintage movie I had seen on German television, called *Feuerzangen Bowle* (Flaming Punch Bowl). It was a lighthearted, humorous story about a privileged and highly educated young man who, because he had received his education from private tutors, had never experienced life in a public school. To make up for this gap in his experience, he disguised himself as a student and enrolled in a public school. The film was basically an account of his experiences and escapades. The lead was played to perfection by Heinz Ruehemann, a dean of German film actors now in his 90s. If life had been as trying for current day teachers as depicted in the film, I could easily understand why my "friend" had suffered a heart attack.

The following day I hiked from Big Meadows to Pass Mountain shelter, a distance of about 18.4 miles, walking almost exclusively along the Skyline Drive, but returning to the Trail when it offered more scenic possibilities or a more direct route.

On the stretch between Stony Man Mountain and Hawksbill Gap, I met an older gentleman, a research meteorologist from Washington, D.C., by profession, but a birdwatcher by passion.

He wore very old sneakers that had rotted apart where the canvas uppers joined the rubber soles, and his stocking feet protruded from both the front and rear of both shoes. His trousers and shirt were stained and rumpled, and his hair looked as though he had just gotten out of bed and forgotten to comb it. In his left front shirt pocket was stuffed a thick pack of worn, dirty index cards on which were recorded notes about various birds. He held several cards in his hands which he caressed fondly with his thick fingers as we talked.

He said he had seen two whitetail bucks hiding among some boulders just down the Trail from where we were standing. "There's all kinds of wildlife out here. All you need to do is keep still and keep your eyes open. Pretty soon you'll see 'em. Most people miss 'em because they're in too much of a hurry."

I moved as slowly and quietly as possible down the Trail in the direction where he said he had seen the bucks. But I didn't see a trace of the deer.

I also met Jack Reeder, a past president of the Potomac Appalachian Trail Club, who, along with three other people, a man and two women, was maintaining the Trail. I told him how much I admired the spirit of the various Trail Club members for their sacrifice and dedication in working on the Trail. I felt it was important for all hikers, and especially Thru-Hikers, to tell the Trail maintainers how much their work is appreciated. I personally suspect that their efforts probably mean more to the viability of the AT as a recreational entity than any other single factor, including the money Congress appropriates for Trail protection. A short time later, I met two women happily engaged in arduous labor, trying to remove an obnoxious tree root that surely had been tripping unwary hikers.

It was late and I was exhausted when I reached Pass Mountain hut. Pat and Erin Keough, a father/daughter team, were already at the shelter. Pat, a large-boned man with a round, ruddy face and smiling blue eyes framed by glasses, spoke with a Bronx accent. He had a crisp Irish wit that initially seemed somewhat incongruous with his very apparent intellectual maturity. That incongruity was quickly explained when he informed me that he was an accountant by profession and worked for the General Services Administration (GSA) as an auditor. Anyone who worked for the GSA in any capacity, but especially as an auditor, had to have a fantastic sense of humor just to survive.

Erin was a very pretty girl, light complexioned like her father, but slight of build, and at first, because of the mature way she acted, I thought she might be Pat's wife or girlfriend. Later I learned she was only 14 years old and realized that her body was just beginning to round out. She took charge of the cooking and had a way of giving orders or asking questions that initially caused me to think she was older than she was. Neither of them mentioned Erin's mother during the conversation. Although it was a glaring omission, I didn't feel comfortable enough with them to raise the subject.

For supper I added some freeze-dried meat to my macaroni and cheese. It was delicious, but it was also highly seasoned with monosodium glutamate, and that night I went into atrial fibrillation. I converted back to my normal rhythm by morning, but since I had not slept well, I awoke with the now familiar washed-out feeling. I decided to take a day off from the Trail to rest. I was close to Elkwallow Gap which was within driving distance of the family home in Berryville, and I decided to ask my sister, Jackie, to pick me up. With that in mind, I headed slowly up the hill.

CHAPTER 24

A Journey Done — Half Way

It was midmorning when I arrived at Elkwallow Gap, and I joined the throng of people already congregating around the picnic area and the gift shop/burger bar concession. After calling home, I ordered two deluxe hamburgers and relaxed on a small grassy knoll near the service station to await my sister.

During the night, thieves had broken into the candy and soda machines near the gasoline pumps, and the filling station manager couldn't begin service until the Park Rangers had processed the crime scene and completed the paperwork. The customers listened quietly and nodded sympathetically as the manager poured out his tale of woe. No one complained, even quietly among themselves, let alone to the manager, as the Rangers went about their business.

The people paid little attention to me, but when I did speak with someone, the responses I received were universally positive and spontaneously friendly. After watching the scene for some time, it occurred to me that I was seeing real Americans, relaxed and freed, at least temporarily, from their work-a-day lives, and I was impressed by their universal good will.

My sister picked me up as planned, and inside of an hour, I was sipping beer in front of the TV. That afternoon I worked out a slack-packing schedule that covered almost 100 miles. I calculated it would require eight days to complete the distance, and by the end of that time I would have covered some 1030 miles, just about halfway in my adventure. It was now the 31st of August, and in another 11 days I would complete my third month on the Trail. Time to come off, I thought, then hastily reappraised my feeling.

I didn't want to make any decisions right then, preferring

instead to see how I felt and how the weather held. I didn't have much hope for the weather. I had had more than my share of rainy weather during the preceding weeks, and the outlook for the coming week promised more of the same.

That evening after supper, I discussed with my sister the possibility of her supporting me while I slack-packed, and she agreed, all except for taking me out to the Trail crossings at 7:00 a.m. in the mornings. For that chore, I enlisted the help of 82-year-old Russell Reeves, a family friend of longstanding, who was visiting my sister and mother. Russ, unlike my sister, was an early riser, so starting the day at 7:00 a.m. wasn't a problem. His only concern was that he wouldn't be able to find his way back after dropping me off, but I showed him on the maps where we would be going and in the end he agreed. Everything appeared set. The schedule I planned was simple:

> 1st day hike from Elkwallow Gap to Compton Gap
> 2nd day hike from Compton Gap to Manassas Gap
> 3rd day hike from Manassas Gap to Ashby Gap, Paris, VA
> 4th day hike from Ashby Gap to Snickers Gap
> 5th day hike from Snickers Gap to Keys Gap
> 6th day hike from Keys Gap to Weverton, MD
> 7th day hike from Weverton, MD to Turners Gap
> 8th day hike from Turners Gap to PA-MD state line

I awoke on the First of September to a heavy rain storm that weather reports indicated would last the day, and having not the slightest inclination to hike in the rain, I decided to take the day off. I reasoned that I needed the extra rest and new hiking boots, and I could use the time profitably to shop in Winchester for a new pair. My old blue-footed boobys had become so thin in the soles that every small rock or root on which I stepped jabbed my foot.

It also rained heavily the next day. After much deliberation, I chose to take it off also, but decided rain or not to start on the following day. I slept badly that night because the sound of the rain spattering on the metal porch roof outside my window penetrated even my unconscious state. I hoped desperately that it would diminish, which it did by morning, but then, just as Russ and I were about to leave, the sky opened up again and it poured. The perplexed look on Russ's face indicated what he was thinking as I loaded my pack into the car. Finally he said it. "You really going to hike in this stuff?"

I nodded with determination. "Real hikers hike in any weather," I lied. Russ only shook his head. Fortunately, the rain slackened to a light drizzle by the time we reached Elkwallow Gap.

Almost as soon as I started hiking up Piney Ridge, I began seeing deer. In the 1.9 miles between Elkwallow Gap and Rattlesnake Point overlook, I counted 18 of them, including a four-point buck. Mostly, they huddled together in small groups, all of them watching as I trudged silently along the pathway. I wondered if they were as tired of the miserable weather as I.

I was able to hike without interruption for the next several days and my slack-packing schedule worked perfectly. I was especially proud of my sister. I had chosen some obscure places as pickup points, but she always correctly navigated to the point and was there on time. Russ, for his part, had no difficulty because I drove to the drop-off points, and he had only to drive home.

The second day was a repeat of the weather of the previous four days, and I was beginning to think the sky would never clear. The high point of the day occurred when I encountered a young spotted fawn coming up the Trail. It moved silently over the rocks, its finely sculpted legs suggesting future speed and power as it climbed effortlessly toward me. I was fascinated by its liquid brown eyes that stared at me in wonderment. It sidled off the path to let me pass but remained so close I could have touched it. I walked for another ten yards then looked back. The fawn was watching me from the same place where I had passed it.

The low point of the day came at the very end of the hike, just before I reached the village of Linden, Virginia. The Trail followed a country road into town, and as I neared the town, the farms and fields gave way to houses, some built within a few yards of the road. As I approached the first house of a row that lined the right side of the road, a large golden retriever came racing in a frenzy down the lawn to challenge my presence. I stayed on the far side of the road from the house, hoping to remain outside the dog's territorial boundaries. The significance of my decision was lost on the dog.

It crossed the gravel driveway without slowing, hit the road snarling and barking, and stopped only when I raised my hiking stick. I sidestepped down the road to keep the snarling dog to my front. It lunged repeatedly at me, but I was able to keep it at bay by jabbing at it with my stick. Almost as soon as the golden retriever had crossed the road, a Doberman Pinscher appeared from behind the house and raced down the incline to reinforce the attack. I thought I might be in real trouble and wished I had my pistol with me. At least, I could have scared the dogs off with it. I backed down the road using my stick to fend off the dogs, at the same time yelling for the owners for help. No one came to my rescue.

The Doberman caught my hiking stick with his mouth, but I swung him to one side in a heaving motion and twisted the stick at the same time so that he lost his hold. Then I tried to nail him with the butt of it. The dog mostly evaded my thrust, but it was enough to buy more time and distance. In the meantime, the other dog tried to get behind me, and I swiped at it with my stick which sent it scurrying backwards. I was eventually able to work my way past the house, and after about 30 yards, the dogs quit their physical attack but continued to bark me off their turf. The adrenalin was still pumping when I reached the little general store on Virginia Highway 5 about 15 minutes later.

The mountains over which the Trail was sited were pretty tame compared to those in Tennessee and North Carolina. The drop-offs into the gaps were fairly steep, but less than 2,000 feet elevation in most cases. After I reached the ridge crest, I could depend on the Trail following a fairly level route with no great changes in elevation so long as it stayed on the ridge crest. Only when the Trail dropped down the mountainside did the hiking become difficult. Then the pathway fluctuated in elevation because of the side ridge arms and draws, and the hiking became a constant series of small climbs and descents. Although none of the changes in elevation where particularly long or steep, they were, nonetheless, tiring because of their sheer numbers. I learned again that fifty 100-foot ascents required as much energy as a steady 5,000-foot climb, perhaps more, because of the fifty 100-foot descents that followed the climbs. That was especially true of the Trail section between Ashby Gap and Snickers Gap.

The Blue Ridge in Northern Virginia consists of a chain of single mountains which stretch like a string of elongated green beads from the Maryland border to the Shenandoah National Park. Consequently, there were abundant views of the Virginia Piedmont to the east as well as those of the Shenandoah Valley which stretched verdantly westward toward the Allegheny Mountains of West Virginia. On the way from Snickers Gap to Keyes Gap, I crossed Devils Racecourse, an ancient stream deposit of steamer-trunk-sized boulders from beneath which could be heard the sound of a hidden present-day stream. The ancient

Confluence of the Potomac and Shenandoah Rivers at Harpers Ferry, West Virginia.

water course must have been very wide, judging from the width of the boulder field that stretched up the mountainside.

On the ridges surrounding Harpers Ferry, West Virginia, re-mained vestiges of the rock redoubts built by Civil War soldiers during the battle for the town. I was impressed by the house-sized boulders and wondered how they had been transported to form the redoubts. The Trail snaked about the rocks, crossed the ridge, and provided several excellent opportunities to view the junction of the Potomac and Shenandoah Rivers and the town of Harpers Ferry. The Potomac flowed easily between the gigantic boulder deposits as it coursed the gap in the Blue Ridge on its way toward Washington, D.C. The Shenandoah River seemed much less formi-dable in that it was very shallow with long stretches of rock ridges showing above the water like exposed ribbing, and the water seemed to flow quietly.

After crossing the Shenandoah River, I climbed the escarp-ment leading to the town heights and passed an old cemetery containing the final resting place of John Harper, one of the de-scendants of Robert Harper for whom the town was named. I

also passed Jefferson Rock, a large flat rock that rested precariously above the valley on red sandstone pillars that, in turn,
rested on a larger rock ledge. This rock was not the original
Jefferson Rock. The original rock was sent to the bottom of a
quarry in 1800 by some soldiers of the Federalist garrison in protest against Thomas Jefferson's campaign to reduce defense ap-
propriations. (How things have changed in the Army since that
time!) A short time later, I passed the fieldstone ruins of St.
John's Church, which was used as a medical aid station by both
sides during the Civil War.

The route I had chosen bypassed the main part of town and,
as a result, I missed the Appalachian Trail Headquarters and had
to return up the hill for a visit. This time I followed Main Street
past the gift shops and old homes that line the streets. It was like
marching through a living history of the United States in the
mid-1800's.

Harpers Ferry is actually a National Historic Park adminis-
tered by the National Park Service, and many of the buildings
dating from the Civil War appear today as they looked then.
Some were undergoing restoration to preserve their 19th century character, while others were undergoing renovation to return them to the style of buildings of that era.

When I arrived at the headquarters, Jean Cashin was sitting
behind the front desk which served as a reception area. Despite
having a telephone "glued" to her ear and responding to questions and requests from others in the office and on the phone,
she greeted me with a warm smile. She took my picture for a
photo album of Thru-Hikers who visited the headquarters, and I
made an entry in the accompanying Trail register. I enjoyed seeing pictures of the people whose comments I had been reading
in the Trail registers during the past three months. I bought
some post cards and note cards and talked with Jean about the
Trail and Thru-Hikers we had known. Then she drove me back
to the bottom of the hill.

I was impressed by the personal attention I received and
have since learned that I was not an exception. Jean had a reputation as a surrogate Trail mother universally admired by all the
Thru-Hikers.

A narrow foot bridge connected to the railroad trestle led
across the Potomac and joined the tow path of the Chesapeake
and Ohio Canal on the Maryland side of the river. (Mostly the
canal was dry or had very little water.) As I headed toward

Shenandoah River at Harpers Ferry.

Shell ruin of St. John's Church at Harpers Ferry.

Weverton, Maryland, it suddenly occurred to me that I had finally left Virginia. I was beginning to think that Virginia was endless. It was 539.9 miles from the Virginia-North Carolina border to the Virginia-Maryland state line. Fully one fourth of the entire AT lies in Virginia.

As I walked down the path that thousands before me had walked, I became aware that I was experiencing a part of history. That realization put me in a reflective mood, and I fell into a meditative state without effort. I reminisced about my development on the Trail, how I had matured from a rank, green hiker, trying to sort out his career choices, to a seasoned Thru-Hiker who had learned something much deeper and much more valuable.

I really had developed spiritually. I no longer harbored panic fears of death. I remembered the time I had suffered my first episode of atrial fibrillation on the Trail at Plum Orchard Gap and the terror that experience had evoked. I thought about the similar experience at Abingdon shelter when I had screamed at the moon, clenching my fists in rage, railing against God. I guessed that to be the turning point. After that episode, I had pretty much taken subsequent episodes in stride.

My climb up Roan Mountain was perhaps the most influential of all my experiences. It came at a time when I had reached my physical and emotional limits and was forced to ask God for help. I had been numb with fatigue both physically and emotionally and had wanted only to make it to a place where I could rest and spend the night. God not only gave me strength that carried me to the top of the mountain, He also provided sustenance.

I remembered fondly the expression on my son's face when he had dropped me off at Nimblewill Gap and the panic I had experienced after he left when I suddenly realized how alone I was. It all seemed so long ago.

A vision of Max Patch and the wave of emotion it evoked welled up in my memory. I again saw the stands of daisies bobbing in the sunlight on the side of the hill and the sea of grass undulating down the ridges. Vision after vision tumbled from memory, all of them bringing a fresh feeling of beauty to mind. Scenes of Long Creek Falls, the Smokies, Dismal Creek Falls, Roan Mountain, Hump Mountain, Round and Jane Balds, Dragons Tooth, Spy Rock, and others all took their places in the parade of images my memory marched by me.

The next day was the 11th of September, and it marked the

Appalachian Trail Conference Headquarters at Harpers Ferry.

completion of my third month on the Trail. I was now over the 1,000-mile mark and was as cocky with experience as I had been apprehensive when I had started. I knew that nothing was going to stop me now.

I paused for lunch at the Gathland State Park where I viewed the monument to Civil War correspondents erected there by George Alfred Townsend, a Civil War correspondent himself, who wrote under the pen name Gath. He had also built a beautiful home on the grounds along with a mausoleum which he intended as his final resting place. Only the foundation remained of the house, and the mausoleum, although in good shape, was empty. Something about the "best laid plans of mice and men" crossed my mind.

I had decided the previous night that the 11th would be my last day on the Trail. I was tired of the physical demands of the Trail, of the climbs, the rain and the discomfort, and I needed to get on with the other things I had planned when I retired. I was tired of the Trail in a physical sense but not in a psychological sense. I knew I would come back to the Trail the following year to complete the second half. I had already made that vow because I had made a personal commitment.

The weather was misting and it was gloomy in the forest when Russ dropped me off at Weverton. Except for talking with a group of school children on a class field trip, I saw no one. The children, all in their early teens, were very interested when I talked about the mountains in the South. I reminisced aloud about Roan Mountain, the Balds, the Smokies, and my encounter with the bear at the Cosby Knob shelter and Max Patch and the Grayson Highlands and the Blue Ridge and Spy Rock Overlook. I was in a satisfied, confident, reflective mood and could have talked for hours. The children listened with rapt attention. Occasionally, I glanced at the teacher to see if I was taking too much time, and the faintly smiling, reflective expression on his face told me he was as interested as the children.

Evidently my talking with the children opened my mind to further reflection on my experiences on the Trail and long after I left the class to continue my journey, images of other experiences flashed across my mind like subliminal messages on a screen. I felt somewhat like an elder statesman, one who had performed his last duty, then rested amid the adulation and thanks of the grateful citizenry whom he had served. It was vain of me to think that way, but I enjoyed it anyway.

I returned to my most recent accomplishments on the Trail, those which involved the development of my spiritual character. I began to assess what I had accomplished during my last three months and traced my progress from basically a materialistic orientation to one in which I began to understand the essence of my spirituality. I had made astounding personal progress.

I wondered if everyone who came on the Trail experienced such drastic changes in their lives. I had been told by my last boss that I would be a different person when I finished the Trail. I wondered what he would think if he were to meet me now. Would he see a difference? Besides a shaggy beard, long hair and a loss of 25 pounds, I was similar on the outside to the guy he knew. But there were also differences!

My body was much stronger from the rigors of the hike, as though the walking had cleansed it of impurities. Does walking also produce a psychological cleansing or a psychogenetic effect which induces spiritual reflection? Does it lead to improved meditative functioning?

I thought again about the idea of balance. Did a healthy

body also produce a healthy spirit and vice versa? I doubted that I could have achieved anywhere near the spiritual progress had I not been walking. I decided the walking cleansed not only my body, but also my mind. It was like I had taken a three-month mental shower, washing away a 50-year accumulation of myths and shadows, and with each successive day I was able to see a little more of my original spirit. I had a lifelong, perhaps an eternal responsibility to continue that effort.

I had hit on another truth — responsibility. It, too, like faith, required work. It was as much a gift as faith because it followed that when I received the gift of faith, I received with it the gift of responsibility. Nurturing faith was God's way of ensuring my commitment to spiritual development. That was my part of the bargain. I was to be responsible to see to it that my faith endured.

I had the tools I needed to continue the development myself. I could continue. God would be there if I faltered, but I had the tools and all I needed was to use them diligently for the purposes for which they had been given. I had a new map for a new journey which would be as exciting as any I had ever undertaken.

The sun broke through the trees with a weakened light, warming the path as I passed by Dahlgren Backpacking Camping Area, a cluster of rustic wooden buildings standing in the shade of the late summer forest. The Trail climbed to Turner Gap, and in the sunlight on top of the hill, I could see the outline of the pickup and my sister waiting.

ON HIKING

Hiking isn't just the fun.
It's not one great commune,
Or walk with nature in the sun
Or in the forest cool.
It's just not deer and hummingbirds,
Nor meadow bursts of flowers,
Nor virgin stands of hemlock trees
Nor vistas from the balds.

There is another side.
It's rain and cold
And sweat-drenched backs
And knife-stab knees from torture climbs.
It's painful hips and shoulder aches
From where the pack straps rub.
It's wrinkled feet from soaking grass
And insect bites and hornet stings,
And swarms of gnats
You wear like halos in the heat.
There's sometime fright
From lightning strikes
That crash upon your ridge.
And walking on with blistered feet
And sometimes deep despair.

And yet, despite the pain
Despite the fear, and plain discomfiture,
There is no other way
To stretch the limits of resolve
And test the romance of the Trail
Against a flagging will.
It is the total sum that means
When someone says, "I've walked it all."

About the Author

Retired Army Colonel Jan D. Curran hiked the 2,000-mile Appalachian Trail from Georgia to Maine (1986-87) to aid in his transition from military to civilian life. In the doing, he not only discovered a worthy challenge but discovered himself on a very personal level.

Born in White Plains, New York, Curran earned a B.A. degree in English from the University of Vermont and a M.S. degree in Education from Niagara University. He entered the U.S. Army, Infantry, in 1956, where he became first a platoon leader, then a company commander, operations and intelligence staff officer, service school and ROTC instructor, military assistance advisor in Vietnam, and installation manager. He served two tours of duty in Vietnam. Later he was assigned to Germany (he can read, write and speak fluent German) where he became Community Activity Commander and Deputy Community Commander in Mainz. During his 13 years of duty in Germany, he had the pleasure of serving for a year directly for then Brigadier General H. Norman Schwarzkopf. General Schwarzkopf is remembered well as Commander in Chief of the U.S. Central Command and all U.S. Forces in Operation Desert Storm.

Curran lives in Naples, Florida, where he enjoys tennis, painting and traveling while continuing to write. Meanwhile, he is particularly active in civic groups devoted to the elimination of waste in government and reduction in taxation and spending.

INDEX

-A-

-B-

-M-

-S-

-T-

[* Places located along the North Carolina-Tennessee border.]

"End of the Trail."

The Appalachian Trail Series
by Jan D. Curran

The Appalachian Trail: A Journey of Discovery
(ISBN 0-935834-66-4, $12.95, Softcover)

The Appalachian Trail: Onward to Katahdin
(ISBN 1-56825-072-X, $14.95, Softcover)

The Appalachian Trail: How To Prepare For & Hike It
(ISBN 1-56825-050-9, $14.95, *Softcover*)

The Appalachian Trail: How To Prepare For & Hike It
(ISBN 1-56825-051-7, $19.95, *Hardcover*)

— Five Ways to Order —

Your Local Bookseller — Ask your local bookstore to order the book you want by providing them with the book's complete ISBN number (see above). Our books are available to booksellers from all major book wholesalers/distributors and by publisher-direct, prepaid S.T.O.P. order.

Telephone — Call, toll free, 1-800-356-9315. MasterCard, Visa, American Express and Discover cards accepted.

Fax — Fax, toll free, 1-800-242-0036. MasterCard, Visa, American Express and Discover cards accepted.

Email — NAIP@aol.com. Please provide: the Quantities and Complete Titles of the Books you want to order; Your Name; the Delivery Street Address (remember, UPS deliveries cannot be made to PO Boxes; deliveries to PO Boxes can be made only by the Postal Service); City, State, Zip; Phone/Fax Numbers; Credit Card Number; Expiration Date; and Your Address (if different from delivery).

Online — http://www.upperaccess.com (Upper Access Books) or http://www.amazon.com (Amazon.com). Both sites carry all our books, and they accept all major credit cards using secured ordering (which means your credit card number is not accessible to the public).